Wilf Wilkinson was born in Leeds in 1921 and educated at Fulneck Boys' School, Pudsey. After three years in a Local Government Office, he was called up into the Non-Combatant Corps in 1941.

At the end of the war he entered London University, first at Richmond College and later at King's College, where he took the B.D. degree and the A.K.C. diploma. He was made Deacon in 1950 and ordained Priest in 1951 at St Albans.

After curacies at Luton and Berkhamsted, he went to Manchester, where for eight years he was Vicar of Woodhouse Park during the building of the William Temple Church. Since 1965 he has been Rector of Clifton, Nottingham, where he is the leader of a Team Ministry.

Biblical theology and psychotherapy have been life-long interests, and of recent years he has been a frequent broadcaster in religious programmes. He is married and has one son.

in the same series

GOOD NEWS IN ACTS introduced by David Edwards
GOOD NEWS IN JOHN introduced by Douglas Webster
GOOD NEWS IN ROMANS introduced by Joseph Rhymer

to be published shortly

GOOD NEWS IN CORINTHIANS introduced by William Neil
GOOD NEWS IN GALATIANS introduced by John Davies
GOOD NEWS IN HEBREWS introduced by Thomas Corbishley

GOOD NEWS IN
LUKE

Luke in
Today's English Version

Introduced by
WILF WILKINSON

Collins
FONTANA BOOKS
in co-operation with The Bible Reading Fellowship

First published in Fontana Books 1974
© Wilfred Wilkinson 1974

Today's English Version of *Luke*
© American Bible Society, New York, 1966, 1971

Made and printed in Great Britain by
William Collins Sons & Co Ltd Glasgow

*To Betty and Mark, wife and son, whose
love is one of my greatest thanksgivings*

CONTENTS

Preface   7

Introduction   9

Part 1: The Coming of the Christ   15

Part 2: Call and Preparation   27

Part 3: The Work in Galilee   32

Part 4: The Way to Jerusalem   62

Part 5: Death, Resurrection and Glory   120

Appendix   158

Luke   165

PREFACE

This book is intended to be a popular commentary, which means that in writing it I have tried to keep constantly in mind the intelligent man or woman who has not had a theological training, though they may be trained in other fields, as so many people are today. The Bible often does not mean very much to such people because they do not know the background material which would light up the text and bring it to life.

I have tried to avoid what seem to me to be the two worst faults of popular Christian books; first that they talk down to the reader, and second that they are extremely conservative and inoffensive, lest they upset anybody, for many ordinary Christians are very touchy about their faith, and easily offended by new thoughts!

With regard to the first point; this book does not talk down to anybody. It is as sound and scholarly as I could make it. It is 'popular' in the sense that it discusses what I imagine ordinary people are interested in, and will find helpful. My deepest hope is that it may make the Bible come alive for those who read it.

With regard to the second point; I have not defended the reader from modern radical thought in biblical scholarship. How could I when my own faith has been so much deepened and strengthened by it in these last twenty years? If we are doing no more than thinking the thoughts of our grandfathers, there is something wrong with us *as Christians*. This is God's world. Science in all its branches belongs to him. Discoveries in many branches of natural science impinge upon our understanding of the Bible, and we should be open to them. The Pharisees whose minds were closed to new thought should be a dreadful warning to us. But it is not only the discoveries of natural science that are important for biblical study. Perhaps even more so, the discoveries of classical scholars, historians and those who study the ancient languages, and the science of manuscripts and ancient texts, shed new light on the scriptures. Our century is once again a time for the kind of adventurous and courageous thinking which the Church showed in the first four centuries of her life.

I would like to ask the serious reader to do what I often fail to do myself! Look up the references to other parts of the Bible whenever they are given. This is a laborious task, but it brings a rich reward, which nothing else can bring.

Every Christian should, I think, possess two translations of the full Bible. First, the Revised Standard Version Common Bible, published in 1973 by Collins. This is the first English Bible since the Reformation to have the blessing of Protestant, Roman Catholic and Orthodox Churches throughout the entire English-speaking world. Along with this, the New English Bible is indispensable. It is the greatest work of biblical scholarship of this century.

Finally, I would like to thank my friend and colleague the Rev. Stephen Oliver for reading my whole manuscript and making many suggestions, nearly all of which I have gratefully accepted. I am glad to have this opportunity of recording my debt to him.

WILF WILKINSON

St Mary's Rectory
Clifton Village
Nottingham

INTRODUCTION

The Author

There is a unanimous tradition from earliest times that the two-volume work of the Acts of Jesus and the Acts of the Apostles was written by St Luke the physician who was one of the travelling companions of St Paul. He is mentioned in Colossians (4:14), 'Luke, our dear doctor, and Demas send you their greetings', and again in 2 Timothy (4:11), 'Only Luke is with me', and in verse 24 of the short letter to Philemon where he sends his greetings, along with Mark, Aristarchus and Demas.

St Luke was a native of Antioch in Syria. He was a cultured man who could write beautiful Greek when the occasion demanded, and could even vary his literary style to suit his subject. For example, the classical style of his opening prologue (1:1–4) gives place immediately to a style with a strongly Hebrew flavour, very like that of the Greek translation of the Old Testament,[1] as he tells the story of the birth of John the Baptist. St Luke is also a careful historian and his work makes good his claim to have 'carefully studied all these matters from their beginning'. (1:3)

The Date of the Gospel

Authors in ancient times did not date their books as we do today, and it is impossible to say exactly when St Luke wrote his gospel. He knew and used Mark, so we must date Luke after AD 64–65. The question is a complicated one, but most scholars would accept a date somewhere between AD 80 and 85 for Luke.

1. Usually called the Septuagint because it was held to have been made by seventy (or seventy-two) scholars.

How St Luke constructed his Gospel

In his introduction St Luke tells us that he had carefully studied all the things concerning Jesus, including the work of others who had written before him, so that he might write an orderly account which would give Theophilus the full truth of all those matters which he had been taught. There is an attractive suggestion that St Luke collected his material and compared his sources during the two years from AD 57–59 when St Paul was in prison at Caesarea awaiting trial.

In composing his gospel, St Luke certainly used Mark. The references in brackets under the paragraph headings in our translation show that clearly. About half of St Mark's gospel is contained in Luke, often in almost the exact language. Again, St Luke largely follows Mark's order in writing his own gospel.

When all the material taken from Mark has been accounted for, there are about two hundred verses consisting mainly of the teaching of Jesus which are common both to Luke and Matthew. In many of these verses the language is so closely similar that we may be almost certain that both writers were using a common document. (For example, compare Luke 10:21–22 with Matthew 11:25–27.) This document was probably written in Antioch (St Luke's home town) about the year AD 50, and consisted mainly of the *teaching* of Jesus. Scholars give it the title 'Q' – from the German word Quelle meaning 'source'. We only know it through the gospels of Matthew and Luke, just as the planet Pluto was only known for many years by the effect it had on the orbit of Neptune. But so many ancient and previously unknown manuscripts of the Bible have been discovered during the last hundred and fifty years that one wonders whether the document 'Q' may one day be discovered.

When everything which St Luke has taken from Mark and from 'Q' is put together, there is still about half the gospel left. This is material which occurs nowhere else apart from Luke, and it is of very special richness and beauty. It includes two of Jesus's greatest parables – the Good Samaritan and the Prodigal Son: the Song of the Virgin Mary (the Magnificat): the Song of Simeon (the Nunc Dimittis): and the story of the Emmaus Road which George Eliot called the most beautiful story in the world. For all this, and for much more of the most precious and beautiful stories and teaching of Jesus, we are indebted to St Luke and to him alone. This may well be the material which he gathered during those two years at Caesarea when St Paul, fobbed off by Felix, waited in the vain hope of getting justice.

St Luke's Purpose in Writing the Gospel and the Book of Acts

St Luke is the only Gentile (that is, non-Jewish) writer in the whole New Testament. He carefully traces the history of the gospel and the Church from its beginning in Galilee and Jerusalem to its arrival in Rome, the capital city of the Empire. In our Bibles the two volumes of his work have become separated from each other by the fourth gospel. This is a pity, for they were certainly written as two halves of a single work. St Luke's aim was to appeal to Gentiles like himself, cultured men of wide sympathies, and to show Christianity as a world religion rather than a mere offshoot of Judaism. The Christ of St Luke's gospel is 'a light to reveal (God's) way to the Gentiles' as well as to 'bring glory to (his) people Israel' (2:32).

A subsidiary purpose may well have been to try to convince the official Roman world, consisting of men like his 'Excellency' Theophilus, that the Empire had nothing to fear from the new religion. Thus, St Luke stresses the way in which Pilate the Roman Governor tried his best to secure the release of Jesus. 'I find no reason to condemn this man,' he says (23:4). Again, after Jesus had been returned to him from Herod, 'I have not found him guilty of any of the crimes you accuse him of. Nor did Herod find him guilty, because he sent him back to us. There is nothing this man has done to deserve death' (23:14–15). In the second half of his work, he shows how

Festus the Roman Governor, in spite of much pressure from the Jews, would not condemn St Paul, but after a full and careful hearing of the charges brought against him, concluded, 'This man has not done anything for which he should die or be put in prison' (Acts 26:31). If Christianity had been able to win the status of a *religio licita* (a legal religion) within the Roman Empire, the whole history of the Church would have been different. But it did not. Instead, it was persecuted off and on for three centuries.

The Special Characteristics of St Luke's Gospel

St Luke has placed the stamp of his own individuality on everything he has written. This does not mean that he has manipulated his material in any dishonest way, but that he has laid his own special emphasis on those things in the story and teaching of Jesus that he wished to bring out and stress.

Thus, Luke has been called the universal gospel. It presents Jesus not as the Jewish Messiah, but as the catholic Christ, the saviour of the world. Whereas Matthew traces the genealogy of Jesus back to Abraham, the father of the Jewish race, Luke traces it back to Adam, the father of all mankind. When they describe the work of John the Baptist, all four gospels quote from chapter 40 of the Book of Isaiah, but only St Luke continues the quotation to include the words, 'All mankind will see God's salvation!' (3:6) St Luke also dates the events in his gospel by reference to the Roman Empire as well as to Jewish life, and he puts the Roman dates before the Jewish ones (3:1), and he ends his gospel on the same world-wide note, 'the message about repentance and the forgiveness of sins must be preached to all nations, beginning in Jerusalem.' (24:47)

Luke is also the Gentile gospel, written for the converts who were pouring into the growing Church. Thus, St Luke normally uses Greek terms instead of Hebrew ones which would not be familiar to Gentile readers (i.e. Master instead of Rabbi; Zealot instead of Cananean), and he does not show much interest in the Old Testament, nor in Jesus as the fulfilment of Jewish hopes for the coming of the Messiah.

Luke is often called the gospel of prayer. More than any other, it shows us Jesus praying – before his baptism (3:21), in solitary places (5:16), spending the whole night in prayer before choosing the twelve disciples (6:12), on the mount of Transfiguration (9:29), and in the final moment as he dies on the Cross (23:46). No less than three of our Lord's parables about prayer appear only in Luke – the friend who came at midnight (11:5–13), the Pharisee and the tax collector (18:9–14), and the parable of the widow and the judge (18:1–8).

Luke is also the gospel of women. The birth stories in Luke are told from the point of view of Mary. Luke gives us the story of Martha and Mary welcoming Jesus into their home (10:38–41). Jesus's tenderness to women is shown in this gospel as nowhere else – to the widow at Nain (7:11–17), to the women who lived a sinful life (7:36–50). St Luke alone tells us about the women who accompanied Jesus and his disciples on their preaching tour through the towns and villages (8:1–3).

Luke is also the gospel of joy. At the beginning there are the angel's words to the shepherds, 'I am here with good news for you, which will bring great joy to all the people.' (2:10) At the end the disciples return to Jerusalem 'filled with great joy, (they) spent all their time in the temple giving thanks to God' (24:52–53 – the last verse in the gospel). St Luke alone gives the three great parables of the joy in heaven over one sinner who repents – the lost sheep (15:1–7), the lost coin (15:8–10), and the lost son (15.11–32). His three great hymns of joy, the Magnificat (1:46–55), the Benedictus (1:68–79), and the Nunc Dimittis (2:29–32) have been used in the daily worship of the Church for many centuries.

Finally, Luke is the gospel of the outcast and the poor, in which Jesus is shown as the friend of tax gatherers and sinners, and despised characters like Zacchaeus (19:1–10). Luke gives the beatitude, 'Happy are you poor: the Kingdom of God is yours!' (6:20) in the more direct, and probably more primitive, form than Matthew (cf. Matthew 5:3), and he alone records the parable of the rich man and Lazarus, Jesus's parable of warning to the loveless rich (16:19–31).

All in all, it is not surprising that Renan, the nineteenth-century French theologian, described St Luke's gospel as the most beautiful book ever written. We must now look at it in detail.

Part 1

THE COMING OF THE CHRIST

Introduction (chapter 1)

St Luke begins his gospel with a delicately balanced paragraph in the style of classical rhetoric. Theophilus (Beloved of God) could be a real name, or it could be a pseudonym to hide the real identity of the Roman official for whom he is writing the book. The title 'your Excellency' suggests a Roman of high rank, and it might have been embarrassing for him to have had a book describing a miscarriage of Roman justice addressed to him by his real name!

The Greek word for 'have been taught' in verse 4 can refer to Christian instruction (as in Acts 18:25), which is the way in which our translation takes it. Or it can refer to a hostile and inaccurate report (as in Acts 21:21 and 24). Thus, according to the way in which we translate it, we can think of St Luke as writing his two-volume work to fill out the instruction which 'Theophilus' had already received when he became a Christian, or as writing to some high Roman official whose identity is kept secret, in order to correct the slanderous and incriminating stories which were circulating freely concerning the Christians, and to try to gain from the authorities a favourable hearing for the new religion. The very formal nature of the greeting, which is so unlike the greetings of Christians to each other, might lend weight to this second view.

The Birth of John the Baptist Announced

Every male Jew who could trace his ancestry back to Aaron was a priest. There were twenty-four such families. Zechariah traced his descent through Abia, one of the grandsons of Aaron. Each of the twenty-four orders of priests offered sacrifice in the temple twice a year

for a week at a time. The whole 'clan' came to Jerusalem
and several families took responsibility each day, casting
lots for the duties which each individual would perform.
The most coveted task was to burn the incense which was
offered each day before the morning sacrifice and after
the evening sacrifice. No priest was allowed to perform
this duty more than once in his lifetime, and many of
them never had the chance at all.

When the moment came, he left his two assistants by
the altar of sacrifice and entered the sanctuary alone.
This was the first room of the temple proper, the ante-
room of the most holy place, which only the High Priest
could enter, once each year. Here in the sanctuary stood
the small altar of incense. When he had burned the
incense, the priest came to the rail dividing the court of
the priests from the court of the Israelites, and blessed
the waiting people.

This must have been a time of intense emotion for
Zechariah. It was the crown of his priestly life. But he
carried a deep personal sorrow. He and Elizabeth were
childless. Amongst the Jews this was regarded not only
as a sorrow, but also as a reproach in the eyes of both
God and men.

We can imagine him entering the mysterious solitude
of the sanctuary, torn by the conflicting emotions of joy
and sorrow. The fragrant incense ascends like a prayer.
He is wrapped in the silence and the sanctity of the place.
In this moment he is ready for God to speak, and the
vision is granted him.

The story is full of Old Testament echoes. The old
priest and his wife remind us of Abraham and Sarah.
Elizabeth's words, 'Now at last the Lord has helped me
. . . He has taken away my public disgrace!' (1:25) recall
the words of Rachel when her son Joseph is born
(Genesis 30:23). The vision of Gabriel and Zechariah's
dumbness recall the visions of Daniel and Ezekiel
(Daniel 10:15, Ezekiel 3:26). The child is to be named
John, which means 'The Lord has been gracious.' He is
to be dedicated to God, and from his very birth will be
filled with the Holy Spirit.

Since the days of Malachi, devout Jews had believed that Elijah, who had not died, but had been caught up to heaven, would return to .prepare the way for the Messiah (Malachi 4:5 and 3:1). John is to be the one who will fulfil the prophecies which had gathered round the name of Elijah.

Before we leave this passage, we may note that many of the women in the Bible whose sons became the great spiritual heroes of Israel are said to have been barren, and to have conceived only after many years of hope and prayer. This is one of the ways in which the Bible writers stress that in the great acts of salvation-history, the initiative always lies with God and not with man. It is God who acts, and God who chooses. Man's part is to wait on him, and to respond with obedience and trust.

The Birth of Jesus Announced

St Luke's birth stories have a perfection of taste and a spiritual and literary beauty which have made them the inspiration of the story and the carols of Christmas for two thousand years. Nazareth is a small town lying in a sheltered valley among the southern spurs of Lebanon. It is about 1000 feet above sea-level, and from the hill to the south there is a magnificent view of many of the places famous in the Old Testament. The visit of the angel Gabriel is full of allusions to the Old Testament. The promises in verses 32 and 33 recall many passages which look forward to the coming of the Messiah (i.e. Isaiah 9:7, Daniel 2:44, Micah 4:7), and verse 37 is a direct reference to the promise to Abraham and Sarah, 'Is anything impossible for the Lord?' (Genesis 18:14)

The word 'girl' (verse 27) is a better translation than the 'virgin' of the older English versions of the Bible, for in the Hebrew which lies behind it, the word means simply 'young woman' without necessarily implying virginity. To be betrothed or promised in marriage was in some ways like being engaged in our society, but it was more legally binding. It could only be dissolved by divorce, and should the man die, the girl was a widow in the eyes of the Law.

The child is to be named Jesus. In the Bible, names have a meaning. (See also p. 21f.) They are more than mere labels. The prophets often foreshadow God's purpose for a man through his name, and a man's name often declares his character. The name Jesus means 'God our Saviour'. The whole of this passage breathes the devout hope of the Old Israel waiting for her restoration under the Lord's anointed, great David's greater son. Jesus will take this hope of the coming of the Messiah and remould it in ways that are so shocking to the religious leaders of his people that they will determine, at all costs, to do away with him.

It was common in the Old Testament for people to ask for a sign, as Zechariah had done (verse 18), but Mary offers a perfect and unquestioning trust and obedience.

The Virgin Birth

Here we must consider the doctrine of the virgin birth, and whether we should believe it literally or symbolically. The question is not whether God could or could not create a child without a human father, for of course he could if he is God. We are inquiring what the Bible writers believed, and why they wrote as they did.

There is only one text which definitely requires that the virgin birth be taken literally. That is the direct statement, 'He (Joseph) had no sexual relations with her before she gave birth to her son.' (Matthew 1:25) In the light of that text, the natural interpretation of the words in Luke, 'The Holy Spirit will come upon you, and God's power will rest upon you' (1:35), is that Mary is to remain a virgin, though without the support of the text in Matthew it could equally well be taken to mean that Jesus would be born by the overshadowing of God's Spirit in the same way that John the Baptist was.

The following considerations have been suggested against a literal interpretation of the virgin birth. (1) St Paul, who is the earliest witness we have to the preaching of the Apostles themselves, never mentions it, and does not seem to know of it. (2) St Mark, our earliest gospel does not mention it – and neither does the fourth gospel which is the latest. (3) Both Matthew and Luke use the text of Isaiah 7:14, 'Behold, a virgin shall conceive, and bear a son, and shall call his name Immanuel (that is, God is with us).' Matthew quotes it directly, and Luke uses it indirectly. But the Hebrew word in Isaiah means 'young woman' without any reference to virginity. It was the Greek translation of the Old Testament made about 250 BC which mistakenly rendered the Hebrew by the Greek word *parthenos*, which means 'virgin'. (4) The genealogies both in Matthew and Luke trace Jesus's ancestry back through Joseph, and it is through Joseph that Jesus is the Son of David. It could well be that St Luke's genealogy originally accepted Joseph in the full sense as Jesus's father, but was later accommodated to the doctrine of the virgin birth by inserting the words here placed in brackets, 'He was the son (so people thought) of Joseph, who was the son of Heli . . .' (3:23) (5) In both Matthew and Luke there is an entirely different atmosphere about the birth stories from the rest of the gospel. In the main part of the gospel Jesus meets hostility, criticism and rejection, and is not recognized for who he is. In the birth stories on the other hand, dreams and an angel, a star and a heavenly choir proclaim him as king and Son of God. This is the language of worship rather than plain history.

The purpose of the doctrine of the virgin birth is to express the mystery of Jesus. In the experience of his disciples, he was utterly transparent to God as no other man had ever been. He brought God to them *completely* in every situation. 'He was the same as God' to them. (Note this very accurate translation in our version of John 1:1 in place of the 'was God' of the older versions.) This was the unshakeable experience of the disciples, and the doctrine of the virgin birth expresses it with perfect beauty.

If we take it literally, we must face the problem of how any being without a human father can possibly be truly and fully man. If we take it symbolically we must face the problem of how a man, just like us in every way, could possibly bring God to us *completely*, in every situation, and be utterly transparent to God in a way that no other man has ever been. Either way, we are left with the mystery of the person of Christ, which is the most glorious mystery of our faith: and must not God always be a mystery to us? If we were able to explain him and contain him within our human minds, he would not be God at all, but just some idol as little as ourselves.

Mary Visits Elizabeth

There are a number of psalms in the Old Testament which are called 'Messianic psalms', because the Jews believed that they referred to the Messiah who was to come. In the first two chapters of Luke there are four songs which are modelled on the old Hebrew verse forms, and which have been called the Messianic psalms of the New Testament. The first of them is the Song of Elizabeth.[1] The other three (the Magnificat 1:46, the Benedictus 1:68, and the Nunc Dimittis 2:29) have been used as hymns in the worship of the Church since at least the sixth century.

'Elizabeth was filled with the Holy Spirit.' This is St Luke's way of describing a sudden gift of prophecy. By all four of these Messianic psalms, he means us to understand that the gospel events which he is going to describe began with a revival of prophetic inspiration, which had been absent for so long in Israel.

The whole of the first section of Luke (chapters 1 and 2) is as exalted and inspired as the Old Testament background from which it comes. We might call these chapters 'theological history', for St Luke's purpose is not to record events in a literal fashion, but to convey the purpose and activity of God which lay beneath the surface of events, and was visible only to those who had eyes to see.

In the literal fact of later history, John the Baptist in his prison sent the agonized question to Jesus, 'Are you the one (who) was going to come, or should we expect someone else?' (7:20) But here, as Mary visits Elizabeth,

1. Although not printed in verse form in most English translations, in the original they have the characteristic arrangement of Hebrew poetry.

'the unborn herald leaps to greet his unborn Lord.' Likewise, whilst we may join with Elizabeth in calling Mary 'blessed of all women', we must not be sentimental. In later years she failed to understand her Son (cf. 2:50, Mark 3:21 and 3:31–35). Her blessedness lay in her unfaltering obedience and trust in God which made her able to be the vessel of his redeeming purpose, and in her unfaltering love for her child, which took her even to stand at the foot of his Cross. The blessed virgin Mary shows perfectly the highest qualities of motherhood.

Mary's Song of Praise

This lovely hymn of praise is saturated in Jewish piety. It is clearly modelled on the song of Hannah (1 Samuel 2:1–10). Almost every sentence in it occurs at some place in the Greek translation of Hannah's song in the Septuagint (i.e. the Greek version of the Old Testament). Like many of the Psalms, it moves quickly and naturally from personal joy and thanksgiving to the exaltation of the whole people of God, and the final verse spans the whole of salvation-history from God's original promise to Abraham (Genesis 12:3 and 22:18) to its fulfilment in the birth of her Son.

The beauty of the Magnificat must not blind us to its revolutionary qualities. Every coming of God is a crisis for men. He scatters the proud people with all their plans. He brings down the mighty from their thrones and lifts up the lowly. He fills the hungry and sends the rich away with empty hands. The coming of Jesus will bring moral, social and economic revolution.

The Birth of John the Baptist

The birth of John was a double joy, first because Elizabeth had at last borne a child, and then, because it was a boy, for the birth of a boy was greeted with much more rejoicing than the birth of a girl. According to the Law of Moses (Leviticus 12:3), a male child must be circumcised on the eighth day and given his name. In the Bible, names are more than mere labels. They point to the character of their bearer, as for instance the name

Jacob (supplanter). They can also be a declaration of faith. At a time when the nation was turning away from God to worship Baals, the parents of Elijah nailed their colours to the mast by naming their son Elijah, which means 'Yahweh is my God.' (See also p. 18.)

Against all expectations Elizabeth insisted on calling her child John, and Zechariah, recovering his speech at that very moment, confirmed her choice. The neighbours saw the hand of God in this and were filled with awe, for when God names a man, he chooses him, and indicates his mission, as when he renamed Jacob the supplanter 'Israel' which means 'Ruling with God' (Genesis 32:28), and when Jesus renamed Simon 'Peter' which means 'A Rock' (Matthew 16:18).

The name John means 'God is gracious.' In this child, then, God will be gracious to his people. Zechariah now bursts out in his great hymn of praise. God is about to fulfil his promise made through the prophets, and even before them in the sacred covenant which he made with Moses and the people of Israel on Mount Sinai; and even before that in the promise which he made to Abraham. All the long centuries of Israel's waiting history are about to be gathered up in God's faithfulness.

We may note that in this hymn, as in the Magnificat, political and religious hopes are woven together, as they are in the writings of the great prophets. We are often told today that religion should not be mixed up with politics. But the will of God is to be done *in this world* and therefore, religion must always have political implications. We cannot allow it to be kept safely inside churches so that men may pursue their sinful ways unhindered!

So, the child grew and lived in the desert until his day came. Solitude has played a part in preparing many spiritual leaders for their work. Elijah and Amos in the Old Testament, and St Benedict and the monks in Christian history all lived away from men, but from their solitude they exercised great influence on the world.

The Birth of Jesus (chapter 2)

St Luke weaves together Old Testament prophecy, secular history and poetic symbolism in his story of the birth of Jesus. The words of Micah (Micah 5:2–5) echo throughout the story as he tells of the woman in labour in little Bethlehem, bringing to birth a child who will be ruler in Israel, whose origins are from ancient days; who will be their shepherd and feed his flock in the strength of the Lord, and be great to the ends of the earth.

St Luke also puts the birth of Jesus into the setting of world history. God brings his promises to fulfilment through the decree of the Roman Emperor Augustus. Like the Emperor Cyrus before him (cf. Isaiah 45:1), Augustus becomes the unwitting instrument of God's salvation. As we might expect, St Luke who was writing for the Roman world is the only gospel writer to bring out this link. We can learn from it that no part of human life, in that day or in ours, is outside the influence of God. He works through the secular as well as through the sacred, and even through men who do not know him.

In addition to prophecy and secular history, St Luke has woven a rich symbolism into his story. The rejection which reached its climax on the Cross began when there was no room at the inn. Shepherds were despised by the Pharisees and doctors of the Law, because their calling made it difficult for them to fulfil their religious duties. St Luke is always interested in the outcast and the poor. The shepherds point forward to the Good Samaritan and the woman who was a sinner, to Zacchaeus and the tax collectors whose response to Jesus is so much stressed in this gospel. The Church of South India has caught the spirit of this passage in its prayer for Christmas Eve.

O God, who before all other didst call shepherds to the cradle of thy Son: grant that by the preaching of the gospel, the poor, the humble and the forgotten may know that they are at home with thee; through Jesus Christ our Lord. Amen.

The shepherds are also a reminder of King David, the shepherd boy, whose greater Son was being born. The chorus of angels express the joy which rings through this gospel and which Jesus said rang through heaven for every sinner who repents.

The Shepherds and the Angels

In the Old Testament, the 'heavenly host', or the 'great army of heaven's angels' as it is translated here, sometimes referred to the angelic courtiers around the throne of God, and sometimes to the stars, which the Jews like all other ancient peoples believed were spiritual beings. According to the Book of Job, 'the morning stars sang together and all the sons of God shouted for joy' (Job 38:7) when God created the earth. St Luke is hinting then that the birth of Christ is a new creation, to be compared with the creation of the world. St John (1:1–14) and St Paul (Colossians 1:16) bear the same witness to Christ.

Jesus is Named and Presented in the Temple

The Law of Moses laid down three ceremonies to follow the birth of a male child. (1) Circumcision on the eighth day, at which the name was also given. The name Jesus is the Greek form of the Hebrew name Joshua which means 'The Lord is Salvation.' (2) In the case of a firstborn there was the rite of redemption (Exodus 13:12, Numbers 18:15). An offering of five shekels (about 75p) was made, which might be thought of as buying the child back from God to whom every firstborn male belonged. This could be done any time after the first month. (3) The mother was unclean for forty days during which she could not enter into any form of public worship. She then brought a lamb and a turtle-dove or young pigeon to the temple to be sacrificed for her Purification. This was an expensive sacrifice, and the poor were allowed to substitute a second dove or pigeon for the lamb. It was this 'offering of the poor' which Mary made for her Purification.

If we read verses 22–24 carefully, it seems that St Luke

has confused the order of these events, and he makes no mention at all of the five shekels to redeem the child. Is this because, being a Gentile, he was not familiar with the finer details of Jewish ceremonial law? Or is he telling us that Jesus was never 'bought back' from God, but was presented totally and permanently to God's service like the child Samuel? (1 Samuel 1:27–28)

The Jews were in a turmoil of longing and expectation for deliverance from Roman domination. Some sought it through political means, and urban guerrilla tactics, as we should call them now. But Simeon and Anna belonged to a small group known as 'The Quiet in the Land' who waited on God in prayer. In the child Jesus, Simeon recognized the fulfilment of God's promises. His song is the last of the four great canticles which St Luke gives us. It echoes the universal note of the great prophet of the Exile (Isaiah 40–55). 'And the glory of the Lord shall be revealed, and all flesh shall see it together.' (Isaiah 40:5). 'I will give you as a light to the nations, that my salvation may reach to the end of the earth.' (Isaiah 49:6)

Simeon introduces for the first time the theme of suffering which will grow and unfold as the gospel develops, and which Jesus himself finally takes up at its very end. 'Was it not necessary for the Messiah to suffer these things and enter his glory?' (24:26) The Messiah must suffer with Israel and for Israel to be her glory. It is typical of St Luke to introduce Anna, and so to put a woman alongside a man. (See also p. 13.) It is also interesting that she has the same name as the mother of Samuel.

The Boy Jesus in the Temple

When a Jewish boy is twelve years old he becomes a 'son of the Law', able to accept for himself the responsibilities and religious duties that his parents pledged him to when he was circumcised. So, this was an important Passover for Jesus and his family. During Passover, members of the Sanhedrin (the great religious council of the Jews) met in public in the temple and discussed theological questions. It was these public discussions which so fascinated the boy Jesus.

The caravans of pilgrims were so large that it was not surprising that it was nightfall on the first day's journey back before he was missed. His reply to Mary's rebuke is significant, 'Didn't you know that I had to be in my Father's House?' The Jews thought of God as the Father of his people Israel, but this personal consciousness of God as *my* Father is a new thing. Jesus's sense of a unique relationship to God is already dawning.

From this point we hear nothing more of Jesus for eighteen long years. It says much for the gospel writers that they did not invent anything to fill the gap.

Part 2

CALL AND PREPARATION

The Preaching of John the Baptist (chapter 3)

Once again as in 2:1 St Luke, who is writing for educated Romans, puts his story in a world setting. He introduces John the Baptist with words so often used in the Old Testament for God's call to a prophet, 'the word of God came to John . . .' All the gospels quote the words from Isaiah 40:3–5, 'Someone is shouting in the desert . . .' but only St Luke the Gentile, writing for Gentiles, continues the quotation to include the words 'all mankind will see God's salvation!' Verses 10–14 also are peculiar to St Luke. Their message of sharing and social justice reminds us of the life of the early Church as he describes it in his second volume (Acts 2:44–46 and 4:32–35). They should come with great power to our twentieth-century world with its wide differences between the rich and poor nations, as well as between rich and poor individuals. We shall meet St Luke's social concern, his care for the poor, and his warnings about wealth, again and again as his gospel continues.

John's picture of his hearers as being like snakes wriggling away from a forest fire is a vivid one. The Jordan ravine was covered with thick scrub, and fires were a common sight; so also was the sight of the wood-cutter's axe leaning against the next tree to be felled. The winnowing-shovel was a great flat-bladed shovel with which the newly reaped corn was tossed into the air. The heavy grain fell to the ground first, the lighter chaff fell separately and was afterwards burned.

St Matthew and St Mark tell us more about John at a later stage in their gospels, but St Luke rounds off the story here, and John does not appear again. It was probably for political reasons that he was imprisoned in the fortress of Machaerus on the shores of the Dead Sea, though according to St Mark his denunciation of Herod's marriage to Herodias was the actual cause of his death (Mark 6:17–29). The sexual immorality of the Herods was almost beyond belief, and was a cause of great scandal to devout Jews. So intermingled were their unions that Herodias was both the sister-in-law and the niece of Herod Antipas. He seduced her in Rome from his half-brother who was her husband, and divorced his own wife to marry her.

The Baptism and Genealogy of Jesus

For roughly eighteen years after the visit to Jerusalem when he was twelve years old (2:41–50), Jesus's experiences of God must have been growing, and he must have been waiting for some word from God to come to him. John the Baptist's ministry was a clarion call to all Israel to repent and be ready for the coming Messiah. People flocked to him, and there was a great movement towards God throughout the whole country. Jesus knew that at last his 'time' had come. We need not worry about how Jesus could undergo a baptism of repentance if he was himself without sin. In being baptized, he made himself one with the people of God, and he responded to the call of God that he felt in his heart. Heaven opened to him, and he heard God's voice saying to him, 'You are my own dear Son, I am well pleased with you.' The first of these two sentences is a quotation from Psalm 2:7, and the second is from Isaiah 42:1. In an amazing way, the whole destiny of Jesus is foreshadowed in these two texts. Psalm 2 was accepted as a description of the messianic king of Israel who would rule all nations. The verse taken from Isaiah is part of the description of the servant of the Lord which reaches its climax in the great description of the suffering of God's servant in chapter 53 of the prophecy.

Jesus will indeed be the king whose kingdom will have no end, but only because he will be the servant who will pour out his soul unto death and in doing so heal the sin of many (Isaiah 53:12). Only St Luke mentions that Jesus was praying when the revelation came to him. In St Luke's gospel, all the great turning-points in the life of Jesus take place in the setting of prayer. (See also p. 13.)

In studying the Bible we have to try to see things through the eyes of those who wrote it, whose outlook and world were in many ways so different from our own. Thus, St Luke would not have been unduly concerned if somebody had complained that the names in his genealogy did not agree with those given in Matthew (Matthew 1:2–16). Each writer wanted to make a particular theological point through his genealogy, and that is the important thing about it. St Luke places it here, straight after the baptism in which Jesus is declared to be the Son of God, to make the point that he is also a real man. Like St Matthew, he traces the ancestry back through the royal line of David (the lineage of the Messiah) to Abraham, the father of Israel. But St Luke, with his universal interest, goes back beyond Abraham to Adam, the founder of the whole human race. Jesus is not only the redeemer of Israel, but the saviour of the world. He is the second Adam, founder of a new humanity. As G. B. Caird says, 'Jesus as Son of God was the fulfilment not only of Israel's destiny but of the destiny of mankind as well. Man was created for the kind of relationship to God that Jesus realized in his own life and so made possible for others also.'[1]

The Temptation of Jesus (chapter 4)

After every great moment of spiritual vision and exaltation there comes the inner struggle of thinking out how it is to be achieved in practice, and lived out in daily life. It was so for Jesus too. When he rose from the waters of baptism he knew that he was the longed-for Messiah and in a unique sense the Son of God. How was he to carry out the work of the Messiah? What did it mean for himself that he was God's own dear Son? For forty days, which is the biblical way of indicating an indefinite

1. *St Luke*, by G. B. Caird, Pelican Gospel Commentary, p. 39.

period of time – 'for weeks!' as we might say – Jesus
explored and rejected one course of action after another,
as he thought out the meaning of his life and work. Many
tempting possibilities presented themselves, only to be
pushed away.

Later, Jesus must have summed up for his disciples
these weeks of thought and spiritual struggle in the three
pictures of the temptations that we are given here. Like
the parables, these pictures bear the stamp of Jesus's
mind, and like the parables, the more we meditate on
them the more depths and unexpected glints of meaning
they reveal to us.

The first temptation was to give priority to meeting
the physical and economic needs of the people – and the
Jews were desperately poor. How can men be expected
to listen to good news about God with hunger gnawing
at their bellies? The second temptation was to be a
political conqueror. It was expected of the Messiah that
he would liberate his people and lift them above their
enemies, and there were thousands of young Jews who
were only too ready to spring to arms. Of course, this
would inevitably involve some compromises, but could
that be helped? And would the end not justify the
means? The third temptation was to work wonders to
make men believe in him, and also to put God to the test
instead of trusting him. 'If you are God's Son', ah yes, *if*!
Don't you need to be sure before you launch out on this
fantastic mission? Aren't you entitled to some proof?
The Rabbis have a tradition that the Messiah when he
comes will swoop down from the pinnacle of the temple.
Both you and they would *know* that you are the Messiah
if you did that. Jesus answers each temptation with a
text from the book of Deuteronomy, thus linking his
own experience with the trials of God's people in the
wilderness (Deuteronomy 8:3, 6:13, 6:16).

Only St Luke adds that the devil 'left him *for a while*'.
The temptations were not a once-for-all experience.
Again and again through his ministry the same basic
temptations assailed Jesus in different guises and dis-

guises. At the very end of his earthly life, at the Last Supper (22:28) Jesus says to his disciples, 'You have stayed with me *all through my trials.*' The Greek word is the same word that is used here for the temptations.[2]

2. I have discussed the temptations more fully in my book *To Me Personally*, Fontana, pp. 45–52.

Part 3

THE WORK IN GALILEE

Jesus Rejected at Nazareth

Galilee was the highland area in the north of Palestine. It was as fertile as a garden and densely populated. Closely surrounded by Gentile nations, its people were the least conservative of the Jews. Here, in the synagogue, Jesus began his ministry. The synagogues were the place where the weekly worship of the people took place. There was no professional minister. The affairs of the synagogue were administered by a board of elders, and by various lay officials.

The Sabbath worship began with the reading of the Shema, 'Hear, O Israel: The Lord our God is one Lord; and you shall love the Lord your God with all your heart, and with all your soul, and with all your might . . .' (Deuteronomy 6:4–9) Then, after prayers, there followed a fixed reading from the Law, and after that a more freely chosen reading from the prophets. The reader would then sit down to expound what had been read. (We talk of a professor as having the Chair of Philosophy, or Classics, etc. – he *sits* to teach his subject.) Any distinguished visitor might be invited by the president to read and expound what he had read in this way. Jesus chooses the words of Isaiah 61:1–2 to which he adds the words, 'to set free the oppressed', etc. from Isaiah 58:6. It was a reading full of the promises which the Jews believed would be fulfilled in the new age which the Messiah would bring in.

He hands the scroll back to the attendant and sits down to teach, beginning with the electrifying words, 'This passage . . . has come true today, as you heard it being read.' Their immediate delight gives way first to doubt as they begin to say, 'Isn't he the son of Joseph?', and then to blind fury when he points to two notable instances where God's favour had gone out to *Gentiles* rather than to Jews. They are not prepared to hear any gospel that is good news for Gentiles! Jesus has touched the core of their rejection of the mission for which God had chosen Israel. They would like to have killed him, but his 'time' had not yet come. He walks through them, and goes his way. We next find Jesus at Capernaum. It is interesting to note that Nazareth is 1300 feet above sea-level. Capernaum is 682 feet below sea-level.

A Man with an Evil Spirit

One of the things which impressed people during the early period of Jesus's ministry was his authority. First in his teaching: the Rabbis supported everything they said by long quotations from various authorities on the Law. Jesus taught with the direct authority of personal inspiration. The same authority was seen in the way he cast out demons. There was no parleying, no long search for a power that was stronger than the evil spirit, whose aid could be enlisted. Jesus simply commanded the spirit 'Be quiet, and come out of him!' and out it came! There is no wonder that everybody was amazed at his authority and power.

Jesus Heals Many People

In the account of the healing of Simon's mother-in-law, the doctor in St Luke shows himself. 'High fever' is a medical term, probably meaning malaria; and they do not simply 'tell him about her' as in Mark. They (literally) 'consult him' about her. Jesus shows the same authority over disease as he had shown over demons.

The Jews reckoned the days not as we do, from midnight to midnight, but from sunset to sunset. It was forbidden to carry any burden or to do any work on the Sabbath. Thus, the people wait until after sunset before bringing the sick to Jesus to be healed. Jesus is reluctant to be hailed as Messiah because the popular ideas of the Messiah are so far apart from his own. To them, Messiah meant a political conqueror who would sweep Rome into the sea and set the Jews up to rule over the Gentiles. To Jesus it means all that is in the servant prophecies in the book of Isaiah. Before he can accept the title of Messiah, he has to teach them what it really means.

Jesus Preaches in Judea

St Luke now mentions the Kingdom of God for the first time in his gospel. This is the central theme in the preaching of Jesus, and he expounds it in parable after parable. Whenever St Luke mentions Judea, he usually means Palestine as a whole – Judea, the land of the Jews – rather than the actual province of Judea itself.

Jesus Calls the First Disciples (chapter 5)

Gennesaret and Tiberius are alternative names for the Sea of Galilee, which is a stretch of water about thirteen miles long by eight miles wide. Because it lies 680 feet below sea-level, it has an almost tropical climate. It teems with fish, shoals of which often appear unexpectedly, thickly covering the water over a large area. In New Testament times, its shores were thickly populated.

St Luke's account of the call of Simon is very different from that in Mark and Matthew. Commentators have noticed how closely it resembles the encounter between Jesus and Peter by the lakeside after the Resurrection (John 21:1–14), and some have wondered if this is the post-Resurrection story, misplaced by St Luke. The gospels are not technical histories, and their writers were not mainly concerned with accuracy of details. But St Luke knew St Mark's gospel, and had indeed studied it carefully, yet he nevertheless chose his own fuller version of the call of Simon and the first disciples. They may well have had contact with Jesus on a number of occasions before their final decision to leave everything and become his disciples.

Whenever men experience a vision of God, they are always exalted and abased at the same time. God's presence is life, and yet it is judgement. In the presence of Jesus Simon feels both the longing to be with him for ever, and also an utter unworthiness. The words, 'Go

away from me, Lord! I am a sinful man', remind us of
the call of the prophet Isaiah (Isaiah 6:1–8).

Jesus Makes a Leper Clean

One of the most terrible things about leprosy was that it
cut the sufferer off from human contact. He was socially
isolated, and spiritually unclean. He had to wear his
clothes torn, his hair dishevelled, and a flap of material
over his mouth. Whenever anybody approached him he
had to cry, 'Unclean, unclean!' He had to live alone
'outside the camp' (Leviticus 13:45). So, the man should
not have approached Jesus at all (see p. 107). But his
hesitating half doubting plea, 'Sir, if you want to, you
can make me clean!' is met by the immediate willingness
of Jesus, 'I *do* want to . . . Be clean!' and suiting the
action to the words, Jesus reaches out and touches him,
yes, actually touches this poor outcast who was untouch-
able to everybody else. How sweet that touch must have
been! Jesus then sends him to fulfil the demands of the
Law of Moses and be formally declared by the priest
cleansed of his disease, and restored to the community
of Israel (Leviticus 14:3–9).

This section ends with another of St Luke's references
to the importance of prayer in the life of Jesus. St Luke
so often stresses that in the life of our Lord there was a
steady rhythm of prayer and activity. The giving out in
healing and teaching was always preceded and followed
by the taking in, in prayer and quietness. In a time like
ours when public worship is neglected, we might also
note that Jesus worshipped regularly in the synagogue
until the opposition became so intense that he was driven
out (e.g. 4:16).

Jesus Heals a Paralysed Man

The Pharisees were a group within Judaism who were
dedicated to the keeping of the Law of Moses in its
utmost detail and to preserving the purity of the Jewish
religion. 'The teachers of the Law', which is St Luke's
name for the scribes, were those who defined what the
great commandments of the Law meant in every circum-

stance of life that could possibly be imagined. For example, they extended the general commandment not to do any work on the Sabbath (Exodus 20:8–11) into thirty-nine main headings of different kinds of activity which could be called work, and each of these categories was sub-divided still further. Thus, to heal a man on the Sabbath was forbidden as a kind of work – unless his very life was in immediate danger. A plain bandage could be put on a wound to stop it getting worse, but not ointment, because that would begin to make it better, and healing was work, and work was forbidden! Legalism like this was bound to clash irreconcilably with the free and compassionate goodness of Jesus. Again, the scribes and Pharisees held that God alone could forgive sins. For any man to usurp the divine prerogative was blasphemy – speaking against God. The words of Jesus to the paralysed man, 'Your sins are forgiven you, my friend', shocked them profoundly.

But they also believed that sin and sickness were indissolubly linked. If a man was ill, it showed that he had sinned. The Rabbis had a saying, 'There is no man healed from his sickness until all his sins have been forgiven him.' Jesus applies their own logic in a devastating way. When the man gets up and takes his bed – healed – he proves by their own arguments that his sins must be forgiven! They are baffled, and defeated, and enraged. One lovely thing about this story is the sentence, 'When Jesus saw how much faith *they* had, he said to the man . . .' None of us comes to God on his own. We have all been brought into his presence by the love and prayer of others, often through many years, who sometimes care more for us than we care for ourselves.

Jesus Calls Levi

The method of collecting taxes left ample room for the tax gatherers to extort extra money from the common people. Their regular contact with Gentiles made tax gatherers continually ceremonially unclean and, therefore, unable to fulfil their religious duties, and those of them who were directly employed by the Romans were 'quislings' into the bargain. Tax collectors were banned from the synagogues and were treated as the dregs of society.

The Pharisees were shocked that Jesus should seek the company of people like this, and even more shocked that he should enter into the very intimate fellowship of *eating* with them. Jesus's reply reveals the fundamental difference of approach between the Pharisees and himself. They avoided contact with sinners lest their own purity should be defiled. Jesus believed that sinners could only be saved by one who would bring the healing power of God's forgiveness to them. A doctor must have contact with his patients!

The Question about Fasting

In Palestine, newly-weds did not go away for a honeymoon. They stayed at home, and for a week kept open house for their guests. During this time all the laws of fasting were relaxed for 'the children of the bridechamber' as they and their guests were called. The disciples of Jesus are children of the bridechamber while he, the bridegroom, is with them, but the day will come when the bridegroom will be taken away, then they will fast. This is the first hint of our Lord's foreboding of death.

The difference between St Mark's 'No one uses a piece of new (i.e. unshrunk) cloth to patch up an old coat' (Mark 2:21) and St Luke's 'No one tears a piece off a new coat to patch up an old coat' (verse 36) illustrates the way in which slight changes appeared in the sayings of Jesus as they were told and retold during the thirty or more years before the first written gospel appeared. The meaning of both sayings is the same, but the image has become slightly different, and in this case less natural in the later gospel (St Luke) for who would tear a piece from a new coat to mend an old one? Wine bottles were made from skins. A supple new skin would stretch as the wine fermented, but if new wine was put into an old skin that had grown hard, it would burst it.

The meaning of the two parables is clear. The new order of the gospel cannot be confined within the old order of Judaism, nor can it be grafted like a patch on to the old order to repair its deficiencies. Here, in Jesus, is something *fundamentally* new, which needs an entirely new vessel to contain it. Jesus demanded a supple and adventurous spirit from his disciples. They had to think new and shocking thoughts, and leave their old ways to become his followers. Christ makes the same demand of us. We are all tempted to cling to the old orthodoxies and to past outlooks. But we need the kind of faith that is adventurous and open to new truth.

Verse 39 is, in fact, an old proverb. It does not appear in the parallel section in either Matthew or Mark (Matthew 9:17, Mark 2:22). The difficulty in interpreting it is that, of course, old wine *is* better than new! Is Jesus just pointing to the fact that people who are satisfied with the old ways are not likely to support change? Or is he sympathetically drawing attention to another truth of life, namely this, that to leave old ways for new always involves a sacrifice which is difficult to make? We leave something which has been good to us for – nothing – at first, for the new thing has not yet come into being for us, it takes time and faith to create it and enter into it.

The Question about the Sabbath (chapter 6)

In a Gentile world, the keeping of the Sabbath was the outward and public sign of being a Jew, and as such was held in very high respect by the Pharisees. In their eyes the disciples were breaking the Sabbath in no less than four ways. (1) By reaping: they plucked the ears of corn. (2) By threshing: they rubbed them in their hands to separate the wheat from the chaff. (3) By winnowing: they blew the chaff away. (4) By preparing food: they did the first three things to make the corn ready to eat. All these four kinds of work were strictly forbidden on the Sabbath, and the penalty according to the Law for profaning the Sabbath was death (Exodus 31:14). They are seeking a capital charge against Jesus and his disciples.

In his conflicts with the Pharisees Jesus, time and time again, goes down to the deep spiritual principles which are the foundation of the Law of Moses, and tries to make them look with fresh eyes at their own Old Testament. Every Sabbath morning, twelve wheaten loaves, one for each of the twelve tribes of Israel, were laid on a golden table on the north side of the holy place in the temple. The bread represented the presence of God, and was called 'The Bread of the Presence'. It was holy, and only the priests could eat it (Leviticus 24:5–9). Jesus reminds them of how David, their great hero, when he was fleeing for his life from Saul, took this sacred bread for himself and his men (1 Samuel 21:1–6). What does this mean? Does it not mean that human need is more important than ritual observance?

The Man with a Crippled Hand

Healing was another form of work, and so this was also forbidden on the Sabbath, unless there was actual danger to life. (See p. 36.) In this incident, Jesus takes the initiative and challenges the watching scribes and Pharisees to accuse him. He cuts the ground from under their feet by asking, 'What does our Law allow us to do on the Sabbath? To help or to harm?' Who is keeping the spirit of the Sabbath better, they whose malicious design is to harm him, or he whose whole intention is to help the man? For Jesus there is no neutral position between good and evil. To fail to do good is to be on evil's side.

Jesus Chooses the Twelve Apostles

Only St Luke tells us that Jesus spent the whole night in prayer before he chose the twelve out of the much larger number of disciples who were following him. (See p. 13.) This is the founding of the new Israel. As the old Israel had twelve tribes each under its 'judge', so the twelve are to be judges in the new Israel. (See 22:30, and footnote on p. 139.) St Luke always calls them Apostles, a term which is rarely used in the other gospels, and which did not truly apply until after the Resurrection. This emphasizes their eventual role in the Church, for the word means 'someone who is sent out', as for instance an ambassador or envoy (cf. St Paul in Ephesians 6: 19–20).

What a mixed group they were – upper-class John and working-class Peter; quisling Matthew and nationalist Simon; withdrawn Thomas and outgoing Andrew. What arguments and tensions there must have been as they rubbed the corners off each other during their journeyings together. But they were held together and moulded together by Jesus. In all this, they are a miniature of what Christ means his Church to be, a fellowship which transcends all natural and human barriers, held together and moulded together by him.

The Sermon on the Plain   chapter 6:17–49

Jesus Teaches   Happiness and Sorrow   Love for Enemies Judging Others   A Tree and Its Fruit   The Two House Builders

'Coming down from the hill with them, Jesus stood on a level place.' It is interesting to note that there is a level platform halfway down the hill behind Capernaum, the town which figures so prominently in the early ministry of Jesus. The rest of this chapter corresponds to the collection of teaching commonly called 'The Sermon on the Mount' in Matthew, chapters 5–7. St Luke's sermon is briefer and somewhat different. He places it immediately after the call of the twelve as a sort of 'inaugural sermon' of the new Israel. It is a description of life in the Kingdom of God. In its fullness the Kingdom belongs to the end of the age, when all things will be brought to their conclusion. But in Jesus, the Kingdom has already broken into this world, and even now the quality of its life can be tasted.

Three characteristics of life in the Kingdom are given. First, it completely reverses the values of the world as it is today. The best commentary on St Luke's beatitudes (verses 20–26) is provided by the more spiritualized version in Matthew 5:3–10. In Palestine in Jesus's time the devout and faithful in spirit *were* poor, it was those who had come to terms with the heathen régime who were well off. The contrast between the blessings and the woes (Happy are . . . and How terrible for . . . in our translation) reminds us strongly of the Magnificat (1:51–55). God will scatter the proud and lift up the lowly. He will fill the hungry and send the rich away with empty hands. There is a permanent truth here. Our present world is largely organized in sinful contradiction to God's will. The coming of God's rule is bound to reverse its values. The followers of Christ must time and time again reject the world's standards and ways, and in doing so face hostility and isolation.

The second characteristic of life in the Kingdom is love. The Greek word for love which is most commonly used in the New Testament is the word *agape*, and this is the first time it appears in Luke (verse 27). In classical Greek it was little used and was a very weak word like our word 'nice'. This made it easy for Christians to take it and fill it with new meaning, and make it the most common word for love in the New Testament. *Agape* is not the warm affection of family life or the love of friends – *philia* is the word for that. It is not the passionate love between sweethearts or between husband and wife – *eros* is the word for that. *Agape* is the settled goodwill towards another person which always seeks his true welfare however he may respond, and is neither changed nor defeated by hatred or evil. It is the love of God, who is good to the ungrateful and the wicked (verse 35) and makes his sun to shine on bad and good people alike and gives rain to those who do right and those who do wrong (Matthew 5:45f). It is the love of Christ who prayed that even those who were crucifying him should be forgiven and be saved (23:34).

'If anyone hits you on one cheek, let him hit the other one too' (verse 29). Matthew reads, 'If anyone slaps you on the *right* cheek . . .' (5:39) Commentators have pointed out that this suggests an insult – a blow with the back of the hand from a right-handed person to strike the right cheek. Matthew also has, 'if someone takes you to court to sue you for your shirt, let him have your coat as well.' (5:40) The image behind Luke seems to be highway robbery rather than the law court, in which the coat is seized first, then the shirt. Professor Lampe suggests that perhaps St Luke did not realize that in Palestine the cloak, which was also used as a covering for sleeping out of doors, was the more important garment.

We are bound to judge *acts*; stealing is wrong, lying is wrong. We are bound to judge *attitudes*; envy is wrong, jealousy is wrong, hate is wrong. But only God can judge *people*, because only he can know all the facts about them; the pains and deprivations in childhood, the in-born weaknesses of temperament which have gone towards making them what they are today.

Behind verse 38, 'a generous helping, poured into your hands – all that you can hold', is the picture of a peasant woman buying grain, pulling out the fold of her robe above the girdle to form a large pocket, and shaking it up in her hands when it seems to be full so that the grain settles and there is room for more.

The third characteristic of life in the Kingdom is obedience, not to a written code, but to a person, to the King himself. By the side of the wadis which run down from the hills to the Sea of Galilee there is often a sandy strip. It is easy to build on, sheltered, and close to the trickle of water – and water is scarce in Palestine. But when the snows melt on Hermon, the trickle of water can become a raging torrent sweeping all before it, and unless its foundations have been dug right down to the rock the house is doomed. It is not approval of his teaching that Jesus wants, nor enthusiastic acclaim nor even reverence, but *obedience*, and it is the storms of life that show the difference between those who have merely paid him lip service and those whose foundations are laid in a deep inner obedience of heart.

Jesus Heals a Roman Officer's Servant (chapter 7)

Roman soldiers play a creditable part in St Luke's writings both in his gospel and in Acts. The words, 'he himself built a synagogue for us', need not mean that he had given the synagogue himself, but more probably that he had been put in charge of the building work. An Egyptian inscription tells us that Roman officers sometimes undertook work of this kind. The man was a centurion, that is, he was in charge of a hundred men, and corresponded roughly to a company sergeant-major in a modern army. He had been attracted by the purity of Jewish religion, and had perhaps attached himself to the local synagogue as a 'God-fearer', without being circumcised or adopting the whole Jewish Law. He knew that a Jew who entered his Gentile household would be ceremonially defiled, and so he asks Jesus, so great is his faith, merely to say the word that will heal his servant from a distance. It is interesting that he recognized that Jesus's power came from obedience to God, as his own power came from his obedience. When he gave an order that was within his obedience to his superiors, the whole power of the Roman Empire flowed through him. He recognized that because of his perfect obedience to God, the whole power of God himself flowed through the word of Jesus. For St Luke, no doubt, the climax of the story is the praise which Jesus gives to a Gentile, 'I have never found such faith as this, I tell you, not even in Israel!' (verse 9)

Jesus Raises a Widow's Son

Unlike the previous section, this story occurs only in Luke. The village of Nain was about two miles from Shunem where Elisha had raised the son of the Shunammite woman (2 Kings 4:18-37). A very similar story of Elijah raising a widow's son is to be found in 1 Kings 17: 17-24. Indeed the words 'Jesus gave him back to his mother' are exactly the same as those in the Elijah story. The word 'coffin' in verse 14 is an unfortunate translation. The word 'hearse' would be a better modern equivalent, or 'bier' as in the older English versions. The Greek word indicates the long stretcher-like pallet on which the body, wrapped in a linen shroud, was carried to the grave. Because of the heat, people were buried within a few hours of death, and always outside the town. Some may have been buried whilst actually in a coma.

To touch the bier made Jesus unclean according to Jewish ceremonial Law. The people hail him as a great prophet because he has done what Elijah and Elisha, two of the greatest of the early prophets, did. But the heart of the story is Jesus's compassion for the widow who had lost her only son.

In view of all that we now know about the irreversible decay of brain cells which takes place within even the first minute after death, some people are inclined to think that this miracle, and the raising of Jairus's daughter (8:49–56), are miracles of raising from a coma rather than from death. The two Old Testament miracles with which the story is so closely linked could well be such; indeed, Elisha's stretching himself upon the child, 'putting his mouth upon his mouth, his eyes upon his eyes', etc., (2 Kings 4:34) reads very much like a description of the kiss of life, and in the case of Jairus's daughter, Jesus himself says that the child is not dead but only sleeping. But whatever conclusion we may come to, there can be no doubt that the early Church believed that Jesus restored to life and health those whom everybody else had pronounced dead.

The Messengers from John the Baptist

Many a man has cracked in solitary confinement. In the loneliness of a prison cell, even one's deepest convictions can seem doubtful. Is this man the Messiah, about whom John has heard such disturbing stories of consorting with tax gatherers and sinners, or has he been mistaken in him? It must have been an agonizing puzzle for John and so he sends two of his disciples to ask Jesus point-blank.

John had soaked his mind in the prophecies in the second part of the book of Isaiah (Isaiah 40–55). Indeed, he defined his whole life and mission in the words of Isaiah, 'I am the voice of one who shouts in the desert: make a straight path for the Lord to travel.' (Isaiah 40:3) His disciples are present as Jesus heals the sick, drives out evil spirits and gives sight to the blind. Jesus's reply to John has a wonderful depth in it. In effect, he says to them, 'Tell John to go back to Isaiah and read 29:18, 35:5, and 61:1 again. Tell him that you have actually seen all this fulfilled.' This demands from John a new look at his great prophet, for John had expected a Messiah who would shovel the wicked into the fire like chaff!

Jesus then speaks to the crowd about John. What had they gone out into the desert by the Jordan to see? A reed bending in the wind? There were plenty of reed beds by the Jordan, but they didn't go out for that, and nor was John a 'reed man' who could be swayed this way and that by every wind of circumstance. Had they gone out to see a man dressed up in fancy clothes? No! Men who dress like that are found in palaces. St Luke shows his dislike of affluence by adding 'luxury' to the source from which he drew this incident – 'those who dress like that *and live in luxury* are found in palaces.' (cf. Matthew 11:8)

They went out to see a prophet, and what they actually saw was one who was more than a prophet, for John was also the messenger spoken of in Malachi 3:1 sent to 'open the way' for the Messiah. But nevertheless, John belongs to the old order, not to the Kingdom – presumably because he has not given full allegiance to Jesus as the twelve disciples have done, but is still doubtful.[1]

Verses 29 and 30 (which are only in Luke) read as though they are an explanation of the general situation at the time, which St Luke is inserting for the benefit of his Gentile readers who are not familiar with Jewish life in Palestine. They also foreshadow the rejection of Jesus by the Jewish leaders, as they had already rejected John.

We now return (verse 31) to Jesus's discourse. This is one of the places where we glimpse Jesus's interest in children, a quality so rarely found in any of the great men of the ancient world. He must have watched them

1. Matthew 3:14 and John 1:29 suggest that John recognized Jesus at his baptism as Messiah. But neither Mark nor Luke give this impression and theirs is probably the earlier and more trustworthy tradition. Neither does Jesus's remark here that the least in the Kingdom of God is greater than he.

closely as they played at weddings and funerals, and
noticed the contradictious ones who would not join in at
anything! That is exactly what the Jews were like. John
was too unsociable for them, Jesus too sociable; John
was too ascetic, Jesus too permissive!

Jesus at the Home of Simon the Pharisee

This was not just a family meal, but a formal dinner-
party at which the guests reclined at table on couches
instead of sitting. Their feet, sandals removed, were
stretched out behind them. When a Rabbi or some other
distinguished guest had been invited it was common for
people other than guests to come in to hear his conversa-
tion, and often beggars would come too, hoping for
scraps of food. This was how the woman who lived a
sinful life was able to gain admission.

Three courtesies were usually offered to a guest. His
feet, dirty from the street in their open sandals, were
washed by a servant. His head was anointed with a drop
of perfume, and his host greeted him with a kiss of peace.
None of these courtesies was offered to Jesus. If the
woman was able to get to Jesus so easily because he was
near the balcony where the steps led up from the court-
yard, he had also been given one of the lowest seats at
the banquet. She saw that his feet had not been washed
and burst into tears, wetting them as she cried. She then
did a very brazen thing for any Jewish woman to do, she
let down her long hair and wiped Jesus's feet with it, and
then proceeded to anoint them from the little phial or
'alabaster' of perfume which women often wore round
their neck.

Simon would never have compromised his ritual cleanliness by allowing that kind of woman to touch him,
and he muttered to himself that if Jesus had really been a
prophet, he would have sensed straightaway what kind
of woman she was, and sent her packing. Jesus must have
overheard Simon's comment, for he tells him the story
of the two debtors, with its question at the end. The
point of the parable is clear. The woman's thankful love
was a sign that she realized how much had been forgiven

her by God. Simon's little love was a sign – not that he had little for which to be forgiven – but that he had not even begun to waken up to the depth of his need and so had not yet experienced God's forgiveness. When he too had received God's forgiveness, love would be born in his heart as well.

Something may have gone before this meal which St Luke has not told us. It was thought to be a meritorious act to invite travelling teachers who had preached in the synagogue to a Sabbath meal afterwards. Had Jesus preached in the synagogue on God's forgiveness, and impressed them all, especially the woman? We shall never know, but it could have been so.

Women who Accompanied Jesus (chapter 8)

Jesus now leaves the area of Capernaum where no doubt he had many friends with whom he could stay, and becomes a travelling preacher. Only St Luke gives us this little glimpse of the way in which he and his disciples were provided for. Here again, St Luke is pointing out the important place which women had in the life of our Lord. (See p. 13.)

The Parable of the Sower

Only three parables are recorded in all three of the synoptic gospels.[2] They are the mustard seed, the wicked husbandmen, and the sower. A careful comparison of the three versions of the parable reveals St Luke's Gentile background beneath the surface. The phrases 'believing and being saved' and 'the time of testing' (verses 12 and 13) were common phrases in the Gentile Church, and the phrase 'in a good and obedient heart' (verse 15) was as common in classical Greek as the phrase 'in this day and age' is in our own time. When God uses a man, even for the high service of writing a gospel, he does not iron out his individual personality and background. God is a respecter of persons!

Jesus's parables are always vivid stories taken from

2. Matthew, Mark and Luke are called 'synoptic gospels' because they take the 'same view' of the life of Christ.

real life. They usually have one main thrust of meaning. What is the primary meaning of this parable? Think of the situation of Jesus and the disciples at the time when he actually told it. Opposition was growing, some of those who had at first followed him were falling away (cf. John 6:66). Perhaps even the twelve were becoming discouraged. 'Look at that farmer,' says Jesus. 'He is well aware that a lot of his seed will be wasted. But he doesn't give way to discouragement. He sows on, because he *knows* there will be a harvest. And I sow on, because in spite of opposition and the falling away of some, God will bring the glorious harvest which he has promised. God will bring in his Kingdom.'

The Purpose of the Parables

The gospels are written in Greek, but Jesus spoke in Aramaic. It is sometimes possible for a skilful linguist to see behind the Greek text to the Aramaic which it translates. We must remember that there were many 'mystery religions' in the ancient world in which spiritual truths were deliberately made obscure to all but an inner circle. Some people in the early Church may have thought that if a parable of Jesus was puzzling, it was because he intended it to be so, but this kind of approach was, of course, foreign to our Lord.

It surely cannot be that Jesus delivered his parables to prevent people from understanding his teaching, as this section seems to imply. On the contrary, their purpose was to illustrate it and make it clear. After a full discussion of this passage and of the Aramaic which lies behind it, Joachim Jeremias offers the following translation: 'God has given you the secret of his Kingdom, but to those who are outside, everything is puzzling, so that (as it is written) they see but do not perceive, and hear but do not understand, unless they turn around and God forgives them.'[3] In other words, the gospel can only be understood by believers. It is bound to remain a riddle to unbelievers.

3. *Interpreting the Parables,* by J. Jeremias, S.C.M. Press, p. 11f.

Jesus Explains the Parable of the Sower

In reading the parables, we can sometimes detect two levels of meaning. There is the original meaning which Jesus himself gave it in the actual situation of his own earthly life. There is also a second level of meaning which the early Church saw in it as they tried to apply Jesus's teaching to their own lives, and to their own situation, which was often different from the situation in which Jesus told the story in the first place. We ourselves sometimes add a third level of meaning as we try to apply the parables to our modern situation, which is different again.

Many scholars believe that this section is an interpretation by the early Church rather than the words of Jesus, because it turns the parable into an allegory. An allegory is a story in which everything stands for something else. The seed on the path stands for those who did not accept the message at all. The seed on rocky ground stands for those whose response is shallow. The seed among thorns stands for those whose faith was choked by the worries and riches and pleasures of this life; and so on, and so on.

In the ancient world, allegory was the universal way of interpreting religious truth. Most of the fathers of the early Church interpreted the whole of the Old Testament in this way. But Jesus delivered parables, not allegories. (See *Interpreting the Parables*, p. 10.) A parable is a story usually drawn from real life, in which the things in the story are what they are in real life – the farmer is a farmer, the seed, a seed, rocky ground, rocky ground and nothing else. But shining through the earthly situation can be seen the truth of God. In the words of the old Sunday School definition, 'a parable is an earthly story with a heavenly meaning.'

So then, the section explaining the parable may well be the early Church applying it as an allegory to its own situation – and why should we not do the same? We might well, each of us, apply the whole parable to ourselves. I am often the hard soil of the pathway, the man whose heart is too hard for the seed of God's word to get in; and I too am the rocky soil with not sufficient depth to stand up to temptation; and I am also the thorny patch, deluded by the rat race and the lure of money and pleasure which choke my spiritual growth. But by God's grace, I may also be the good ground, where the seed, in spite of all the difficulties, will one day bear fruit for him.

Such an interpretation turns the story into a quite different allegory from the one which the early Church made of it, and it illustrates the danger of allegorizing. By allegorizing, you can make a parable mean almost anything! So we must be aware of the danger and always have in mind the primary meaning which Jesus himself meant his parables to have.

A Lamp under a Bowl

This saying appears with small but very interesting differences in Matthew: 'No one lights a lamp to put it under a bowl; instead he puts it on *the* lamp-stand, where it gives light for everyone in the house.' (Matthew 5:15) But in Luke, Jesus says, 'No one lights a lamp and covers it with a bowl . . . Instead, he puts it on *a* lamp-stand, so that people will see the light as they come in.' (8:16)[4] The background of the saying in Matthew is the Jewish one-roomed peasant cottage, where the only lamp was put in the middle of the room. But the background of Luke is the wealthy Roman villa where there were a number of lamps, one of which was put in the porch at night to light people coming in from the street outside.

Pithy sayings of Jesus like this one seem to have circulated amongst Christians without their original setting being remembered. Thus, St Matthew uses it to illustrate the point that Christians must let their light shine out before men; whereas St Luke uses it to illustrate the point that the truth cannot be suppressed, nor the lie concealed for ever. Everything will finally be revealed in its true colours.

In verse 18 Jesus states one of the great laws of life.

---

4. Our translation is not quite accurate here. The Greek text of Matthew clearly reads 'the', and of Luke 'a'.

The more we use our gifts, the more they will increase. The less we make of them, the less we shall have, until we have nothing.

Jesus's Mother and Brothers

Mark 3:21 and 3:31–35 suggest that Jesus's family did not understand him and thought that he was beside himself. Jesus says quite clearly that natural relationship to him in itself avails nothing, whether it be his own people the Jews, or his own people his family. If they reject him, they put themselves outside the sphere of salvation. The relationship that avails is the spiritual relationship of obedience and trust. It is those who hear the word of God and obey it who are most truly his mother and brothers.

We should take the words 'Your mother and brothers' (verse 20) literally. In support of the doctrine of the perpetual virginity of the blessed virgin Mary, it has sometimes been argued that they were children of Joseph by a former marriage, or that they were cousins of Jesus. But there is no scriptural warrant for this. The plain meaning of Matthew 1:25 is against it ('But he had no sexual relations with her before she gave birth to her son'), and Mark 6:3 gives the names of Jesus's four brothers and also mentions that he had sisters.

Jesus Calms a Storm
Jesus Heals a Man with Demons

These two stories seem to us to be of a quite different kind from each other. The first is a nature miracle. With our knowledge of meteorology, many people today find it difficult to accept it literally. The second is a miracle of psychological healing. With our knowledge of psychiatry, many people today find it much easier to believe this literally. But to St Luke and his readers there was no such division, the two seemed to be both of a kind, for they were both examples of Jesus's authority over 'chaos': the first in nature, the second in human nature.

In the Old Testament the sea is the symbol for all the forces of chaos and evil which are not yet under the rule of God.[5] Psalm 65 links God's power over nature with his power over human nature:

> who dost still the roaring of the seas,
> the roaring of their waves,
> the tumult of the peoples.

Man was intended by God to be lord over nature (Genesis 1:26, Psalm 8), but he has forfeited his lordship by sin. Jesus is perfect Man, and through him the divine power which brings order out of chaos can be seen triumphantly at work. This, it seems, was what both these incidents meant for St Luke and his original readers.

On the natural level there are many interesting details in the two stories. The Sea of Galilee is over 600 feet below sea-level. It is noted for sudden storms which are caused by the wind rushing down the steep ravines cut by the rivers which act like funnels, drawing the cold air down from the highlands above. Suddenly the lake is a boiling cauldron, and then, just as suddenly, it is calm again. It is interesting to notice how the disciples' rebuke to Jesus in Mark 4:38, 'Teacher, don't you care that we are about to die?' is softened in Luke, which was written some twenty years later, when reverence for the risen and ascended Lord had increased in the Church.

Some Christians will believe that Jesus rebuked the storm and stilled it; others that he stilled the storm of fear in the hearts of the disciples, and that the storm on the lake subsided quickly and unexpectedly from natural causes as it often does in Galilee. We must show charity to each other in things like this, and not judge each other's faith or lack of it.

The site of Legion's healing was probably the modern village of Khersa on the east side of the lake, which was mainly Gentile country (e.g. the inhabitants kept pigs – the pig was an unclean animal to the Jews). The man was what we might call today a violent schizophrenic. He

5. Note that in St John's vision of heaven in Revelation 4:6 the sea which is before the throne of God is 'like glass'; i.e. perfectly stilled. At the end of Revelation in 21:1 the sea is no more. 'Then I saw a new heaven and a new earth; for the first heaven and the first earth had passed away, and the sea was no more.' (RSV Common Bible)

had perhaps been driven out of his mind as a child by witnessing the frightful atrocities of the Roman legion which put down the rising of Judas of Galilee in AD 6. The Romans crucified almost two thousand young Jews in Galilee. That could have been why he now called himself Legion. Or could it be that he felt so utterly bad that he felt there was a whole legion of devils inside him? He lived among the burial caves, which in popular imagination were the haunt of demons and unclean spirits.

Seeing Jesus, he casts himself down with a cry, hailing him with the Gentile title 'Son of the Most High God'. Jesus demands his name. To know the name of a person or spirit meant to have power over him (cf. Genesis 32: 27–29). His reply is 'Legion'. A legion was a Roman division of 6000 troops! It is a pity that our translation reads 'mob'. Not every word in the Bible needs modernizing! In any case, whatever a Roman legion was, it was not a mob. The discipline and precision of the Roman legions was one of the wonders of the ancient world.

Pigs are unclean animals to the Jew – a suitable haunt for devils. They are also easily frightened when they are herded together. They may well have panicked at Legion's screams and cries, and dashed over the cliff edge to destruction. It was also popularly believed that the only way to destroy a demon for ever was to drown it in deep water.

Contrary to his usual practice of forbidding those he had healed to publish it, Jesus tells Legion to go back home and tell what God has done for him. This may have been because he was a Gentile, living in a community which had not got any false ideas of the Messiah to unlearn. Significantly, the man goes through the whole town, telling what *Jesus* had done for him.

Jairus's Daughter and the Woman Who Touched Jesus's Cloak

During this part of his ministry Jesus had no privacy. Wherever he went he was besieged by human need. The synagogues were ruled by a committee of elders. Jairus

was the president of one and had the duty of controlling
its worship. At this time when the synagogues were being
closed to Jesus, and opposition to him was hardening,
it must have taken some courage and perhaps some
pocketing of his pride for Jairus to seek Jesus's help.

It makes no difference to Jesus that the request comes
from a man who is a prominent member of a group that
is out to destroy him. Jesus really does love his enemies
and do good to those who hate him (6:27). Entering the
house, he takes with him only Peter, John and James,
the three who formed the inner circle of the disciples.
The little girl may not have been dead. If we take literally
the words of Jesus, 'she is only sleeping', she was not.
St Luke, writing for Gentile readers, omits the lovely
Aramaic phrase in Mark, 'Talitha cumi', with which he
lifts her up.

Many commentators have noticed how sensitive Jesus
was to the feelings of the parents who needed something
practical to do to be able to contain their emotions –
'Give her something to eat.' In contrast to the command
to Legion to spread the news of what God had done for
him, now that he is back in a Jewish environment, Jesus
commands them not to tell anybody what has happened.

The woman who touched Jesus's cloak probably
suffered from menorrhagia, a continuous menstrual flow.
St Luke the doctor softens Mark's comment that in spite
of spending all that she had on doctors, she got worse all
the time! The most terrible thing about this distressing
complaint was that it cut her off from all social contact
and from all public worship too. She had to live her life
isolated from people and feeling isolated from God
because she was continuously ceremonially unclean, and
she made anybody she touched unclean like herself
(Leviticus 15:19–30). That was why she crept up behind
Jesus and discreetly touched one of the four tassels which
every devout Jew wore at the corners of his cloak to
remind him of the commandments of God (Numbers
15:37–41).

She must have been terrified when Jesus turned round
and asked who touched him. But so sensitive was he

that he had distinguished the deliberate touch from the casual pressure of the crowd. Every contact with human need cost Jesus something. He was giving out. It was in times of prayer, often while the disciples were still asleep, that he renewed his resources in communion with his Father.

It is a mark of love that he does not let the woman go away unknown and unhealed in spirit, guilty perhaps at the wrong thing she had done to him by touching him. He draws her into a warm relationship with himself (note the affectionate address to her, 'My daughter') and bids her go in peace. He restores her in soul as well as body.

Jesus Sends out the Twelve Disciples (chapter 9)

There are at least three reasons why Jesus sends the twelve out on their missionary tour. (1) There comes a stage in the training of any pupil when he has listened and watched long enough, he can only learn more by doing it himself. (2) There are indications that in spite of the crowds and the popularity, the beheading of John the Baptist gave Jesus a deep sense of foreboding and urgency. (3) In view of the crowds and their continual demands on him, Jesus himself could not hope to cover the whole territory of Israel, especially if his time was to be short.

There is a sense of urgency about the mission. They are not to go equipped for a long tour and they are not to spend time on those who reject them but are to say in effect, 'You have elected to be as the heathen', and pass on. This is what shaking the dust off their feet amounted to (verse 5). When a Rabbi returned to Israel from a foreign journey, he shook off the last particle of Gentile soil from his shoes in order to avoid bringing heathen dust into the Holy Land of Israel.

Herod's Confusion

The missionary tour must have raised a great furore because the talk of it was so widespread that it reached Herod. He had only just disposed of John the Baptist, and now there was another of these religious leaders to come to terms with! His desire to see Jesus for himself is mentioned again by St Luke later (23:8).

Herod seems to have been a man who was 'interested in religion' in a casual sort of way (cf. Mark 6:20). But he could not be brought to face God. The revolutionary changes in his life and morals which taking God seriously would have demanded of him were too much, so he stayed at the level of discussing religion to avoid its challenge. He has many successors in our own day!

Jesus Feeds the Five Thousand

Both Matthew and Mark say that Jesus took his disciples to a lonely place when they returned from their mission. But St Luke says 'to a town named Bethsaida' (verse 10), and yet, only two verses later (verse 12) they are asking Jesus to send the crowd to the nearby villages to get food 'because this is a lonely place'. Torrey suggests that St Luke mistook the Aramaic word for 'fields' or 'open country' for the very similar word for 'city', so that we should really read that Jesus took his disciples to 'the open country round Bethsaida'.

Bethsaida was just outside the jurisdiction of Herod and it may well have been for safety's sake that Jesus went there. He is not to be trapped unwittingly by Herod and imprisoned as John had been, to be done away with later at the tetrarch's whim. When Jesus goes to Jerusalem to die, it will be because he knows that his time has come. The initiative will be his and his alone.

The feeding of the five thousand is the only miracle recorded in all four gospels. This is surely a sign of how important this story was to the early Church. Many people today find it difficult to interpret the story literally for both scientific and religious reasons. With our present knowledge of the natural world it is difficult to believe that matter can be multiplied like this, and from a religious point of view it is difficult to see how such superhuman power can be reconciled with the full humanity of Jesus.

It is interesting that nowhere in the story is it directly

said that Jesus multiplied the bread. The suggestion of miracle only comes indirectly with the gathering-up of the fragments. Some scholars think that it was a *sacramental* meal in which each received a morsel of bread, as at holy communion. In favour of this view, we may note that in Mark, the earliest gospel, the language of the story is very close indeed to the words of the Last Supper (cf. Mark 6:41 with Mark 14:22) and with the practice of the early Church at the breaking of bread where the president gave the elements to the deacons to distribute amongst the worshippers, as Jesus here gives the bread to the disciples to distribute.

Others think that the miracle was a miracle of *sharing*. Inspired by Jesus, everybody shared what he had, and there was more than enough for all. Others again take the story literally as a miracle of multiplying five loaves to feed five thousand.

But whatever our position, we must not think that the divinity of Jesus in any way depends on whether or not he performed miracles. We believe that he is the Son of God because of the life of perfect love to his Father and to all men whether friends or enemies, which he led even to death, yes, and death on a Cross. That is the real miracle about our Lord Jesus Christ (cf. Philippians 2:5–11). Neither must we miss the rich overtones which are the most important thing about this story. It looks back to God's deliverance of his people from Egypt when Israel was fed by manna in the wilderness (Exodus 16:12–15). The account in the fourth gospel stresses this aspect again and again (John 6:31, 48–51, 58). It also looks forward to the fulfilling of all things in the new age of the Messiah. This new age was frequently pictured as a banquet (e.g. Isaiah 25:6–8) and it is a symbol which Jesus himself often used in his preaching (e.g. Luke 13:29 and 14:16–24). Here in the open country as he bids farewell to his Galilean supporters before turning his face to Jerusalem and the Cross, Jesus breaks bread with them in a sacramental foretaste and pledge of the Messianic feast which will be consummated 'when he comes' (1 Corinthians 11:26).

Peter's Declaration about Jesus
Jesus Speaks about His Sufferings and Death

St Luke's statement that Jesus was praying when his disciples came to him is a clear indication that he is about to introduce something of critical importance (see p. 29) in the life of Jesus. In spite of the way in which Jesus has contradicted so much of the universally accepted expectations of what the Messiah would be like, the twelve have come to the firm conviction, 'You are God's Messiah.' This must have been a moment of great exaltation for Jesus. He is now able to go on and take them a crucial and shocking stage further. The Messiah must suffer and be rejected and be put to death. St Luke omits what both Matthew and Mark tell us, that Peter immediately took him to task about this and received one of the sharpest rebukes in the gospel. The disciples have still much to learn about their master and about the Messiah.

In verse 23 St Luke alone adds the words 'every day' to the command to 'take up his cross . . . and follow me'. 'My servant will be with me where I am,' says Jesus at this point in the fourth gospel (John 12:25–26). The closer we draw to our Lord, the more deeply we shall be made one with him. We shall be with him in his suffering, sharing with him the pain and burden of the world's sin, and finally we shall be with him in glory, sharing his Kingdom.

The saying about saving one's life and losing it (verse 24) occurs no less than six times, and is in all four gospels. This is a sign of its importance. It is one of the great and universal spiritual truths. The parent who tries to cling to his growing children loses them; the husband who is possessive of his wife destroys their relationship. What we hoard and hug to ourselves we lose. What we adventure for God we keep. It is in letting go, in losing ourselves that we find ourselves, and life eternal.

The Transfiguration

Once again St Luke alone tells us that Jesus was praying

when he was transfigured. St Luke never loses an opportunity of stressing that all the great moments in the life of Jesus, and all his great decisions, take place in the setting of prayer; they spring out of his communion with God.

The Transfiguration must have been an awesome mystical experience both for Jesus and for the disciples. It had the directness of living experience, and conveyed countless undertones of meaning within itself. It carried its own conviction and needed no explanation or confirmation. Our way of entering into it is to try to understand some of the many undertones of meaning which were conveyed directly in the vision itself to Jesus and the three disciples.

In Moses and Elijah, the Law and the Prophets, that is, the whole of Jewish religion, are brought together. All that has gone before in God's dealings with his people is to be gathered up in the decision to go to Jerusalem which Jesus is now taking. They talk to him about his dying (the actual Greek word used is *exodus*) which he will soon fulfil in Jerusalem. Indeed, by his death Jesus will accomplish a greater deliverance even than Moses did in the exodus from slavery in Egypt, for Jesus will deliver us from the slavery of our sins.

The baptism of Jesus had been marked by God's voice confirming him at the beginning of his ministry. Now as he realizes that the fulfilment of his work as Messiah must be to die in Jerusalem, the same voice commissions him again as he turns his face to the Cross.

For the disciples the Transfiguration must have been a wonderful confirmation of their growing faith in Jesus. There was the cloud, which in the Old Testament always symbolized the presence of God. There were Moses and Elijah, two of the greatest figures in Israel's history, both of whom were associated with the coming of the Messiah, and who together symbolized the whole of Israel's religion – Moses the Law, and Elijah the prophets. Peter, practical down-to-earth Peter, wants to build three tabernacles, as Israel had built a tabernacle in the wilderness to enshrine the glory of God. But a vision cannot be held, it must always be realized in everyday life, and this vision must be realized through suffering and death for Jesus and eventually for them too, for as he promised, 'My servant will be with me where I am.'

Jesus Heals a Boy with an Evil Spirit

St Luke has very much abbreviated the vivid story in Mark. Jesus comes down from the mount to a scene of confusion and defeat. The father is disappointed, the disciples are defeated, the boy is unhealed. The account of his condition is a classic description of epilepsy.

In the words, 'How long must I stay with you? How long do I have to put up with you?' (verse 41) we can detect the sheer human weariness of Jesus, and the spiritual strain that he was undergoing, preoccupied as he was with the terrible prospect of the Passion that lay ahead. One of the great temptations of Christians from the earliest days has been to play down the full humanity of our Lord and to make him into a supernatural figure who 'knew it all beforehand and walked six inches above the ground'. This temptation is seen even as early as the gospels themselves, because looking back from the vantage point of the Ascension, they sometimes write as though things which only became clear afterwards were clear at the time of their happening. But they were not. Life unfolded to Jesus as it unfolds to us, and he walked by faith as we walk by faith. He was a real human being who grew tired as we do, and when he was under great strain sometimes found people difficult to bear with, as we often do. Little phrases like the one here allow us a glimpse of the completely and perfectly human Jesus.

For the vivid details of the healing of the boy the reader must turn to Mark 9:14–27, which fills out St Luke's abbreviated version and makes adequate comment on it.

Jesus Speaks again about His Death

We might wonder how the disciples can have been so obtuse! But it is amazing how people can be unable to take in what they don't want to hear, and quite unable to understand even simple truths which contradict their cherished and deeply held beliefs. St Luke offers the suggestion that God himself must have hidden it from them so that they could not understand.

Who Is the Greatest?

Nothing shows the gulf between Jesus and his disciples more clearly than this incident. To him, greatness lay in humble and self-forgetting service. Their hearts were set on power and precedence – who comes first. Jesus's own words in John 5:44 provide a perfect comment on this section: 'You like to have praise from one another, but you do not try to win praise from the only God; how, then, can you believe?'

Who Is not against You Is for You

This section offers us a lesson in tolerance. There were many exorcists in Palestine who claimed to cast out demons by the aid of some good and more powerful name or spirit, and the name of Jesus was being used in this magical way. The history of the Church has often been marred by the exclusiveness which insists that anybody who is not of our denomination does not belong to the true Church, or, anybody who does not think exactly as we do 'is not saved'. We might well compare the saying here, 'Whoever is not against you is for you', with a very similar (but very different!) saying later in the gospel, 'Anyone who is not for me is really against me; anyone who does not help me gather is really scattering.' (11:23) We might well apply the first saying to other people – are they actually working against Jesus? If not, they are our allies; and the second saying to ourselves – if I am not actually for Jesus, then I am really against him.

Part 4

THE WAY TO JERUSALEM

In Matthew and Mark it is almost possible to plot the journey of Jesus on the map. But the next ten chapters in Luke are a rich source of teaching, and particularly of that precious material which is given to us only by St Luke. Between here and 18:15 (the point at which St Luke returns to Mark's framework of events) there are no less than thirteen parables which are only in this gospel. Among them are the two greatest parables Jesus ever told, the Good Samaritan and the Prodigal Son.

From time to time there is a reminder that Jesus is on the fateful journey that ends in Jerusalem – St Luke mentions this to maintain the dramatic tension, but his main interest is in the teaching not the travelling. In any case, he was probably not familiar with the detailed geography of Palestine, and it would certainly not be important to his Gentile readers.

A Samaritan Village Refuses to Receive Jesus

The word 'exodus' for Jesus's death in the Transfiguration story reminds us of Moses; so now the words 'taken up to heaven' remind us of Elijah, the other one who was with him on the mount, for according to 2 Kings 2:9–11 Elijah did not die, but was taken up to heaven in a whirlwind.

The bitter feud between the Jews and the Samaritans had many roots, racial and political as well as religious. The rival temples, one on Mount Gerazim and the other in Jerusalem, each claimed to be the one true sanctuary of the Deuteronomic Law (Deuteronomy 12) and were symbols of the hostility between them. The Samaritans were especially hostile to pilgrims going through their country to Jerusalem. For this reason, Jewish pilgrims going from Galilee usually avoided Samaria and went the longer way round through Perea. Pious Pharisees would not defile themselves with Samaritan soil anyway! Jesus makes an offer of friendship in wanting to visit the Samaritan village, but when they realize that he is on his way to Jerusalem, they spurn him and will have nothing to do with him. James and John want to call down fire from heaven – another reminder of Elijah who called down fire on the troops of the King of Samaria (2 Kings 1:9f). But the way of Jesus is not to call down God's curse on his enemies but to love them and die for them. Some later manuscripts of Luke add at the end of verse 55 the words: 'and he said, "You do not know what manner of spirit you are of; for the Son of man came not to destroy men's lives but to save them." ' Scholars tell us that these words are not part of the gospel as St Luke originally wrote it. But whether they are or not, they have the authentic ring of Jesus about them.

The Would-Be Followers of Jesus

This section is dominated by the urgency of the journey to Jerusalem. The first man is bidden to count the cost of following Jesus, who has 'no place to lie down and rest'. St John uses the very same Greek word for the final rest on the Cross when Jesus 'bowed his head' and died (John 19:30).

The second man wants to wait until his parents die, and then, free of family responsibilities, he can follow Jesus. But the work of the Kingdom is too urgent for that, and even the sacred ties of family life must come second to the demands of God (cf. Matthew 10:37).

The third example is not given in the parallel passage in Matthew. The saying about the plough sounds almost like a proverb. Ploughs in Palestine had only one handle, and it required a man's whole attention and energy to cut a straight furrow through the hard soil.

Jesus Sends Out the Seventy-two (chapter 10)

St Luke alone tells us of the mission of the seventy-two, who are not heard of again in the gospel story. Many manuscripts give the number as seventy. In other parts of the Bible too there is often uncertainty between seventy and seventy-two. It was a highly symbolic number. It is a number that means world mission. (How appropriate to St Luke the Gentile!) Seventy (or seventy-two) scholars had translated the Old Testament from Hebrew into Greek which was the universal language of the ancient world. The Jews believed that there were seventy-two nations on the earth – twelve, the number of the tribes of Israel multiplied by six, which was the 'worldly' number.

It is also the number that means helpers. There were seventy members of the Sanhedrin, the Supreme Jewish Council. Moses had appointed seventy (or seventy-two) assistants to help him to administer the affairs of the children of Israel as they journeyed through the wilderness to the Promised Land (Numbers 11:16–17). Now, Jesus is looking symbolically outward to every race of men and like a second Moses is sharing the burden of his work.

The instructions given to the seventy are almost the same as those given to the twelve (9:1–6) but with the extra note of urgency that they are not to stop to greet anyone on the road. Much time is wasted in the Near East in elaborate salutations. They are to heal the sick and to preach. Their message is to be that, 'The Kingdom of God has come near you.' The Kingdom of God was the central theme of Jesus's own preaching. They are not to spend time on those who will not welcome them (cf. 9:4–5).

The Unbelieving Towns

Every approach of God to us is a crisis. (*Krisis* is the Greek word for judgement.) His drawing near brings peace and new life if we accept it. But if we do not, it becomes a judgement, for our very rejection of his grace puts us further from God than we were before. Chorazin and Bethsaida are worse than Tyre and Sidon, for God has drawn close to them in Jesus and they have by and large rejected him. Tyre and Sidon would perhaps have repented like Nineveh did when God's word came to her (cf. Jonah 3:5).

The Return of the Seventy-two

While the Seventy-two were away, Jesus in a vision saw Satan falling like lightning, defeated. It was a common belief that the world and especially the Gentile world lay under the dominion of Satan (cf. 4:5–7). This was a vision of the future, for it was on the Cross that the powers of evil were totally and finally defeated. It may too have been a vision of the final consummation of all things in the age to come (cf. Revelation 12:8–9). The success of the seventy-two was only a foretaste of victory.

The words, 'Rather be glad because your names are written in heaven' (verse 20), refer to the practice of posting up outside an ancient city the names of its inhabitants. It was believed that God himself kept such a register (cf. Exodus 32:32, Isaiah 4:3, Daniel 12:1). To have one's name written in heaven meant to have a secure place in the age to come.

Jesus Rejoices

This section is of great theological importance. Some people have argued that with the passing of the years, the early Church turned the prophet Jesus of Nazareth into a divine figure, Jesus the Son of God. St Paul has sometimes been held mainly responsible for this transformation.

There was certainly a growth in the Church's understanding of Jesus, and without doubt the Jesus of the fourth gospel (the last to be written about AD 100) is a much more exalted figure than the Jesus of Mark (the earliest to be written about AD 65). But here, coming from St Luke's source which is known as 'Q' (the source which he shares with Matthew), *which is even earlier than Mark*, is a statement of the unique Sonship of Jesus, so clear that it might well have come straight from the pages of the fourth gospel (cf. John 3:35, 6:46, 14:9, 17:10). Furthermore, it has about it the rhythm of Hebrew poetry which suggests that it existed even earlier than the first translation into Greek.

Jesus had been conscious of a special relationship between himself and the Father at least since his baptism. He had lived in complete obedience to it. Now, it comes to full flower, and he realizes the perfect and *unique* unity that exists between himself and God (cf. John 10: 30) and how completely God has entrusted his eternal purpose into his hands. The time that prophets and devout kings of many generations had longed for is now here, and the disciples are blessed indeed to experience it.

The Parable of the Good Samaritan

'A certain teacher of the Law . . . tried to trap Jesus.' The Greek word means rather 'to put to the test' than 'to trap'. He wanted to try Jesus out on a theological point which was a common subject of discussion amongst Rabbis and teachers of the Law. It was widely held that the two commandments, to love God and to love one's neighbour, summed up the whole Law. But the Rabbis argued endlessly on two points. First, could any of the 613 commandments in the Law be considered weightier or greater than the rest, and second, exactly who was included in the term 'neighbour'? Did it include Gentiles? Did it include enemies?

The lawyer is not really seeking information. He wants to start a theological discussion which will test Jesus as an expositor of scripture. But Jesus is not to be led into a theological discussion that is unrelated to life. He first throws the man's question back, and he shows straight away that he had known the answer to it before he asked it! When he continues to ask for a definition of just who is one's neighbour, Jesus tells him a brilliant story which brings him face to face with a question he had not asked, namely, 'To whom should I be a neighbour?' The answer of the story is: to anybody whose need makes a claim on my love. Let us look now at the details of the parable.

Jerusalem is 2300 feet above sea-level. Jericho is 1300 feet below sea-level. So, in just over twenty miles, the road falls 3600 feet. The man was certainly going down from Jerusalem to Jericho! On either side of the road the country is honeycombed with narrow defiles and twisting wadis, which make it an ideal haunt of bandits. It was known as the Bloody Way. It is not surprising that the man was robbed and beaten up and left lying half dead by the roadside.

That was what posed the problem for the priest. Was he dead or not? If he was, and even his shadow passed over the body, the priest would be ceremonially unclean. If he touched the man, and he proved to be dead, the priest would be unable to perform any of his religious duties for a week. The man looked dead, and so, rather than take the risk, the priest passed by on the other side of the road, where not even his shadow would cross the body. The Levite did the same thing, and for the same reason. They both put ritual purity before human need.

Popular stories often have three characters in them – like the Englishman, the Scotsman and the Irishman, and the stress usually falls on the last one. Again, there are many well-known 'threes' that go together, and when anybody mentions the first two, our minds automatically supply the third – e.g. navy, army and (of course) air force. In the same way, when our Lord mentioned priest and Levite, all his hearers would be expecting Israelite to follow. So, the ordinary Jewish layman, the Israelite, is to be the hero of the story! Imagine the pleasure of the crowd. Priest and Levite are to be taken down a peg! Imagine their pleasure, and imagine their anger when the third character proves not to be an Israelite but of all people a hated Samaritan![1] When Jesus asks the lawyer which one had been a neighbour to the injured man, he will not even use the word Samaritan, but replies, '*The one* who was kind to him.'

The Samaritan when he came poured oil and wine into the man's wounds. This is a typical medical note on St

1. In the time of Jesus, relations between the Jews and Samaritans had become more embittered than ever. Some time between AD 6 and 9 during Passover the Samaritans had defiled the temple in Jerusalem by strewing dead men's bones in its courts, thus making it unusable for worship on the greatest feast of the year. See also p. 62.

Luke's part. Wine was a popular antiseptic, and oil was used to soothe and promote healing. The words 'put the man on his own animal', together with his obvious familiarity with the innkeeper, suggest that the Samaritan was a merchant of some sort who carried his goods on one ass or mule and rode a second beast himself.

There are still the remains of an ancient inn on the Jerusalem-Jericho road. The wording of the Greek text can well be taken to suggest that he actually sat up all night with the man. On the following morning, he leaves two denarii – two days' wages for a working man – with the innkeeper, with the promise that when he comes back that way he will pay any further expenses. His credit was good, no doubt because he was 'a regular' and often stayed overnight on his journeys.

We take the parable to be a command to love our neighbour with a practical and self-sacrificing love. We are right, and all down the centuries it has been an inspiration for social care and compassion. But was that what Jesus himself meant by it when he originally told the parable? If it was, why did he not choose an ordinary Israelite as everybody expected he would, as the hero of the story? Why choose a hated Samaritan and thereby invite the hostility of his hearers?

The reason may well be that it was the narrow nationalism of his fellow countryman that Jesus wanted to highlight. The Jews in Jesus's time would have felt no obligation whatever to help any of their traditional enemies - such as the Romans or Samaritans, or indeed any Gentile of whatever race. These people were not neighbours! By taking as the hero of his story a Samaritan who was prepared to be a neighbour to one of his worst traditional enemies, Jesus wanted to shock his hearers out of their narrow and exclusive nationalism. 'You go, then, and do the same' means 'treat anybody of any race and any nation (and any colour!) as a neighbour'.

Jesus Visits Martha and Mary

Having just recounted a parable which praises 'practical

Christianity', St Luke skilfully follows it with a story which balances it.

Mary, sitting in rapt attention, is absorbed in listening to Jesus. Generations of Christians have seen in her a model of the contemplative life of prayer and meditation. Martha and the Good Samaritan on the one hand, and Mary on the other, illustrate the twofold rhythm of the spiritual life in which service and prayer both have their place. Our Lord himself is the perfect example of the balance between the two. (See also p. 55.)

It is important to notice that Mary is not praised at the expense of Martha. The monastic life is not 'better' than the secular life, as was argued from this text in the Middle Ages. Jesus defends Mary against Martha's attack. Nor does Jesus rebuke Martha for her practical temperament. The gentle rebuke is directed at her fussy anxieties and her self-pity. To renew her spiritual resources she needs what Mary is determined to have.

Jesus's Teaching on Prayer (chapter 11)

Once again St Luke shows us Jesus at prayer. Rabbis often gave their disciples model prayers, and the twelve ask Jesus to do the same for them. The Lord's Prayer as it stands in Luke is shorter, less Jewish and less rhythmical than in Matthew. The version in Matthew is more liturgical. It has been smoothed and polished by some years of use in the worship of the Jewish Christian Church.

'Father' is the Aramaic word *Abba* which was a child's normal way of addressing his father. It was our Lord's uniquely intimate and childlike way of addressing God. 'May your holy name be honoured' – in Hebrew the name meant much more than merely what a person was called. It expressed and stood for his whole character and personality. Compare, for instance, 'I have manifested thy name to the men whom thou gavest me out of the world' (John 17:6, RSV Common Bible) with our present TEV translation of the same verse, 'I have made you known to the men you gave me out of the world.' God's name is his whole nature and purpose. It is kept holy when his nature and his purposes are known and reverenced. 'May your Kingdom come' – God's Kingdom is not a territory as when we say 'throughout the length and breadth of the kingdom'. His Kingdom is his rule in the hearts of men – God's reign. His kingship is here now, and perfectly in Jesus like a tiny piece of leaven in the lump of humanity, or like a tiny mustard seed. But it must grow and become a tree in whose branches the birds of the air can make their nests (13:18). It is interesting to note that 'the birds of the air' was a way of referring to great empires such as Babylon and Assyria.

'Give us day by day the food we need' – the Greek word translated 'day by day' is only found here and in the Lord's Prayer in Matthew (6:11). There has been a great deal of discussion as to exactly what it means. It was once found in an old papyrus manuscript (which has since been lost!) where it clearly referred to rations served out the night before for the coming day.

'Forgive us our sins, because we forgive . . .' – the forgiveness of our sins is linked with our forgiving everyone who has done wrong to us. This is hard teaching, for when we have been deeply wronged and hurt it is an agony to forgive those who have wronged us. We find it beyond our power. But the gospel will not allow us any escape. 'I may forget but I can never forgive' will not do. The cleansing joy of knowing God's forgiveness ourselves, and the pain of forgiving others who have sinned against us, are inseparably joined together like the two sides of a coin.

'And do not bring us to hard testing' – the Jews believed that the end of this age and the coming of the new age of the Messiah would be marked by the full revelation of anti-Christ, and a time of the most intense suffering and convulsions of the whole world order such as had never been known before (cf. 21:25–28). But this would herald the final triumph of God's Kingdom. The early Christians (and perhaps Jesus himself) expected this to come in the lifetime of the original disciples (cf. 1 Thessalonians 4:15–17). It is to this final test that this sentence in the Lord's Prayer originally referred. So, in the New English Bible, and in the new translation of the Lord's Prayer made for use in public worship by an international committee of all the main Christian denominations, the wording used is 'do not bring us to the test', and it is this final time of trial that they have in mind. But the great and final time of trial need not exclude the 'hard testing' which each one of us must undergo, and from which we shrink and pray to be delivered, as our Lord himself in the garden of Gethsemane shrank from the hard testing of the Cross and prayed that he might be spared it (22:42–44).

Many writers have pointed out that the Lord's Prayer begins with adoration which is the mountain peak of prayer, and continues with concern for God's will and God's Kingdom, and then after all that, turns to our own needs. This is the right order for prayer.

The Friend Who Came at Midnight

There is a lovely touch of humour about this parable. Travellers in Palestine often journey late to avoid the scorching midday heat. When the man arrives, the day's baking has all been eaten. But in the east the law of hospitality is sacred, the guest must be provided for, and so, late as it is, his host goes to a neighbour to borrow bread.

The Palestinian cottage was just a one-roomed house, earth floored with a raised platform at one end. At night the family put their sleeping mats on the raised part and lay down in a row close together for warmth. The domestic animals were brought into the lower part and the door was shut and bolted with a long iron bar going right across it through iron rings. There was no electric light. It would be impossible to get up without waking the whole family, not to mention the animals. So the man replies, 'Don't bother me! The door is already locked, and my children and I are in bed.' But the neighbour is not to be put off so lightly. He carries on knocking until it is obvious that the only way to quieten him is to get up and give him what he wants! Jesus's hearers must have smiled at the humour of the situation. Jesus ends the story with the words, 'Ask, and you will receive; seek, and you will find; knock, and the door will be opened to you.' Ask, seek, knock – in the Greek, these three words are present imperatives, and the important point about a present imperative in Greek is that it is a command to *continuous action*. Keep on asking; keep on seeking; keep on knocking; as the man in the parable did.

The root meaning of the word 'parable' is to put one thing by the side of another. One can do this either to show how much alike the two things are (as Jesus often does in his parables of the Kingdom), or to show how much they differ from each other. In this parable, Jesus is doing the second thing, he is pointing the contrast between the unwillingness of the man who was knocked up and the willingness of God who loves his children. 'As bad as you are, you know how to give good things to your children. *How much more, then,* your Father in heaven will give good things to those who ask him!' (Matthew 7:11) St Luke has changed Matthew's 'good things' to the best gift of all, 'give the Holy Spirit to those who ask him'.

Jesus and Beelzebul

The word Beelzebul is not found anywhere outside the Bible, and there are different spellings of it in different manuscripts (e.g. Beelzebub). In New Testament times it meant 'Prince of the devils' and stood for Satan himself. Its origin is amusing. Baal-zebhul was the god of the Philistine town of Ekron. The name meant 'Lord of the House'. The heathen Baals were fertility gods, whose worship was supposed to ensure good harvests. The writer of the book of Kings with a rather nice sense of humour called the god of his enemies not Baal-zebhul but Baal-zebub, which means 'Lord of Flies' (2 Kings 1:2). Baal-zebbul meant 'Lord of Manure', which added to the joke!

Jesus's reply to his opponents is so clear that it hardly needs comment. (1) Do they really think that Satan is destroying his own kingdom by fighting against himself?

(2) What about other exorcists whose work they applaud? Why don't they accuse them of being in league with the devil? (3) Must it not be by God's power (literally the finger of God[2] – cf. Exodus 8:19) that he overcomes demons, and doesn't that show that the Kingdom of God has already broken through the power of evil?

In verse 22 our Lord may well be taking up the proper meaning of the word Beelzebul (Lord of the House) which his critics have used. The Lord of the House can only be dispossessed of his property when one stronger than he comes and attacks him and defeats him.

The Return of the Evil Spirit

To the ancients, the whole world was peopled by evil spirits which might enter into you and inhabit you. They were thought to roam especially through desert places where they screamed and howled (hence the phrase 'a howling wilderness'). So, when an evil spirit went out of a man it was thought to travel over dry places seeking somewhere to rest. If it could not find anywhere it returned, and if it found its old house clean and all fixed up and *empty*, it might easily bring seven other spirits (note the perfect number seven to indicate the complete possession by evil which follows) and reoccupy its old home.

It is strange that St Luke omits the word *empty* (cf. Matthew 12:44). Only if the house is empty can it be re-occupied. The lesson of the parable is very close to verse 23 above, 'Anyone who is not for me is really against me . . .' Nobody can be neutral in the war of God against the powers of evil. If the vacuum is not filled by God it will inevitably be filled by the devil. It also teaches the futility of a negative religion which casts out this, and forbids that. There must be an in-filling of positive goodness as well.

2. Matthew reads 'by God's Spirit'. St Luke never uses the phrase 'Spirit of God' or 'God's Spirit'. For St Luke, the Holy Spirit is always connected with Jesus; preparing men for his coming into the world: fully incarnate in him during his earthly life: and filling his followers after Pentecost.

True Happiness

The woman pays Jesus a conventional and extravagant compliment. 'Your mother is a fortunate woman to have a son like you.' Jesus replies with an unexpected seriousness which must have brought the woman up short.

The Demand for a Miracle

The Jews were always asking for miracles as a 'sign' from God. As St Paul says, 'Jews want miracles for proof, and Greeks look for wisdom.' (1 Corinthians 1:22) The only sign they will get, says Jesus, is the sign of a prophet preaching repentance, which is what Jonah was. The Gentile population of Nineveh turned from their sins at Jonah's preaching (Jonah 3:4–5). The Gentile Queen of Sheba came from the ends of the earth to hear Solomon's wisdom (1 Kings 10:1–13), but God's own people for all their religious observances will not recognize God's call to them when it comes through one greater than either Solomon or Jonah. On the Day of Judgement they will be accused by Gentiles!

Matthew 12:40 gives a different and probably later explanation of the 'sign of Jonah'. The early Church quickly made a link between Jonah's three days and nights in the belly of the fish, and Jesus's rest in the sepulchre. But St Luke's application is much closer and truer to the actual situation during the earthly life of Jesus.

The Light of the Body

A number of sayings about light have been collected together here. The first may have referred to Israel who had covered God's light up to preserve it for herself instead of putting it on a stand so that all the Gentiles could see to come in from the darkness outside. (See also comment on 8:16 on p. 50.) The saying about clear and bad eyes can be transposed from the physical to the spiritual plane, for the word for 'clear' also means sincere, or generous, and the word for 'bad' can mean churlish, mean, or stingy. A sincere and generous spirit brings light to a man's whole life. But if his spirit is churlish or mean, the very light that is in him is darkness.

Jesus Accuses the Pharisees and the Teachers of the Law

This section looks very much like a collection of criti‐cisms which Jesus made against the Pharisees and teachers of the Law on a number of different occasions, for various parts of it occur at many different points in Matthew, Mark and Luke (see Matthew 23:1–36, Mark 12:38–40, Luke 20:45–47, and Matthew 15:17–20, Mark 7:14–23).

The Pharisee was surprised that Jesus had not washed before sitting down to eat, not because Jesus's hands were dirty but because he had not performed the ritual washing which had to be done in a precise and rather complicated way, using no less than one and a half eggshells full of water!

Verses 39–41 are rather obscure in meaning. They may mean 'a better way of keeping your pots clean in God's sight would be to use them for feeding the hungry, a moral duty which you neglect in favour of your cere‐monial scrupulosity.' Matthew's version, 'You clean the outside of your cup and plate, while the inside is full of things you have got by violence and selfishness' (Matthew 23:25), makes a better comparison between the outside and inside of the cup than Luke's reading does.

Verse 42: the Law said that a tenth of the harvest should be given back to God. (Leviticus 27:30 – our word tithe comes from the same root – tenth.) The main crops of corn, wine and oil were intended, but the Pharisees went to the length of tithing even seasoning herbs like mint and rue.

Verse 43: the Pharisees liked to be on show in the best seats in the synagogues, and to be greeted with deference and respect in the street. This is all too modern and 'close to home' to need any comment! But the point about the graves does need explanation. To touch a grave made a Jew unclean for seven days and so debarred him from all religious worship (Numbers 19:16). They therefore marked graves by whitening them so that people could avoid them. Jesus says that the Pharisees are like unmarked graves, people come into contact with them, and without knowing it they are defiled, because their influence is a bad influence,[3] and they teach a false view of God and of religion.

Verse 45: Jesus accuses the teachers of the Law of making religion a burden that is too heavy for all but a very few to bear. With the great mass of complicated religious duties and regulations which one had to fulfil to keep the Law this was quite true and, furthermore, instead of offering any positive input of help to the ordinary people, the teachers of the Law only increased the burden with ever new duties to fulfil.

Verse 47: no doubt the scribes and Pharisees claimed to honour the great prophets and to show that they did so by building and maintaining beautiful memorials to them. But with an ironic and clever shift of viewpoint, Jesus accuses them of sharing in the wicked work of their ancestors. 'Your fathers killed them, and you provide the graves!' The culmination of all the wickedness of all the centuries from the death of Abel which was the first murder recorded in Jewish scripture (Genesis 4:8) to the murder of Zechariah, which was the last (2 Chronicles 24:22) has now been reached. The day of reckoning for it all has come. The present generation must either repent and turn completely to God, or pay the price of it all. In the event they set their seal on the sorry tale of history by rejecting God's only Son and adding his murder to all the rest.

Jesus's final charge against them is of obscurantism. They were supposed to expound the scriptures to the people. But all they did with their labyrinthine extensions and legalism was to make them so obscure that ordinary people could not understand them – and they lost the main point of the scriptures themselves in the process.

A Warning against Hypocrisy (chapter 12)

In St Luke's gospel Jesus hardly ever speaks to his

---

3. Compare Matthew 23:27 for the rather different criticism that they are like whitewashed tombs which look fine on the outside but are full of corruption within.

disciples alone; the crowd, as here, is always somewhere in the background. He tells them to be on their guard against the yeast (or leaven) of the Pharisees. Yeast is a silent and all-pervading ferment which affects the whole lump of dough through and through. In the Bible it nearly always refers to an evil influence rather than a good one (cf. 1 Corinthians 5:8). We might compare it with the influence which advertising or the mass media exercise on us today: all-pervading, largely unconscious, yet affecting our standards of value and our whole outlook.

In Luke, the 'yeast' of the Pharisees is their hypocrisy. (Notice that in Matthew 16:11-12 it is their *teaching*.) The word hypocrite is so often hurled at Christians that we might well look at what it really means. First, a hypocrite is not somebody who fails to live up to his ideals. If a man lives up to his ideals, they are too low and it is time he found some better ones! Again, it is sometimes thought that a hypocrite is somebody who 'acts a part' like a play actor, because the Greek word *upocrites* has as its classical Greek background the Greek drama. But the way to find the meaning of New Testament words is not to trace them back through classical Greek, but through Aramaic, and beyond that, through the Greek of the Septuagint[4] to the Hebrew of the Old Testament.

To find the meaning of 'hypocrite' we must look carefully at the ways in which Jesus used it, because it is Jesus who has brought it into prominence. In Jesus's use of it the essence of hypocrisy is found in three things. (1) In being more concerned about what other people think than about the truth itself; trying to project a good image, and preserve one's respectability at all costs. The hypocrite is concerned about 'appearances'. He wants his goodness to be seen by men. Examples of this are in Matthew 6:2, 6:5, and 6:16. The Pharisee wants it to be *seen* that he is making a generous gift to charity, that he says his prayers, that he is keeping the fast. (2) In being

4. The translation of the Old Testament into Greek, made about 250 BC supposedly by seventy (or seventy-two) scholars, for the Jews of the dispersion.

outwardly religious, but inwardly profane and ungodly. As Isaiah said (29:13), 'this people draw near with their mouth and honour me with their lips, while their hearts are far from me.' The example of this is Matthew 23:27. Jesus says that the Pharisees are like whitewashed graves which look nice from the outside but within are filled with corruption. (3) In being self-satisfied and self-admiring, sure of one's own goodness. The example of this is in Luke 18:9–12 where the Pharisee parades his goodness before God in his prayers and gives thanks that he is not like the tax collector. Hypocrites are not as plentiful in the Church as they were two generations ago, for it is now neither fashionable nor profitable to be a churchgoer!

Whom to Fear

'I tell you, my friends'; this is the only occasion in the first three gospels where Jesus calls the disciples 'friends' (cf. John 15:14–15). The Greek text of verse 5 reads, 'I will show you whom to fear: fear *him* who after killing has the authority to throw into hell.' Who is meant by 'him'? Is it God, or is it Satan? Our translator has decided that it is God. But many commentators think that 'him' refers to Satan, because Jesus never tells us to be afraid of God, and it is in any case such a contradiction of God's detailed care and love which are spoken of in the very next verse. On the other hand, there are those who say that 'him' refers to God, before whose might and majesty we should have a sense of awe and reverence which amounts to a 'holy fear' and which cleanses the soul of all other fears:

> Fear him ye saints and you will then
> Have nothing else to fear.

It would have been better if Dr Bratcher had left the matter open as the Greek and other English versions do by translating 'him' instead of 'God'.

The word for hell is *Gehenna* in the Greek (literally Ge-Hnnom, valley of Hinnom), and this is the only mention of it in the whole of St Luke's gospel. The valley of Hinnom near Jerusalem had been defiled by human sacrifice in the time of the wicked kings Ahaz and Manasseh (2 Chronicles 28:3, 33:6, Jeremiah 32:35). It had long been used for burning the city's rubbish, and so it became a fitting symbol for the destruction of evil by perpetual fire.

Confessing and Denying Christ

The New Testament gives no support to the sentimental idea that 'We're all going the same way really, and we shall all be all right in the end.' Our attitude to Christ in this life has an eternal significance. Christ is the truth as well as the way and the life, and if the truth is that we have denied him, that is the only truth that he can tell concerning us. Both Matthew (12:32) and Mark (3:29) link the sin against the Holy Spirit with the incident where Jesus is accused of casting out demons by Beelzebul the prince of the demons (see comment on 11:14 on p. 72, and without doubt this is where it rightly belongs. The sin against the Holy Spirit is to call what is manifestly good, evil, and to ascribe what is clearly the work of God to the devil. It is to see the sick healed and madmen made sane, and then say, 'This is the work of Satan.' While such complete and determined moral blindness lasts there cannot be any forgiveness, whether it is in this life or in the next. This is not because God is unwilling to forgive, or because there is a sin that is too great for his love to meet, but because such a man has convinced himself that sin is righteousness and so is unable to repent and ask for God's forgiveness. Nobody who is conscious that he has sinned, and wants to be forgiven, has committed the sin against the Holy Spirit, and nobody who wants to be forgiven is unforgivable. Jesus goes on to promise that the Holy Spirit will be with his disciples in their hour of need. Even under persecution they are not to be anxious for God keeps faith with those who keep faith with him. The words with which to witness to him will be given when the time comes.

The Parable of the Rich Fool

Wills had to be drawn up in accordance with the detailed provisions of the Law of Moses, which defined the rights of the eldest and of other members of the family. So, a dispute about a will was a matter of both religious and secular argument. There was a strong feeling in Jewish society against splitting up a family property into separate parts. In this case the elder brother obviously wanted to leave the inheritance undivided. This may well be what is praised in Psalm 133:1. 'Behold, how good and pleasant it is when brothers dwell in unity!' There is perhaps a hint of the difficulty it caused for servants when they had two or more brothers over them in such an estate, in Jesus's saying, 'No one can be a slave to two masters; he will hate one and love the other; he will be loyal to one and despise the other.' (Matthew 6:24)

Jesus had proved himself to be brilliant and unusual in expounding the scriptures and the man no doubt hoped that he might get some help from him. It may be that Jesus detected greed beneath the request, for he goes on straightaway to say to the crowd, 'Watch out, and guard yourselves from all kinds of greed', but for whatever reason he refuses to be drawn into squabbles about property. His concern is with the *true* life of man, and 'a man's *true* life is not made up of the things he owns, no matter how rich he may be.' How much our affluent, covetous, discontented and advertising-ridden society needs to ponder that!

The parable which follows is another of those which come from the rich store of material which is special to St Luke. As William Barclay points out, the rich man seems to be completely self-centred. The whole of the dialogue that goes on in his mind is packed with 'I', 'my' and 'self'. (Myself, himself and yourself all refer to him!) God said, 'You fool!' In the Bible, the fool is the man who by his practical way of life denies God's existence (Psalm 14:1). The crisis of death lays bare his essential poverty.

To the end of time the parable will apply at its face

value to every man, for we all must die and there are no pockets in a shroud! But in its actual setting in St Luke's gospel we should perhaps interpret it in a different way, taking it as of one piece with all that follows as far as verse 46. It is then a parable about the crisis of the Kingdom. The Messianic age is breaking into this world in the coming of Jesus with a crisis as absolute as the crisis of death. 'The Kingdom of God has already come to you' (11:20), and it shows up as clearly as death the real and the unreal in men's lives. On this understanding of it, it is one of the 'eschatological' parables, that is, a parable which is concerned with the coming of the Kingdom, or the last things (Greek, *eschatos* = last).

Trust in God

The rich fool put possessions before his real life because he had so many of them. But it is equally possible to put possessions before one's real life by continually worrying because one has so few of them. The real cure for worry is to put God's Kingdom first in our lives and our personal and material needs second. Those who do will find that God provides for his children's needs. They will also discover that their needs are much fewer and simpler than the world supposes. The pure poetry and beauty of this paragraph shine through every translation. We understand it not by detailed explanation but by being caught up and inspired to see the world and life through the eyes of Jesus.

Riches in Heaven

St Luke places this section immediately *after* the beautiful paragraph on trust in God and freedom from anxiety. St Matthew on the other hand places it *before* that paragraph, with the sayings about the light of the body in between (cf. Matthew 6:19–23). St Luke has put the sayings about the light of the body a whole chapter earlier (11:33–36). This shows us something about the way in which the teaching of Jesus has come to us. We have not got any verbatim record of his words on any occasion, such as a modern tape recording would supply,

which could be played back time and time again without
any variation, as for instance Sir Winston Churchill's
wartime speeches can still be played back. The teaching
of Jesus comes to us through the minds of men who
loved him and pondered his words for many years
before they were written down. Each remembered them
in his own way and according to his own background and
personality. It is like light shining through a tinted lens.
We see both the original light and the tint which the lens
has given to it. St Luke has a strong ascetic element in
his make-up, and also a deep compassion for the poor.
These qualities can often be seen in his writings.
Matthew's 'Do not save riches . . . here on earth'
(Matthew 6:19) is in Luke 'Sell all your belongings and
give the money to the poor.' In his second volume, he
tells us how the earliest Christians actually did that
(Acts 2:44–46).

Watchful Servants

In this section there are two parables; verses 35–38, the
watchful servants, and verses 39–40, the thief in the night.
A third parable follows in the next section. The theme of
all three is watchfulness and preparedness.

In Palestine the long robe which formed the common
dress was gathered up and fastened tightly into the girdle
for work or any energetic action.

When a bridegroom went to fetch his bride he left
servants at home who had to be ready to receive him
when he returned from the wedding feast, at whatever
time it might be. The reference to the master girding
himself and waiting on his servants rings rather strangely.
It reminds us of Jesus washing the feet of his disciples at
the Last Supper (John 13:4).

The little parable of the thief in the night is also found
in Matthew 24:43 (where the time – night – is suggested).
The Greek word for 'break into' is interesting. It means
literally 'to dig through', and that is exactly what thieves
often did for it was easier to dig through the mud wall of
the house than to break in by the door. The disciples are
to be watchful.

Perhaps originally the various parables about watchfulness referred to the impending climax of Jesus's life, namely death for himself and intense suffering for his disciples, which Jesus knew must come and through which the Messianic age would dawn – the baptism he knew he had to be baptized with. But later the early Church reapplied them to their expectation of the Second Coming (see next section below). In an amazing way so much of our Lord's teaching which originally was for particular people in particular situations has also a universal relevance, to all times and all people. This parable is an example. So many of the great spiritual crises and opportunities of life seem to come unexpectedly like a thief in the night, and so often, looking back, we realize that they found us wanting. The parables of watchfulness will apply to every disciple of Christ in every century until God brings this world to its end.

The Faithful or the Unfaithful Servant

This parable may originally have been spoken by Jesus against the scribes and Pharisees who had been set over God's household to teach the Law and care for his people. They had misused their responsibilities, and now the hour of reckoning had come.

The early Christians expected Christ to return in glory in their own lifetime. As the years went by and Christ still did not return it is easy to understand how they applied parables such as this to their own situation. 'My master is taking a long time to come back' (verse 45). Compare this with the words in the second epistle of Peter, which is one of the latest books in the New Testament, 'He promised to come, didn't he? Where is he? Our fathers have already died, but everything is still the same . . .' (2 Peter 3:4)

The words 'cut him to pieces' in verse 46 could well be a misunderstanding of an Aramaic word which means 'cut him off' – compare our modern phrase to cut somebody out of a will, or 'cut him off with a shilling'.

Jesus the Cause of Division

In the Bible fire is a symbol of testing and of judgement (cf. 1 Corinthians 3:13). John the Baptist had used it of the coming Messiah who would 'burn the chaff in a fire that never goes out' (Matthew 3:12, Luke 3:17). In another image Jesus says, 'I have a baptism to receive' or better, 'to be baptized with' (Common Bible translation). In the passive voice the word means to be submerged, or to be overwhelmed.[5] As the Psalmist says, 'All thy waves and thy billows have gone over me.' (Psalm 42:7) 'I have come into deep waters, and the flood sweeps over me.' (Psalm 69:2) Jesus wishes that the fire was already kindled and that the terrible baptism that is going to overwhelm him was over. We glimpse here something of the strain and anguish of soul which our Lord was suffering at this time.

Jewish literature was full of predictions of the woes which would overwhelm the world as a prelude to the establishment of God's Kingdom. Nobody except Jesus dreamed that the Messiah himself must pass through those deep waters. But Jesus knew it, and the longing to complete his work struggled with the shrinking from suffering and from judgement which he knew Israel would bring on herself in rejecting him (cf. Luke 23:28).

In verse 51 St Luke changes Matthew's 'I did not come to bring peace, but a sword' (Matthew 10:34) to read 'Not peace, I tell you, but division.' St Luke is writing to commend the Christian faith to the rulers of the Roman Empire. The last thing that he would want Theophilus to think would be that Jesus came to spread revolution!

Family divisions were an outrage to Jewish morals but they were expected as part of the intensified evil which would precede the end of the age.

Understanding the Time

The people who listened to Jesus were so good at interpreting the signs of the weather, why were they so blind

5. Active voice =to baptize; passive voice =to be baptized.

to the signs of the times? Jesus seems to have viewed the rejection of himself as Messiah and political disaster for Israel as being closely linked together.

They thought of the coming of the Messiah in terms of national pride and worldly greatness and being set up to rule over the Gentiles. Jesus calls them, in the light of their own scriptures, to think again and to reconsider their calling as God's people in terms of love and humble service. Their rejection of his way can only lead to disaster for the whole nation. 'If you only knew today what is needed for peace! But now you cannot see it! The days will come upon you when your enemies will surround you . . . They will completely destroy you and the people within your walls.' (19:42–44)

Settle with Your Opponent

Jesus underlines the urgency of the situation. A debtor who cannot pay should do his best to settle the matter even at the last minute on the way to court rather than face being jailed for debt. It is as late as that for Israel!

Turn from Your Sins or Die (chapter 13)

St Luke was a historian. It is not surprising that he has taken care to preserve these two incidents which have links with contemporary events in Palestine in the time of Jesus's ministry, though unfortunately we have no other record of them.

Feelings always ran high in Jerusalem at Passover-time when thousands of pilgrims came to offer sacrifice in the temple and Pilate more than once quelled disturbances with ferocious severity.

He had undertaken to improve the water supply of Jerusalem, which badly needed doing, and decided to finance it out of certain temple revenues. This provoked a storm of protest amongst the Jews, and many of the Pharisees held that men who took wages for working on the project were robbing God. The collapse of the tower which overlooked the Pool of Siloam might well have been connected with this work. It would quickly be forgotten, like a mine disaster in modern times which hits the headlines for a day or two and then passes into limbo. Jesus may well be commenting here on the disaster which was on everybody's lips at the time, and St Luke, hearing about it when he was collecting material for his gospel seized on it at once and preserved it for us. (See also p. 10f.)

The theology behind the two incidents is very important. The orthodox Jewish view was that suffering and misfortune were a direct punishment for sin. As Eliphaz said to Job, 'who that was innocent ever perished?' (Job 4:7) or as the Psalmist wrote, 'I have been young and now am old; yet I have not seen the righteous forsaken or his children begging bread.' (Psalm 37:25) The view lingers even today in the way in which people say when misfortune comes upon them, 'I don't know what I've done to deserve this!' Jesus denies this view of sin and punishment. Their death was not a punishment, and it does not prove that they were worse sinners than those who escaped the misfortune. But he goes on to say that if the nation does not repent of its sins and turn from the course it is pursuing, the whole nation will perish as these few men did. Jesus's insight into the political situation was proved true within a very few decades when in AD 70 the Romans made a final end of things and Titus razed Jerusalem to the ground and destroyed the Jewish State.

Sin always brings suffering, but we cannot argue the reverse, namely that suffering is always a punishment for sin. All Frenchmen are Europeans, but it does not follow that all Europeans are therefore Frenchmen!

The Parable of the Unfruitful Fig Tree

The theme of this parable is the same as that of the two previous stories – repentance – but there is an added urgency about it. For Israel, this is the last chance to bear fruit or be cut down like the fig tree. In Palestine fig trees were often planted among the vines. The fruit of a tree could not be taken for three years after planting (Leviticus 19:23), so the tree in the parable was already six years old. A fig tree absorbs a specially large amount of nourishment and so tends to take away from the surrounding vines. The use of manure or fertilizer is never mentioned in the Old Testament, so clearly the gardener is prepared to go to very special lengths to try to save it. This is a parable of mercy and judgement. In spite of God's longing to save Israel and willingness to take every possible measure to do so, if she continues on her present course judgement must come, and the hour is very close.

Jesus Heals a Crippled Woman on the Sabbath

It is unusual to find Jesus teaching in a synagogue at this stage in his ministry. Most synagogues had banned him long ago! The issue at stake is the same as in the healing of the man with the withered hand in 6:6–11. If the woman had been ill for such a long time, the Pharisees argued, Jesus could quite well have waited until the morrow when he could have healed her without breaking the Sabbath. It is interesting to note that the official does not attack Jesus directly, but takes it out on the congregation – as perhaps he was wont to do!

The logic of Jesus is simple but devastating. The Law allowed domestic animals which had been fastened up overnight to be loosed and fed and watered on the Sabbath. What about this daughter of Abraham,[6] much more than an animal, who had been fastened up for eighteen years – not just overnight. Should not she be released on the Sabbath?

St Luke has a very fine and complex mind and there are deeper levels to this story. In the Greek, there is a play on words between 'bound' and 'free' which it is very difficult to reproduce in English. She is *bound* by Satan so that she is bent. Jesus breaks Satan's bonds and *frees* her so that she can straighten herself and praise God. This is the Kingdom of God breaking in, the

6. It is unfortunate that Dr Bratcher translates the warm Greek, 'Daughter of Abraham', by the cold word 'descendant'. He does the same thing again, equally unfortunately, in the story of Zacchaeus (19.10).

Messiah overpowering Satan and releasing his prisoners (cf. 11:14–22, and especially verses 21 and 22).

The Greek word *dei* which is used in verse 16 for 'Should she not' be freed from her bonds on the Sabbath is an extremely important word in St Luke. It is sometimes translated 'was it not necessary' or 'must' or 'it had to be'. It always denotes a divine necessity, something imposed by God himself through which his plan of redemption would be carried to fulfilment. St Luke uses the word no less than ten times in connection with Jesus. The first is at the beginning of the gospel when the boy Jesus says to his parents, 'Didn't you know that *I had to be* in my Father's house?' (2:49) and the last is at its very end when the risen Christ says, 'everything written about me in the Law of Moses, the writings of the prophets, and the Psalms *had to* come true.' (24:44)

The Parable of the Mustard Seed

This parable is found in each of the first three gospels (cf. Matthew 13:31–32, Mark 4:30–32). The smallness of the mustard seed was proverbial, though modern botanists tell us that it is not actually the smallest seed in the world. Full grown it becomes a bush up to twelve feet high, and there are often birds flying around it because they like the little black seeds.

In Matthew and Mark it is the contrast between the smallness of the seed and the size of the full grown bush which is stressed. But St Luke does not even mention the smallness of the seed. He is concerned to draw out a different lesson from the story. The Kingdom of God will become a tree in which the *birds of the air* can build nests. In the Old Testament, a large tree is often the symbol of a great empire, and the birds of the air are the different nations which find shelter and protection under its rule (cf. Ezekiel 17:22f, 31:6, Daniel 4:12). We know also that the Rabbis sometimes referred to the Gentiles as 'the birds of the air'. Here, then, we have St Luke the Gentile, writing for the Gentile world, drawing out the truth that the Kingdom of God is for all the nations of mankind.

The Parable of the Yeast

The leaven was a small piece of dough from the previous baking which had been left to ferment. It was then mixed with the new dough to make the whole lump rise. Leaven in biblical thought nearly always stands for an evil influence (cf. 12:1, 1 Corinthians 5:6–8, Galatians 5:7–10). Jesus boldly uses it here not for the power of Satan, but for the power of God.

So many illuminating – and no doubt true – lessons have been drawn from this short parable by preachers! The Church must go out in the world and Christians must mix in among non-Christians to do God's work. The Kingdom of God spreads slowly and silently, but irresistibly throughout the world – or throughout society. The lump of humanity can only be changed by a power coming in from outside like the leaven that is put into a lump of new dough. Wherever the gospel is preached it sets up a bubbling ferment. All these interpretations have truth in them, and it illustrates the sheer brilliance of Jesus that he can put such many sided truths into a mere couple of sentences. But what did Jesus himself mean to stress in the actual situation in which he gave the parable? Perhaps he meant to point to the *certainty* of great and irresistible growth from the small and apparently weak beginnings of his ministry. The yeast is now in the dough and nothing can prevent the ferment from going through the whole lump.

The Narrow Door

The question of whether many or few would be saved was much discussed among the Rabbis. Jesus refuses to enter into idle theological speculation, but points to the urgency of entering into the Kingdom now, while the door is still open. The theme of urgency and crisis is one which occurs over and over again in Luke. The time will come when it will be too late. The door will have been shut and the banquet begun. It will be no use then making flimsy claims to casual association with Jesus long ago, 'You taught in our town.' If they did not turn from their

evil ways, nor take the opportunity when it was offered,
it will be too late. The door will not be opened.

As it stands the parable obviously refers to the Jews.
They thought that their inclusion in God's Kingdom would
be automatic just because of their race. They also thought
that the exclusion of the Gentiles was certain. Gentiles
would be just chaff for the burning when the Messiah
came! But they will find, says Jesus, men and women
from the east and the west and the north and the south
(cf. Revelation 7:9f) sharing with Abraham, Isaac,
Jacob and the prophets in the great banquet of the
Messiah – and they will be kept outside. Those who are
last now will be first then, and those who are now first
will be last.

The words, 'People will come from the east and the
west, from the north and the south, and sit at the table
in the Kingdom of God', occur in Matthew, but at the
end of a different story (cf. Matthew 8:11–12), that of
the healing of the Roman officer's servant. This gives us
an interesting glimpse into the way in which the gospels
were written. After the Resurrection there was a period
of thirty years or more during which stories and pithy
sayings of Jesus were treasured and passed round by
word of mouth, but not yet written down. The healing
of the Roman officer's servant was one such story
(Matthew 8:5–13, Luke 7:1–10). The saying about people
coming from the east and the west, from the north and
the south to sit at table in the Kingdom of God was one
such saying. St Matthew very appropriately attached the
saying to the story of the healing of a Gentile's servant.
But St Luke chose to attach it to the parable of the
narrow door – again, very appropriately.

The way in which God committed even the record of
the life and teaching of his only begotten Son to the
memories of men and the ordinary processes of human
thought, and the situation of the first century is very
wonderful; far more wonderful than if by some miracu-
lous contradiction of all the laws of human nature he
had used men as typewriters to provide an inerrant
record. (See p. 47.)

Jesus's Love for Jerusalem

We read in Mark 3:6 that some Pharisees joined with Herod's party to plan the death of Jesus. But this was an extreme alliance and there must have been other Pharisees whose antagonism to Herod was far greater than their antagonism to Jesus. It would seem to be some of these who warned Jesus against Herod.

To the Greeks the fox was a symbol of sly cunning as it is to us. But in the biblical background it is a symbol of destructiveness; and the Rabbis in Jesus's time used it to signify a worthless and insignificant man. Herod shared all these characteristics!

'I must be on my way today, tomorrow, and the next day . . .' Three days was a conventional phrase for a short period of time (cf. Jonah 1:17 – three days and nights in the belly of the fish). The 'finishing' of Jesus's work is near. The Greek word means fulfilment or accomplishment. It is the word that is used in his final cry from the Cross, 'It is finished.' (John 19:29) But it is not the will of Herod that will bring things to their fulfilment; it is the will of God, and the time will be God's time (cf. John 7:6f). Until then, 'I must be on my way,' says Jesus. This is another of the great 'musts' of St Luke's gospel. (See p. 88.)

The lament over Jerusalem is full of echoes of the Old Testament. It was expected that the Messiah when he came would gather the scattered children of Jerusalem (Isaiah 31:5, 60:4, Zechariah 10:8–10). To be safe under the wings of God was a familiar Old Testament image (Ruth 2:12, Psalm 57:1, 61:4, 91:4).

In the parallel passage to this one in Matthew 23:37–39 Jesus has already entered the city on Palm Sunday and so the words, 'You will not see me until the time comes . . .' would seem to refer to the Second Coming. But here in Luke, they refer more naturally to the entry into Jerusalem on Palm Sunday.

Jesus Heals a Sick Man (chapter 14)

After morning service in the synagogue was a popular time for inviting guests. All cooking was done beforehand so as not to break the Sabbath. The man with dropsy need not have been deliberately planted to trap Jesus.[7] He could have been somebody who had come in like the woman with the ointment at the house of Simon the Pharisee. (See p. 46.) The issues at stake are the same as in earlier Sabbath healings. (See p. 36.) From the Pharisees' point of view healing was work, and work was forbidden on the Sabbath, therefore to heal was to break the Sabbath. Only urgency (i.e. the immediate danger of death) could excuse such a breach, and the man was clearly not in any immediate danger. To Jesus the claims of charity and humanity are supreme, and to fulfil the claims of love has priority over all ritual observance. In verse 5 there is considerable variation between different manuscripts of the gospel. Some read 'a son (*uios*) or an ox'; others read 'an ass (*onos*) or an ox'; others again read 'a sheep (*ois*) or an ox'. Although the manuscript evidence for reading 'a son or an ox' is strong, the reading 'a sheep or an ox' seems more likely because there is a parallel between 'sheep and ox'; both were domestic animals for which the owner was legally responsible. Normally, he would pull them out even on the Sabbath. If he were a very strict Pharisee and the animal were not dying, he might let food down to it until next day, or find a Gentile to pull the animal out for him!

Humility and Hospitality

Invitations to a formal dinner were usually issued and accepted well in advance. But the guests did not set out until a servant came to tell them 'Come, everything is ready.' There was a strict etiquette about the seating, and they sorted themselves out according to its rules without difficulty, but when the host came in to salute them, he might well call one guest to a higher place by his side

7. In verse 2 the word *hudropikos* is another of St Luke's medical words.

which meant that somebody had to go down, perhaps even to the lowest place! We can imagine Jesus smiling as he tells this tale, and the company smiling as they hear it. But St Luke says that it is a *parable* – an earthly tale with a heavenly meaning, in the words of the old definition, and so we may think of it as illustrating the great reversal which will take place in the coming Kingdom of God. Many of those who are first now will be last then. Whoever makes himself great will be humbled and whoever humbles himself will be exalted. (Note that St Matthew gives this saying in a completely different setting, Matthew 23:11–12.)

In the next paragraph (verse 12) Jesus stresses two things, the first is kindness to the poor and the second is one of his most distinctive ethical principles, namely to do good and to give spontaneously out of a loving heart without any thought of a reward or getting anything back in return. This is how God gives, and when we give like this we are true sons of the Most High (6:33–36). This is the true life of the Kingdom and those who begin it on earth will reap the reward of enjoying it for ever in heaven.

The Parable of the Great Feast

Perhaps the atmosphere had become a little strained by this time! One of the guests tries to break the tension by a little pious platitude. 'How happy are those who will sit at the table (i.e. be invited to dinner) in the Kingdom of God.' Only somebody who felt sure of his own seat at the heavenly banquet could make a comment like that! Jesus takes him up seriously. Is he sure that he will want to accept the invitation to that particular banquet when it comes? And if he does, is he sure that he will like the company he will find there? Jesus then tells the story of the great feast – or would it not be better named the story of the contemptuous guests?

To accept the general invitation and then refuse the summons at the time of the meal was extremely discourteous and amounted to an insult to the host. The first two excuses are from well-to-do men. One was in a good enough position to buy land, and the other must have been a very wealthy man to buy five yoke of oxen.[8] With regard to the third man's excuse, only men were invited to a banquet in Palestine, never women. The newly married man did not want to leave his young wife alone.

We may, if we wish, apply the parable to our own day and think of those who put God's call second to their possessions or their business interests, or family commitments. But we must not miss the primary meaning which Jesus himself gave it. God's invitation to his Kingdom has been given to the Jews, and now the moment has arrived. Jesus is the servant issuing the summons, 'Come, everything is ready!' But the pious Jews are throwing it back in God's face. All right, they have had their chance! Jesus is turning to the tax gatherers and sinners. But still there is room. The Gentiles too are to be invited to come in on equal terms with the chosen people. It is interesting to note that this second command to go out to the country roads and the lanes *outside the city* (i.e. to the Gentiles) is only recorded in St Luke's version of the parable.

The phrase in verse 23, 'make people come in' ('compel' in the older versions), was disastrously interpreted by St Augustine and the Church in the Middle Ages to justify using force and persecution to make people accept the Christian faith. Of course, it does not justify this at all. Oriental courtesy demands that even a poor man should modestly resist the invitation until he was taken gently by the hand and pulled into the house.

The permanent teaching of the parable is that there is an open invitation into the Kingdom of God. Those who are excluded are excluded by their own refusal to accept it – and this is a real and serious possibility.

The Cost of Being a Disciple

St Luke was a highly educated Gentile who could write fluent and beautiful Greek. We might well expect that

8. A decent-sized farm in Palestine was as big as two yoke of oxen could plough.

he would iron out any Semitic turns of phrase or thought from his early Aramaic sources. On the contrary, he always shows a profound respect for the material which comes to him, and is most careful to preserve its original turns of thought and phrase. 'Whoever comes to me cannot be my disciple unless he hates his father and his mother . . .' is an interesting example of this. Hebrew had no way of saying, 'I prefer this to that.' Instead, it had to point the contrast by saying, 'I love this and I hate that.'[9] St Matthew paraphrases the sentence to read, 'Whoever loves father or mother more than me *is not worthy of me.*' But St Luke retains the original Hebraic way of expressing it. Even one's family must come second to him, says Jesus. He makes claims on men which only God has any right to make.

There is a striking contrast between the way in which the Church today approaches men and the way in which Jesus approached them. 'All welcome,' says the Church. 'Our demands are not really very difficult or unpleasant. We don't ask very much and if you don't like them, we can surely meet you halfway!' But Jesus says, 'I must come absolutely first. The Kingdom means a Cross for me, and you must be prepared for it to mean that for you as well. Don't respond too lightly. You had better count the cost very carefully first.'

Worthless Salt

The salt which has lost its taste links well with the two men in the preceding section whose zeal and ability failed. Salt in the east was used as we use it, to season food and to preserve it, but it was also used as a fertilizer. We must understand this saying in conjunction with the variants in Matthew 5:13 and Mark 9:50. The disciples are to be a purifying, preserving, flavouring and fertilizing influence on society. If *they* lose these qualities, where else can they be found? How can they be replaced?

9. 'Jacob I loved but Esau I hated' (Romans 9:13 citing Malachi 1:2–3). See also Genesis 29:30–31, and Deuteronomy 21:15 where the Common Bible has changed the word 'hated' in the old Authorized Version to 'disliked'.

The Lost Sheep and the Lost Coin (chapter 15)

St Luke often puts parables in pairs, and this is not the only occasion when he makes a pair out of a parable about a man followed by one about a woman. (Cf. 11: 31–32 and 13:18–20.)

It was when he was with the 'lost', that is, the tax gatherers and other bad characters, that Jesus told these stories to the Pharisees who complained that 'This man welcomes outcasts and even eats with them!' (to eat with a person being an extremely close form of fellowship in Jewish society). In the Greek, the word for 'This man' is contemptuous – 'this chap – or this fellow'. It is hard to convey the contempt in English.

A hundred sheep was a medium-sized flock. The shepherd is not well enough off to employ a watchman (cf. John 10:11f). Every night he would count his sheep as he put them in the fold, for there were jackals and mountain lions and other dangerous animals abroad in the hill country. The suggestion here is that he has just counted them and there is one missing. So leaving the flock in the care of those who shared the fold with him, he sets out, tired as he is, to find the one that is missing. The words 'puts it on his shoulders' describe a daily happening in the Near East. When an animal has strayed and got lost it often lies down dejectedly. The best way to carry it is across the shoulders with its legs held in front of the chest.

The lost coin was probably part of the woman's head-dress which was bedecked with ten silver coins on a silver chain. This formed part of her dowry and was often a woman's most precious possession which she did not lay aside even at night. It was also a token of her marriage and so corresponded to the wedding ring in our times. She must have been a poor woman if she had only ten drachma in her head-dress (a drachma is worth about 10p in modern coinage). She lights the lamp not because it is night, but because there is so little light in the one-roomed peasant house which had only one tiny window –

and often not even that. The floor was hard, beaten earth covered with dried reeds and rushes. She hopes that as she sweeps, it might glint or tinkle as it moves.

One of the new things in Jesus's teaching about God is that God takes the initiative and goes out to seek sinners. The Pharisees believed that God would receive sinners when they repented and turned back to him. But that was up to them! They, not God, must take the initiative. Jesus's reply to those who criticize him for welcoming outcasts and even eating with them is, 'I am doing what God does. He goes out to seek sinners and bring them home, just because they are *his* and he wants them, just as a shepherd wants his lost sheep and will go out to find it; just as a woman will turn the whole house upside down to find a coin from her wedding circlet, because it is precious to her and she wants it.'

The other thing which Jesus stresses is the joy of God when a sinner is found. The phrases 'joy in heaven' and 'the angels of God rejoice' are both roundabout ways of referring to God himself. The Jews out of reverence often referred to heaven, or the angels, as a way of avoiding the direct use of 'God'.[10]

Note the use of the future tense in verse 7, 'there *will* be more joy . . .' The reference is to the last judgement.

The Lost Son

There are many background details to this the greatest of all the parables of Jesus which we must look at before commenting on its teaching.

A man could will his property to his sons for them to receive after his death, in which case it had to be divided strictly according to the Law of Moses. On the other hand, he could divide it during his lifetime, in whatever way he wished without regard to the Law. But unlike a will, which could be changed, division during his lifetime was irrevocable. The sons would enter into possession of

10. The name of God was so sacred that it was never spoken. All we have are the consonant letters JHVH but nobody knows how the word was pronounced. It may have been JeHoVaH or more likely perhaps JaHVeH. It is usually printed in English versions as LORD.

the land straight away, but the income from it belonged to the father so long as he lived.

The younger son could reasonably expect to do better by setting himself up in business in a foreign city than by staying on the overworked farmland of Palestine. In Jesus's time emigration was common. There were about four million Jews scattered over the Roman Empire, as against only half a million who lived in Palestine. But the lad's spendthrift habits, together with a severe famine, bring him to ruin. To work for a Gentile taking care of pigs which were unclean animals to the Jews represents the lowest depths of degradation. Hunger and the thought of food make him determine to go home and to ask to be received back not as a son, but as a hired servant. Hired servants were the lowest grade of servant which existed. They were hired and fired by the day, and had not even a slave's standing in the household.

Seeing him a long way off, his father throws dignity to the winds and runs out to meet him. (A mature man never runs in the east!) He flings his arms round him and greets him with a kiss. The boy begins the speech he has prepared, but before he is halfway through his father interrupts him to command that the best robe be brought – a sign of honour: that a signet ring be put on his finger – a sign of authority and that he is an heir: and that shoes be put on his feet – a sign that he is a free man; slaves went barefoot. (Cf. the Negro spiritual 'All God's chillun got shoes' – there will be no slaves in heaven.)

When they get home the fatted calf[11] is killed and a feast begins. The father's exclamation of joy 'Because this son of mine was dead, but now he is alive; he was lost, but now he has been found' is pure Hebrew poetry. (Cf. Psalm 103:10–12 for a similar poetic parallelism.)

The elder brother coming in from the fields hears the rejoicing and calls one of the house boys to find out what is going on. J. A. Findlay remarks on the stiff and superior Greek which St Luke uses at this point. He will not go in. But the father, again forgetting his dignity, *goes out to*

11. Fatted calf rather than prize calf (verse 23). It was an animal that was forcibly fed for the table.

him just as he had gone out to meet the younger son, and pleads with him to come in. The elder brother's reply is very revealing. 'All these years I have worked like a slave for you.' This is not the relationship of a son to his father! 'But this son of yours . . .' – the whole phrase is contemptuous (cf. Matthew 20:12, Luke 18:11, Acts 17:18) and he will not call him 'brother' – '. . . wasted all your property on prostitutes . . .' The elder brother supplies that out of his own mind. There has been no previous suggestion that the younger son had been sexually immoral. How often we project our sins and temptations on to other people! 'My son' hardly expresses the affection in the father's reply. He uses an intimate and endearing Greek word *teknon*, 'My dear boy . . . everything I have is yours.' This was literally true for the farm legally belonged to him. 'We had to have a feast and be happy . . .'

The last great touch in the parable is that it does not tell us how the elder brother responded to his father's appeal. It leaves *us* to finish the story. It is a pity that the parable was ever named (by elder brothers!?) 'The Prodigal Son' or 'The Lost Son'. It is a parable about a loving father and his *two* sons, as is clearly stated in the opening verse of it. The hero of the story is the father, and *both* sons are equally lost.

In a marvellous way, it gathers up the two parables which come before it. The sheep was lost out in the wilderness like the younger son in the far country. The coin was just as completely lost inside the house itself, like the elder brother at home on the farm. We must remember that Jesus told the parable in response to the grumbling of the Pharisees that he welcomed outcasts. It is addressed to the Pharisees, the elder brothers. The prodigals are coming home; the spiritually dead are coming to life, and Jesus like the father in the story is going out to meet them and welcome them. He challenges his critics to recognize themselves in the joyless self-righteous and unforgiving elder brothers and to turn from their hardness of heart, and be merciful as God is merciful. He also warns them that if they do not turn they will cut themselves off from the heavenly Father as the elder brother did, and remain by their own choice in the darkness outside.

The Shrewd Manager (chapter 16)

For many people this is the most difficult of our Lord's parables because, on the face of it, it seems that Jesus approves of dishonesty. Ingenious attempts have been made to show that the manager was not dishonest, but was only remitting his own commission on the deal.[12] Suffice it to say here that with the exception of one or two of the longer stories like the Good Samaritan, or the Prodigal Son, the parables of Jesus are always spotlights, not floodlights. That is, they focus on just one or at most two truths and highlight them, and we are not meant to press the other details of the story, for they are just background material, intended to remain in the shadows.

So here it matters not whether the manager is honest or dishonest. Jesus singles out his energetic and decisive action for approval, and draws attention to the fact which is permanently (and sadly) true, that worldly men are often more keen about the things of this world than godly men are about the things of God. A second lesson, drawn by Jesus himself, is that the manager invested in friendship. He realized that friends are more important than cash! The meaning of verse 9 may simply be that we are to use worldly wealth to make friends who will welcome us beyond death. But in view of the very common practice of referring to God in a roundabout way, out of reverence (see p. 97), it is likely that the real meaning is, 'Use worldly wealth to make *God* your friend, so that when it gives out, he may welcome you to the eternal home.' Some manuscripts read *eklipete*, 'when *you* give out', not *eklipe*, 'when *it* gives out'.

Verses 10–13 are a collection of pithy sayings of Jesus which may or may not have been given at the same time

12. Detailed discussion is beyond the scope of this commentary. An excellent treatment can be found in *Companion to the New Testament*, by A. E. Harvey, p. 267; *St Luke*, by G. B. Caird, p. 185; and in *The Parables of the Kingdom*, by C. H. Dodd, Fontana, p. 26.

as the parable, but St Luke appropriately places them here. They can be thought of as variations on the theme of the parable like variations on a theme in music. A man's behaviour in small matters is a guide to his fitness for greater responsibilities; and our stewardship of this world's wealth, which does not belong to us but is only lent to us on trust (cf. 1 Timothy 6:7), is a guide to whether we are fit to have the true wealth of the kingdom of heaven.

Money is one of the great rivals with God for man's allegiance and service. We cannot, says Jesus, divide our loyalties between God and money in a 'both . . . and' kind of way. It is 'either . . . or'. Either we serve God to salvation, or we serve money to our spiritual ruin (cf. 1 Timothy 6:8–10).

Some Sayings of Jesus

St Luke is hardly fair in accusing the Pharisees of loving money. They were not as avaricious as the Sadducees, or as many of the tax gatherers for that matter, though they did regard prosperity as a sign of divine favour. But Jesus is right in accusing them of wanting to look right in men's sight. (See p. 77f.) Once again he points to the fundamental opposition between the world's values and the values of God. Though the Pharisees are religious men, yet they think as the world thinks.

Verse 16 stresses the 'new thing' that has come into the world with Jesus, and the verse has the universal note (*everyone* forces his way in) that is characteristic of St Luke.

Verse 17 reads strangely when we remember the way in which Jesus challenges the scribes and Pharisees on the Law of the Sabbath and on ceremonial cleanliness. But Jesus accepted the religion of the Old Testament as the revelation of God. He did not destroy the Law but made clear its true depth of meaning, and he did this often by scraping away the traditions of men which had overlaid it and obscured it. The words 'smallest detail' in our translation refer to the 'serifs', that is, the little lines at the top or bottom of a letter which distinguished certain Hebrew letters which were very like each other.

In verse 18 we have an example of Jesus's handling of the Law. There were two schools of thought on divorce in the time of Jesus. According to Deuteronomy 24:1, a man could divorce his wife 'If she finds no favour in his eyes because he has found some indecency in her.' There was great argument about what this rather vague statement meant. The school of Shammai held that it meant unfaithfulness and nothing else. But the school of Hillel (another famous Pharisee) held that if she was a bad cook, spoke to a strange man, or if she spoke slightingly of his relations in his hearing, or if she offended in many other trivial ways, it would constitute sufficient grounds to give her a bill of divorcement and send her away.

Taken by itself, this verse seems to suggest that Jesus is laying down an even stricter law than Shammai. But Jesus is not a legislator who gives laws and rules. He always goes deeper and shows the intention of divine love which underlies a law. We shall understand this short verse best if we see it in the light of the longer passage in Matthew 19:3–8. Jesus says that the Law of Moses allowed divorce because of the hardness of men's hearts. When men's hearts are hard, marriages always break down, and then the Law must step in to regulate the situation, to protect both society and the parties themselves. But when God created us male and female, the intention of divine love was a lifelong partnership. Anything less than this is a falling away from God's ideal. But only in the kingdom of heaven where love rules, and hearts of stone have been turned into hearts of flesh, will the ideal be realized in life. (Cf. Ezekiel 11:19.)

The Rich Man and Lazarus

St Luke has a particular compassion for the poor, and so it is not surprising that he (and he alone) has preserved this parable for us. It is the only parable in the gospels in which a character is given a name. Lazarus is the Greek form of the Hebrew name Eleazar, which means 'God is his help', and indeed Lazarus was well named for in the story nobody but God did give him any help! Tradition has given the name Dives to the rich man. (Dives is simply the Latin word for rich man.)

In a few strokes, the brief description of Dives gives a vivid picture of extreme luxury. He dresses in the most expensive finery, and feasts *every* day. Guests at a rich man's table wiped their fingers during the meal on lumps of bread which they then threw away. Those reclining near the windows would toss them out into the street where beggars like Lazarus would be waiting to eat such scraps. Lazarus seems to have been a beggar because he was a cripple, for he had to be brought to the rich man's door.

As Dives's lot is pictured as the ultimate in luxury, so Lazarus's lot is vividly sketched as the ultimate in poverty; 'Even the dogs would come and lick his sores.' In the east, the pariah dog is an unclean and avoided animal. But at death, the roles are reversed. Lazarus becomes the guest of honour at the heavenly banquet.[13] The rich man is in pain in Hades. The word Hades usually means 'the place of the departed' without any reference to reward or punishment, and is the equivalent of the Hebrew 'Sheol'. But round about the time of Jesus it was sometimes used to mean Gehenna, the fiery place of punishment, and it seems to be so used here.

'Send Lazarus to dip his finger in some water and cool off my tongue.' The rich man has not learned much. He still expects to be waited on! But it is to his credit that when he is told that this cannot be done, he wants to save his brothers from sharing his own fate. He thinks that if someone rose from the dead and went to them, they would certainly repent. But Abraham replies that if they will not heed the teaching God has given them through the Law and the prophets, they will not be convinced by someone returning from the dead. St Luke and the early Christians must have been very keenly aware of the truth of that, for Jesus had risen from the dead but the Jews were not persuaded.

13. Older versions speak of him as being 'in Abraham's bosom'. Guests reclined at table and the one 'in his host's bosom' was the guest of honour reclining next to him. Cf. John 13:23.

We are sometimes tempted to think that the original disciples were on better terms than we are. They actually *saw* Jesus, and heard him, and lived with him. How fortunate they were! We are tempted to say with the writer of the children's hymn:

I wish that his hands had been placed on my head,
That his arms had been thrown around me,
And that I might have seen his kind look when he said:
Let the little ones come unto me!

                                        (Jemima Luke)

But this fails to understand the need for faith. They had no advantage over us. It was as easy for them to explain away the miracles, or attribute them to Satan, or to reject him, as it is for us – and many of those who saw Jesus in the flesh did so. It needed the eye of faith to see the glory of God in the face of Jesus Christ just as much then as it does now.

We should not place too much weight on the details of the after-life given in the story. They are really just background material taken from a popular folk-tale of the time.

This parable teaches what Jesus has taught in other places, namely the reversal of earthly values and situations which will take place in the kingdom of heaven. It also invites our judgement on the selfish and callous luxury of Dives in face of the poverty and suffering of Lazarus. And here it must prick our consciences, for we are Dives, all of us in western society, dressed in expensive clothes and feasting in great magnificence every day, while at our gate – nay, in our very living-room, on the television – is Lazarus sick in India, and starving in Africa, and we do nothing about it.

Sin (chapter 17)

St Luke introduces here three sayings which have no real connection with each other, but which may have come to him together from his source called 'Q' which seems to have consisted mainly of the sayings and teaching of Jesus. (See p. 10.)

Verses 1–3a: to drown a demon in deep water was popularly believed to be the only way to destroy it completely. Jesus seems to have been unique in the ancient world in his love for children and his interest in them. They no doubt followed him as children in the east still follow any unusual person. But instead of ignoring them as other Rabbis did, Jesus welcomed them. He put his arms round them (Mark 9:36 and 10:16). He watched their games with interest (7:31–34). He held them up as an example to adults and said that the kingdom of heaven belonged to such as them (Matthew 18:2–4). He said that anyone who welcomed a child in his name welcomed him, and not only him, but God as well (Mark 9:37). Jesus has revolutionized men's attitude to children, and his spirit is a continuing inspiration of child care in all its forms.

Verses 3b–4: untold damage and misery is caused in personal relationships because so often causes of friction and offence are not dealt with by being faced openly and honestly, and then healed by repentance and forgiveness. Instead, time is allowed to dull the sharpness of the pain until the whole thing can be forgotten. But in truth it is not forgotten, but buried alive in the deep levels of the mind where it goes on festering like an abscess that has never been drained, poisoning the continuing relationship. The saying 'time heals' is one of the most untrue of all popular sayings.

In these two short verses there is a whole philosophy of personal relations: the direct confrontation; the cleansing repentance; the healing forgiveness; and the tireless goodwill to go on doing this as often as may be necessary. Seven is the perfect number, and 'seven times' means 'as often as is needed'.

Faith

Once again St Luke refers to the disciples by the title Apostles which does not really belong to them until after the Resurrection. (See p. 39.) Jesus replies to their request that he will make their faith greater with a saying which is a vivid and poetic way of illustrating that apparently impossible things can be achieved by faith. The mustard seed is one of the smallest of all seeds and the mulberry tree one of the most deeply rooted and difficult trees to dig up. For the tree to pull itself up and plant itself in the sea would not be just one impossibility but two! That is a measure of what can be achieved by even a grain of real faith in God.

In the light of the very similar sayings in Matthew 21: 21–22 and Mark 11:21-24 which have 'hill' instead of 'mulberry tree', we are bound to wonder whether St Luke has slightly mixed up this vivid illustration, or perhaps has telescoped two sayings of Jesus together, one about a tree and another about a hill, for as one commentator says, to plant a mulberry tree in the ocean seems a singularly useless proceeding! St Paul's comment, 'I may have all the faith needed to move mountains' (1 Corinthians 13:2), supports Matthew's and Mark's rendering of the saying. But the meaning of either version is clear, and is perfectly captured in the verse:

> Faith mighty faith the promise sees,
> And looks to that alone;
> Laughs at impossibilities,
> And cries: It shall be done!

A Servant's Duty

This parable is delivered against the idea that we can pile up merit before God, or put God in our debt by good works. Its meaning hinges on the relationship of slave to master. The slave himself, and every moment of his time, was wholly and completely owned by his master. He could not possibly put his master in debt to him. Likewise, all that we have and are comes from God, and we belong to him. In that sense, slavery is an accurate illustration. But the basis of our relationship with God is different. It is one of a father's love on one side, and a child's response of love and trust in return, and here again, 'earning' or 'establishing merit' cannot enter into it.

Jesus Makes Ten Lepers Clean

The description of leprosy in Leviticus (13 and 14) suggests that a number of skin diseases were included under the general term leprosy. The worst terror of the disease was the ritual uncleanness which it carried. The leper was not allowed to have any contact with the person or possessions or dwelling of any other Jew. He was totally isolated from society and must have felt isolated from God as well, for he was cut off from the worship of both synagogue and temple. (See p. 35.)

So, the lepers stand at a distance and shout to Jesus. He tells them to go and let the priest examine them to certify that they are cured. Those of them who were Jews would have to journey all the way to Jerusalem. The Samaritan would go to the rival temple on Mount Gerazim. It made a tremendous demand on their faith for them to go like this. The healing miracles of Jesus are never acts of magic performed without any necessary response on the part of the subject. Miracles happen when the love of God is joined to the responding trust of man, as it is here.

It is puzzling that Jesus should complain that nine did not come back to give thanks, for he had himself sent them on the long journey to Jerusalem. We must be content to leave this question unanswered, for we are not given enough information to decide it. The gospels do not give us the kind of video-recording fullness and accuracy which would answer questions like this. Indeed, the setting of the whole story is somewhat of a puzzle. Jesus has been on his way to Jerusalem for eight chapters, and should long ago have left Galilee. If he is now between Samaria and Galilee, he is farther away from Jerusalem than he was at 13:22. The point we must always keep in mind is that the gospels are not biographies of Jesus. They sometimes disagree about the context of various sayings of Jesus, and about the order of events in his life. This is because the gospel writers never aimed at detailed accuracy of this kind. Indeed, in the ancient world it would have been impossible to achieve it anyway. They were written with only one purpose in view, 'that you may believe that Jesus is the Messiah, the Son of God, and that through this faith you may have life in his name' (John 20:31). They fulfil this purpose to perfection. We can put the point in another way. The gospels are not photographs, they are portraits. A photograph is absolutely accurate, a portrait is often not accurate. But a portrait by a great painter reveals more of the real character and personality of the sitter than a dozen photographs. The gospels are portraits, and their writers are artists indeed.

Perhaps the special interest which St Luke the Gentile had in recounting this healing was that in it Jesus commends the eager thankfulness of a Samaritan. It shows the love of Jesus going out beyond the confines of Jewry, and is thus a foretaste of the mission to the whole Gentile world.

The Coming of the Kingdom

The Jews in the days of Jesus were earnestly looking for a new order that would be brought in by the sudden act of God, and would reverse the unjust fortunes of this present age. They believed that it would be preceded by a time of terrible suffering. The early Christians also believed that they were living in the midst of the final act of God's drama of redemption. The whole world might be brought to its conclusion tomorrow – or even today – by the return of Christ in glory. The first letter to the Thessalonians (c. AD 50), which is perhaps the earliest writing in the New Testament, gives a vivid picture of this immediate expectation. (See especially 4:13–5:11.)

The sense of puzzlement and disappointment when the Day of the Lord did not appear as the years went by is reflected in the latest of the New Testament writings, the second letter of St Peter. (See especially 3:3–9.) This letter was written perhaps as late as AD 125, and was certainly not written by St Peter himself, for he died some sixty years earlier during the first of the great persecutions of the Church under the Emperor Nero.

Undoubtedly Jesus had foreseen the destruction of Jerusalem which took place in AD 70, and he warned the Jews of the judgement they were bringing down upon themselves. Scholars differ about the extent to which Jesus expected the end of the whole world and his return in glory during the lifetime of the original disciples. But whatever the truth of that may be, it is clear that the early Christians collected together his sayings about the doom of Jerusalem, and also about the coming Day of the Lord, the final triumph of God's Kingdom. They seem sometimes to have mixed the two events together in their collections.

These sayings were gathered into two great blocks of teaching in the earliest sources of the gospels. One block is in Mark 13, and the other at the end of the lost source 'Q' which we only know through those parts of it which are included in Matthew and Luke. St Luke reproduces here the collection as it stood in 'Q' with some small additions of his own. Later, in chapter 21, he will reproduce the collection in Mark, once again with his own special additions to it.

What are we to say about the Day of the Lord and the coming of Christ in glory? From New Testament times onwards there have always been sects who say that it is upon us at any moment, and even pretend to give the date. They describe it in vivid and literal terms. But Jesus said that he did not know the day or the hour; that lay within the Father's choice alone (see Mark 13:32–33). All speculation therefore is idle. We are to get on with the Lord's work so that whenever he comes we shall be found ready (cf. Matthew 25:1–13). We are also to have a firm trust that God will bring us to our fulfilment, and his whole world to its fulfilment, in his own way and in his own time. Then, all things will be summed up in Christ (cf. 1 Corinthians 15:24–28). Further than this we cannot go, and do not need to go.

The Parable of the Widow and the Judge (chapter 18)

In the Old Testament widows and orphans are symbols for the poor, the weak and the defenceless. The judge was not necessarily a man who would pervert justice, though bribery was (and is) rife in the east. The difficulty was often delay, and a bribe was given simply to get the case heard. H. B. Tristram, in *Eastern Customs in Bible Lands*, p. 228, quotes an exact modern parallel to this story from the court at Nisibis in Mesopotamia. The judge was surrounded by secretaries and the court was full of people trying to get a hearing. The wise ones slipped a bribe to a secretary and their case was soon called. All through the proceedings a poor woman raised a great clamour and refused to be silenced. She had apparently done this for many days. Finally the judge demanded impatiently what was the matter with her. It was a simple case, and to get rid of her he gave judgement on it before the end of the session.

This parable teaches the same lesson as the story of the friend who came at midnight (11:5f), namely that we must keep on praying and never become discouraged. The argument is by contrast. If a judge who does not care for a widow seeking justice can be pestered into hearing her case, *how much more* will God who *does care* for his children vindicate them? But St Luke has placed the parable immediately after the eschatological (i.e. concerning the end of the age, the last things) section (17:22–37), and it seems clear that in this setting he means it to be an encouragement to Christians who were becoming discouraged by persecution and because their hope that Jesus would quickly return in glory was not being fulfilled. They must continue to pray and to believe that God will judge in favour of his people who cry to him day and night. 'But will the Son of Man find faith on earth when he comes?' The Greek of verses 7 and 8 can be taken in more than one way. Instead of 'Will God not judge in favour of his own people who cry to him for help day and night? *Will he be slow to help them?* I tell you *he will judge in their favour and do it quickly*', the New English Bible reads, 'Will not God vindicate his chosen, who cry out to him day and night, *while he listens patiently to them*? I tell you, *he will vindicate them soon enough*.'

The Parable of the Pharisee and the Tax Collector

'Jesus also told this parable to people who were sure of their own goodness and despised everybody else.' In the telling of it, Jesus no doubt had the Pharisees in mind. But to be sure of one's own goodness and despise everybody else is the besetting temptation of all religious people!

There were three special hours of prayer, 9 a.m., 12 p.m., and 3 p.m. It was widely believed that prayer offered in the temple itself was particularly effective and meritorious, so many of the Jews came up at these hours to pray in its courts. People normally stood to pray and prayed aloud in a low voice. The Pharisee stood apart by himself - physically cut off from everybody else, just as in his prayer he cuts himself off from everybody else spiritually. ('I thank you, God, that I am not . . . like everybody else . . . I am not like that tax collector.') In addition to living a good life he is zealous in his religious observance. He fasts twice a week. The Law only demanded one fast a year, on the Day of Atonement. But pious Jews fasted on Mondays and Thursdays, which were believed to be the days on which Moses had ascended and descended Mount Sinai. He also gave a tenth of all his income. The Law required the tithing of main crops only (Numbers 18:21, Deuteronomy 14:22). But the Pharisee tithed in addition even garden herbs such as mint, anise and cummin. He was satisfied with himself!

The tax gatherer by his very profession was outside the Law. He stood at a distance. The characteristic attitude of prayer was with hands and eyes uplifted to heaven. But he does not venture to raise even his eyes, and with his hands he beats on his breast, overwhelmed by the sense of his separation from God, and beseeches God's mercy. This man, says Jesus, and not the Pharisee was in the right with God when he went home. St Luke rounds the story off with a saying which occurs in other places (i.e. 14:11, Matthew 23:12). God will humble the great and exalt the humble. The passive 'will be humbled . . .

will be made great' is a way of avoiding using the divine name out of reverence. (See p. 97, footnote.)

Religious though he is, and good man though he undoubtedly is, the Pharisee is farther from God than the tax collector. His real interest is in himself, not in God. He is full of himself! 'I' and 'my' occur no less than seven times in his short prayer. His trust is not in God but in his own religious achievements and supposed righteousness.

He cuts himself off from everybody else, especially from 'that tax collector', and despises them. As J. A. Findlay points out, 'We cannot cut ourselves off from other men even in our prayers without cutting ourselves off from God.' He compares himself with other people which is always a useless thing to do. Perhaps the most serious thing about his spiritual state is that he is entirely satisfied with himself and therefore is not capable of any further spiritual growth; and because his heart is centred on himself and not on God he is never likely to become dissatisfied with himself. What a terrible plight to be in!

The tax collector on the other hand is not as good a man as the Pharisee, but he is closer to God because he has seen himself as he really is in the light of God's holiness, and has cast himself on God's mercy. The words of Psalm 51, 'A broken and a contrite heart, O God, thou wilt not despise', are fulfilled in him.

Jesus Blesses Little Children

At this point, St Luke returns to the gospel of Mark which he has not used since 9:50. He takes from Mark the stories of the blessing of the children, and the rich man. Both are concerned with the conditions of entering the Kingdom of God.

It is interesting to note the way in which St Matthew and St Luke play down the human emotions of Jesus which are shown so much more clearly in Mark, our earliest gospel. There was a tendency in the early Church, which increased through many centuries, to exalt the divinity of Jesus at the expense of his humanity. In Mark, Jesus is angry with the disciples for stopping people from bringing their children (Mark 10:14), and in Mark, Jesus takes the children in his arms and places his hands on each of them (Mark 10:16). St Luke does not record either of these warm human emotions.

What are the characteristics of childhood that we must have if we are to enter the Kingdom? First, and most important, the willingness to receive what we have not earned and cannot deserve. A child receives like this every day. It is only when we grow up that we live in a world where we have a duty to earn things – and the other side of that coin, a right to demand things. Second, the willingness to be dependent on God as a child is dependent on his parents. Third, trust; we must learn to rely on God and trust him as a child relies on his parents and trusts them. Fourth, openness; children have no prejudices which make their minds closed and prevent them from accepting new truth.

The Rich Man

Once again St Luke omits the details in Mark which show emotion – that the man *ran up* and *knelt* before Jesus, and that Jesus looked straight at him *with love* (Mark 10:17 and 21). Jesus turns the man's rather fulsome greeting away from himself to God. His answer to the question, 'What must I do to receive eternal life?' is 'Keep the commandments', that is, follow the religion which God has given to his people. The man has tried to do this from his youth but still has a sense of unfulfilment and dissatisfaction. St Paul in his pre-Christian days would have confessed to the same emptiness, and also to the truth that the harder one tries the worse the situation becomes. Jesus sees right into the man's soul, and knows that the thing which stands between him and full commitment to God is his wealth. Let him give that up, and join the disciples and he will find the fulfilment he is longing for. But he is very rich and the renunciation is too much for him. He had run to Jesus with such eagerness, now he goes slowly away.

We should not try to soften our Lord's remark about the camel and the needle by saying that because in Greek *kamelos* means a camel, and *kamilos* a rope, that perhaps rope is the better reading to go with needle. Nor must we talk about the tiny side gate in Jerusalem called the Needle's Eye, through which a beast can only squeeze when it has been stripped of its load. Jesus loved poetic hyperbole, vivid and exaggerated images for the sake of emphasis, and the gospel writers have no doubt remembered his saying quite accurately.

This incident does not teach that it is impossible to be a true follower of Christ unless we give all our money away first. Jesus diagnosed that in the case of this particular man, the thing which stood between him and God was his money. It may not be so with everyone, other things can come between men and God. But wealth is especially dangerous, because it focuses our affections on the things of this world ('your heart will always be where your riches are', Matthew 6:21), and it tempts us to trust in it rather than in God (cf. 12:13–21). It also inculcates attitudes of status and power over others which are the very opposite of the humility and self-sacrificing service which must be seen in the sons and daughters of the Kingdom. Wealth may not be evil in itself, but it is spiritually one of the most dangerous things in the world.

Peter points out that the disciples have given up everything, and Jesus replies with a paradox which Christians have proved all down the centuries, that when we give up anything for God, we find that we receive from him more than ever we have given. In losing our life for him we find it.

Jesus Speaks a Third Time about His Death

St Matthew is interested in the fulfilment of *prophecies* and often quotes texts from the Old Testament. St Luke is interested in the fulfilment of *prophecy*. Jesus had seen into the very heart of the scriptures, and the eternal truths which were written there were actually being lived out in him. His deep insight into spiritual reality enabled him to see what *must* happen. It was inevitable that his own people would hand him over to the Romans to get rid of him, and he was convinced that it was equally inevitable that God would vindicate him.

Perhaps we find it hard to understand how the disciples could be so stupid as not to know what Jesus was talking about. But men's power not to see what they cannot bear to see is astonishing. A man who is slowly dying of cancer and is afraid of death will interpret each deterioration as 'a temporary setback' until those nursing him wonder how he can possibly be so blind to the truth.

Jesus Heals a Blind Beggar

The long period of journeying towards Jerusalem which began at 9:51 is now drawing to its close. Jesus and his disciples seem to have joined a company of pilgrims going up to the city for Passover (the 'crowd passing by' in verse 36). It was common for those who could not go up to a festival to line the road as a pilgrim company passed through a village or town to see them pass by and to wish them godspeed on their pilgrimage. The blind man (Mark tells us he was called Bartimaeus, Mark 10:46) hears the commotion and asks what is happening. They tell him that Jesus of Nazareth is passing by.

He immediately hails Jesus by the Messiah's title 'Son of David' – the only time in the gospels when Jesus is addressed by this title. Was it this cry which put into words what many of the pilgrims must have been thinking? And was it the talk that Bartimaeus set going that was responsible for Jesus entering into Jerusalem as the Messiah was expected to enter, when they arrived at the city a few days later on Palm Sunday? (Cf. Zechariah 9:9–10).

Rabbis often taught as they walked, and we can imagine the crowd who were around Jesus hanging on his every word. They cannot hear what he is saying for the clamour Bartimaeus is raising, and he is roundly told to shut up and be quiet. But he only shouts even more loudly, 'Son of David! Have mercy on me!' In the Greek, a much stronger word, literally 'to scream out', is used for his second cry. Jesus stops and orders that Bartimaeus be brought to him. St Luke omits Mark's vivid details

that he *threw off* his cloak and *jumped up* (Mark 10:50).
We must notice how Jesus insists on his full co-operation
and that he shall fully commit himself to faith. (See p. 107.)
'What do you want me to do for you?' It was obvious!
But Bartimaeus must say it himself and believe it in the
saying. 'I want to see again.' Then come the sweetest
words he has ever heard, 'See! Your faith has made
you well', and with them the sight he longs for. It is
a characteristic touch of St Luke to end the story with
the praise of the crowd. Praise rings right through St
Luke's gospel, from the praise of the blessed virgin Mary
in chapter 1 to the praise of the disciples in the last verse
of its final chapter.

Jesus and Zacchaeus (chapter 19)

This is yet another story from the rich store of material
which only St Luke has preserved for us. The Jordan
valley from the Lake of Galilee in the north to the Dead
Sea in the south is for the most part dry and barren. But
at Jericho which lies close to the mountains of Judea
twenty miles from Jerusalem, there is a spring which
irrigates fields and orchards, making it a green jewel in
the desert. Jericho was famous in the time of Jesus for its
palms and balsam groves which perfumed the air for
miles around. Its dates and balsam were exported to all
parts of the Empire. It was also the principal eastern
frontier town of Judea, and was a busy centre of com-
merce and travel.

Zacchaeus was a superintendent of taxes. The Roman
government farmed out the collection of taxes to the firm
which could offer the highest revenue from a given area.
These firms made their money partly by exacting more
than was due (often grossly overcharging) and partly by
investing the money in business ventures before paying
it over to Rome.

Zacchaeus was probably the head of such a firm. The
word *architelones* which is used to describe him occurs
nowhere else in Greek literature, or in the New Testament
either, so it is difficult to be sure exactly what his position
was. But he was certainly rich, hated, and despised! It

took no small amount of courage for him to make himself conspicuous in a crowd, and it involved a total loss of dignity for him to run on ahead and climb a sycamore tree. But like Bartimaeus he was determined to see Jesus, and nothing was going to put him off. What did he expect when Jesus looked up at him? A prophet's stinging denunciation probably. But to his amazement Jesus asks if he might be his guest. As W. R. Maltby says, 'For one friend Jesus made that day, he must have lost a hundred when he chose Zacchaeus to be his host.' Dr Bratcher translates verse 3 in a way which makes it clear that it was Zacchaeus who was the little man. But the Greek could equally mean that it was Jesus who was a little man. Compare the Common Bible translation, 'he sought to see who Jesus was, but could not, on account of the crowd, because he was small of stature.'

It was always open to a tax gatherer to be restored to respectable Jewish society if he repented and made restitution to those from whom he had exacted more than was due. To cover the cases he could no longer remember, he was required to make a donation to charity. Zacchaeus offers to give half his wealth to the poor – much more than could possibly be required; and in any known case to restore not only the amount plus one fifth which the Law required (Leviticus 6:1–5), but the much greater amount required in cases of robbery and destruction of the property (Exodus 22:1). This is generosity indeed! Jesus refers to him by one of the most cherished titles any Jew could bear, he is a 'son of Abraham'.[14] What a wonderful sense of his own value that title on the lips of Jesus must have given him! All this happened because instead of shunning him as the righteous people did, Jesus deliberately sought his company.

The Parable of the Gold Coins

Scholars are agreed that two separate stories have become intermingled in this parable. There is first the story of the nobleman who went away to a far country

---

14. Dr Bratcher unfortunately uses the more impersonal 'descendant' of Abraham, as he does at 13.16.

to be made king. Jesus's hearers would be quite familiar with the details of this story. When Herod the Great died in 4 BC he divided his kingdom, leaving the province of Judea to Archelaus his son. Archelaus went to Rome to persuade the Emperor Augustus to appoint him king of Judea. But the Jews hated him so much that they sent a delegation of fifty men to oppose his election. Augustus did appoint him, though not with the title of king. On his return to Palestine, Archelaus slaughtered his opponents!

St Luke says that Jesus told this parable to those who expected 'that the Kingdom of God was just about to appear'. The teaching is clear, and it applied equally to those in the early Church who expected Christ to return in glory at any minute. There will be a long delay. But Christ will return, having entered into his Kingdom, and then his enemies will come under judgement.

The second parable about the ten servants (though only three of them have any importance in the story) fits well into the long period of absence in the first story with which it is interwoven. Each servant is given a mina, which was equal to a hundred denarii and therefore worth about ten pounds in our currency. This is much less than the 'talent' of Matthew's similar parable, which was worth 10,000 denarii (cf. Matthew 25:14–30). The first two trade successfully, but the third does not. In St Luke's version he wraps it in a napkin which was an irresponsible thing to do. According to Rabbinic Law, had it been stolen he would have had to make good the loss. In St Matthew's version he buries it in the ground, which was the safest thing to do with it, and in Rabbinic Law, released him from liability. But as far as the teaching of the parable is concerned, the point is the same in each case. He hoarded it, and did not increase it.

On our Lord's lips, this parable was no doubt spoken to the Pharisees and other pious Jews. They 'built a hedge about the Law' to keep it safe, and to avoid any contamination of themselves or of the truth God has revealed to Israel by contact with sinners or the Gentile world. But in doing so they are not, as they think, giving back to God what belongs to him, carefully preserved. They are defrauding him. They should risk their spiritual capital by trading with it in the wide world so that they might increase it for God.

St Luke ends the story in verse 26 with one of Jesus's wise general sayings, 'to every one who has, even more will be given; but the one who does not have, even the little that he has will be taken away from him.' This saying makes an apt ending to the parable.[15] It is also given in other contexts in Matthew 13:12, Mark 4:25, and Luke 8:18.

15. Many of the issues connected with this parable have only been touched upon here for reasons of space. A detailed discussion will be found in *The Parables of the Kingdom*, by C. H. Dodd, Fontana, pp. 108–114. For a modern application of the parable see my *To Me Personally*, Fontana, p. 20.

Part 5

DEATH, RESURRECTION
AND GLORY

The Triumphant Entry into Jerusalem

The distance from Jericho to Jerusalem is about twenty
miles, and the road climbs 4000 feet in that distance, to
the crest of the Mount of Olives. The great prophets of
Israel had not only spoken their message, but had often
given extra emphasis to it by acting it as well in dramatic
form. On one occasion, for instance, Jeremiah had
walked through the streets of Jerusalem wearing an ox's
yoke as a proclamation that Judah must come under the
yoke of the king of Babylon (Jeremiah 27:1–11). Jesus's
entry into Jerusalem was an acted message of this kind.
All four gospels record it, but each writer brings into
sharp focus the special thing which he wants to highlight.
St Luke, for example, does not mention the palms and
other branches which were symbols of festivity and
rejoicing. Instead, he highlights the spreading of the
disciples' cloaks on the road in front of Jesus which was
the gesture of acclaiming a king. Instead of quoting the
Zechariah prophecy, 'Here is your King who comes to
you in gentleness, riding on an ass . . .' (Zechariah 9:9),
he quotes Psalm 118:26, one of the 'Psalms of Ascent'
used by pilgrims coming up to a festival, 'God bless him
who comes in the name of the Lord!' but he inserts the
word king and adds the words, 'Peace in heaven and glory
to God!' which remind us of the angel's song at Bethlehem.

The Rabbis said that if Israel was worthy the Messiah
would come with the clouds of heaven, if unworthy,
riding on an ass. Jesus deliberately enters Jerusalem as
Messiah, riding on an ass, in fulfilment of Zechariah's
prophecy:

Rejoice greatly, O daughter of Zion!
Shout aloud, O daughter of Jerusalem!
Lo, your king comes to you; triumphant
and victorious is he, humble and riding on an ass,
on a colt the foal of an ass.
I will cut off the chariot from Ephraim
and the war horse from Jerusalem;
and the battle bow shall be cut off,
and he shall command peace to the nations;
his dominion shall be from sea to sea,
and from the River to the ends of the earth.

(Zechariah 9:9–10)

It is not surprising that the Pharisees complain about what must have seemed to them an almost blasphemous demonstration. Jesus rejects their complaint in the words of what seems to have been a proverb in those times, 'If they keep quiet, I tell you, the stones themselves will shout.'

Jesus Weeps over Jerusalem

As Jesus came over the Mount of Olives the whole city of Jerusalem lay spread out before him across the Kedron valley. This was one of the most beautiful and impressive views of the city. It was dominated by the immense and magnificent buildings of the temple, above which was Herod's citadel which overlooked the city from its highest point. The name 'Jerusalem' means 'vision of peace', and this is the subject of Jesus's lament. He foresaw that the proud nationalism of the Jews and their continual pin-pricking of the Roman power by uprisings and petty rebellions could have only one end, the total destruction of the city. By the time St Luke wrote his gospel, this destruction had already taken place, for in AD 70 the Roman armies under Titus razed Jerusalem to the ground. So beautiful was it that, according to Josephus the Jewish historian, Titus himself wept as he gave the order for its destruction.

Jesus Goes to the Temple

St Mark tells us that Jesus went straight to the temple but, as it was already late, returned to Bethany for the night. On the following morning he returned to the temple and cleansed its courts of the money changers (Mark 11:15–19). St Mark also gives us a fairly clear sequence of events for Holy Week. St Luke on the other hand does not give any clear indication of the days up to Maundy Thursday. He also abbreviates the account in Mark of the cleansing of the temple. Is this because he thought it might have made a bad impression on the high Roman official for whom he was writing his gospel? Theophilus might think that it was an act likely to ferment rioting and that in the very sensitive situation which always existed at Passover-time, Pilate and the authorities had been right to act with extreme severity. The cleansing of the temple may well have been another acted parable. Support for this view is given by the fact that in the account in the fourth gospel (John 2:13–17) the Greek word for the whip which Jesus made is a diminutive word which could be translated 'a little whip'.

In driving out the money changers and dealers in pigeons from the temple court, Jesus was making two protests at the temple trade. First he was protesting at the commercialism which used worship itself to make money out of the worshippers. The various coinages which were current in Palestine had to be changed, and at a high charge, into temple coinage to pay the temple tax of half a shekel per year which every male Jew had to pay. Again, animals for sacrifice certified as 'without spot or blemish and fit for sacrifice' (Leviticus 1:3) were sold in the temple. A worshipper could buy a pair of doves for about 5p outside in the city. But they would probably be declared unfit for sacrifice by the temple inspector. They would cost anything up to 75p from an official booth in the temple court!

Jesus's second protest was that this market place had been set up in the court of the Gentiles, the outermost of the temple courts, and the only one which Gentiles were allowed to enter. So what had been intended by God as a house of prayer for all peoples had been effectively closed to any nation except the Jews; and it had been turned into a hideout for thieves into the bargain. It is strange that St Luke the Gentile who normally takes every opportunity to emphasize the universality of the gospel should break off the quotation 'My house will be called a house of prayer . . .' before the words 'for all peoples' (cf. Mark 11:17 and Isaiah 56:7). But the temple had ceased to exist when St Luke wrote his gospel, and the nations were finding their way into the Church, not the temple of the old order.

The chief priests and the Pharisees would have liked to kill Jesus, but it is not easy to take a popular hero unless it is done by stealth, or unless he can be discredited in the eyes of the people first. This is what they now set out to do.

The Question about Jesus's Authority (chapter 20)

This question, which is the first of a number of attempts to trap Jesus, is put by a deputation which represented the various groups who formed the Sanhedrin, which was the supreme religious council of the Jews. They were not really seeking an answer to their question. Their minds were already closed and made up. They only wanted to find a means of getting rid of him. Thus, if he claimed the direct authority of God's Messiah, he could be charged with sedition against Rome, for was not the Messiah a king? If on the other hand he did not make any Messianic claims, the crowds would soon lose interest in him. Jesus's counter-question exposes their moral cowardice, and their discussion of how to answer him shows clearly that they are not concerned to discover the truth, but only to retain their own position and to find a means of getting rid of him. In these circumstances, there is absolutely no point in Jesus discussing his authority with them, and he refuses to do so.

The Parable of the Tenants in the Vineyard

The parables of Jesus were stories drawn from real-life situations which were within the experience of his hearers, and this one is no exception. In Jesus's day, Palestine was an occupied country. There were many absentee landlords, foreigners who owned large estates which they leased out to tenants, who paid a proportion of the annual yield to the absentee owner. There was a great deal of discontent and smouldering rebellion amongst the peasantry, and it is more than likely that rents were sometimes withheld and that the landlord's agents were received with hostility when they came for their dues. If the heir to a property of this kind died, it might well be declared 'an ownerless property' in which case it would pass to the first person able to establish a claim. Here, without doubt, possession would be nine points of the Law, as the old saying has it. In the turbulent years which led up to the general revolt of AD 66, refusal of rent followed by violence and even murder of the agent might well have taken place, together with the hope that if they killed the owner's son, the tenants might get possession of the vineyard (verse 14).

The direct lesson of the parable on Jesus's lips seems to have been that as the original tenants in the story will be cast out of the vineyard, and it will be given to others who will give the owner his due share of the harvest, even so, the Jewish religious leaders are being dispossessed by God, and the Kingdom is being given to those who are responding to Jesus, the common people and the tax collectors, and beyond them, the Gentiles.

But the story is rich in associations with the Old Testament symbolism of Israel as God's vine, or vineyard, and especially with the great song of the vineyard in the book of Isaiah (Isaiah 5:1–7) which was known to every Jew, and we can see the gospel writers changing the parable here and there, to bring out the similarity with Isaiah's song. In it, Israel is the vineyard and God is the planter and cultivator of it, who looked for it to yield grapes, but after all his care it yielded only wild grapes.

St Matthew and St Mark have made the opening of the parable more like Isaiah 5 by adding details about the digging of the winepress and the building of a watch-tower. None of these details are in Luke. St Mark has made the story more like the history of Israel by saying that the owner sent *many* servants to the tenants to receive his dues, 'and they treated many others the same way, beating some and killing others' (Mark 12:5). St Matthew has changed Mark's order of the killing of the son and the throwing of his body out of the vineyard to read in the reverse order, 'So they grabbed him, threw him out of the vineyard, and killed him' (Matthew 21:39), because this order brings the story more closely into line with the death of Jesus who was taken outside Jerusalem to be crucified.

Thus the original story of Jesus is given a new slant, more like an allegory,[1] and with a rich meaning for the early Christians. The whole history of God's dealings with Israel is now mirrored in it, and one of the most popular 'proof texts' from the Old Testament which Christians used in their arguments with the Jews now forms an ideal conclusion to the story:

> *The stone which the builders rejected as worthless*
> *Turned out to be the most important stone.*
>
> (Psalm 118:22)

St Luke alone adds another text which Christians often applied to Jesus, 'Everyone who falls on that stone will be cut to pieces; and if the stone falls on someone, it will crush him to dust.' (Cf. Daniel 2:34, Isaiah 8:14.) Some late manuscripts of Matthew include this verse, but it was not in the original text of Matthew. That is why Dr Bratcher prints it in Matthew 21:44, but in square

---

1. In a parable there is one chief point of likeness between the story and the meaning, and all the details of the story are exactly what they are in real life – a stone is a stone, a loaf is a loaf, etc. But an allegory is a kind of description in code, in which everything in the story stands for something else, and every detail has its special meaning.

brackets. It was probably first written in Matthew by a scribe who was familiar with Luke.

The Question about Paying Taxes

When Archelaus was deposed in AD 6 Judea, Samaria and Idumea were taken under direct rule by the Roman Emperor and administered by a procurator. At the same time, a poll tax (or 'head' tax) of one denarius per year was levied on each male adult from 14 to 65 years old. This caused the most intense anger amongst the Jews. It seemed to be the final proof of their loss of freedom and subjection to Rome. In Galilee there was a serious uprising under Judas the Galilean (mentioned in Acts 5:37) which was crushed by Rome.

The poll tax, then, was an extremely sensitive issue. Pilate would act quickly and finally against anyone who advised people to withhold the tax; and a Jewish crowd might act even more quickly against anyone who advised them to pay it! Jesus seems to be caught on the horns of a dilemma without hope of escape. The flattery with which the hired men approach him makes them doubly despicable. Jesus asks them to produce a denarius. 'Whose face and name are these on it?' If it was a recently minted coin it would bear the face and name of Tiberius Caesar. This must have made them uncomfortable, because in the ancient world the coinage was held to be the personal property of the king who issued it, and to accept his coinage meant to accept his authority. So they are really answered already, they have accepted Caesar as king and therefore must obey his laws. 'Well, then, pay to the Emperor what belongs to him, and pay to God what belongs to God.' Did Jesus mean pay the tax, or did he mean give Caesar's property back to him and get it out of Palestine? With superb quickness of wit, Jesus has escaped from their trap. But the genius of his reply is that it is more than just a trick answer to a trick question. Jesus here proclaims the principle which has ever since governed the relationship of Christians to the State, namely that we have a duty to the State, to obey the civil power, to be good citizens and to serve the community in which we live. But all authority comes from God and is under God, and is responsible to God, and our first duty is to him. If, therefore, the State becomes evil, then Christians must resist it to the death if need be in the name of God, to whom alone our first and absolute allegiance is due. (Cf. Romans 13:1–7 and 1 Peter 2:13–17 where this principle is worked out in greater detail.)

The Question about Rising from Death

The Sadducees were small in number compared with the Pharisees, but they were very wealthy and very powerful. They were the old priestly aristocracy, the ruling class. In religion they were extremely conservative. For instance, they only accepted the first five books of the Old Testament (called the Pentateuch) as fully authoritative, because these books were believed to have been written by Moses himself. They rejected the later belief in the resurrection of the dead which the Pharisees accepted, on the grounds that there was no evidence for it in the Torah, that is, the Law of Moses as contained in the Pentateuch. (See Acts 23:6–10 where St Paul sets the Sanhedrin in confusion by taking his stand as a Pharisee on this issue.)

They approach Jesus now with a question about the law of levirate marriage, which they had framed in such a way as to reduce the idea of the resurrection of the dead to absurdity. According to Deuteronomy 25:5–10, if a man died childless, his brother should marry the widow and beget a child with her, who in Law would count as the child of the dead man, 'so that his name might not be blotted out of Israel'. The Sadducees thought that their imaginary (and almost impossible) example of seven brothers dying childless in this way made the idea of resurrection absurd. Whose wife will she be when the dead are raised?

Jesus makes it clear that the physical aspect of sex and the earthly institution of marriage that goes with it do not apply in the life to come. But he then goes farther and, arguing in the Rabbinic way – meeting them on their own ground – suggests that belief in life beyond death is implied in a passage from the very Torah which they accept as infallible. In Exodus 3:6 God declares to Moses, 'I am the God of your fathers, the God of Abraham, the God of Isaac, the God of Jacob.' God could only have said this if they were still living; otherwise he must have said, 'I am the God who *was* the God of Abraham, and Isaac, and Jacob.' This kind of reasoning may not carry much weight for us today, but to the Sadducees who treated every word – nay, every letter – of the Law literally, and as infallible, it must have been devastating. Some of the scribes who were present were so impressed that they congratulated Jesus.

The Question about the Messiah

Jesus has survived all their attacks and his enemies have admitted defeat. He now asks them a question. Scholars have shown that the book of Psalms was written by various authors at various times. But in the time of Jesus it was universally believed that David was the author of the whole book, and our Lord would not have been perfectly human if he had not shared the beliefs of his time in matters like this. The most popular title for the Messiah was 'Son of David', and the popular picture of the Messiah was that of a warrior king like his forefather David, who would sweep the Romans into the sea and set up the chosen people as rulers of the earth.

Psalm 110 was taken to be a psalm about the Messiah, written of course by King David. What Jesus is saying to the people is 'You call the Messiah "Son of David", and he is, but is this idea big enough to include all the truth about him? In this psalm, David calls him *Lord*. What do you make of that?'

Jesus himself drew into the idea of the Messiah the divine figure of the Son of Man from the book of Daniel (Daniel 7:13) who would share the very throne of God; and the suffering servant from the book of Isaiah (Isaiah 53) who would pour out his soul unto death, and bear the sins of many.

We today face exactly the same temptation as the people who were listening to Jesus, to think that *we know*, that our doctrines and formulations *contain* God. They don't, they only reach out towards him. We must always be open to new truth and to have our understanding of God enlarged. This is sometimes a very painful process!

Jesus Warns against the Teachers of the Law

Jesus's first complaint against the scribes is their ostentation. When they were at prayer or performing certain of their scribal duties, they wore a specially long version of the Talith, the Jewish outer garment. Jesus accuses them of liking to walk about as well in their long scribal robes, so as to be noticed by people.

His second complaint is their love of superiority. The rule was that a man must salute his superior in the knowledge of the Law. The scribes loved to be greeted and have their superiority acknowledged in this way in the market place. It was becoming the custom in the time of Jesus for the elders to sit in front of the congregation in the synagogue, facing the people. They love this, says Jesus – and the best places at feasts as well (cf. 14:7–14).

The reference to taking advantage of widows is obscure. It could perhaps refer to taking large sums of money for offering prayers on their behalf. There have been periods in history when the Christian Church itself has not been guiltless in matters like this!

The Widow's Offering (chapter 21)

The court of the women was the second court of the temple, the next court inwards from the court of the Gentiles. In it stood the thirteen trumpet-shaped alms boxes, into which people put their offerings. The lepton (literally 'the thin one') was the smallest coin in value that was minted, worth less than a farthing. It was forbidden to offer one lepton in the temple. So the widow was making the smallest permitted offering when she put in two lepta.

But the richness of a gift is first the spirit in which it is given. A gift can be given casually or grudgingly or meanly, or it can be an expression of the love that is in the heart of the giver. The second richness of a gift is the sacrifice which it involves, its cost to the giver. The widow gave 'all she had to live on', that is, her whole daily wage. Gifts which are made from love, and with sacrifice, are precious to God whatever their value in cash may be.

Jesus Speaks of the Destruction of the Temple

The building of the new temple was begun by Herod the Great in 20 BC. It was still unfinished in the time of Jesus, but it was already one of the wonders of the ancient world. The pillars of the porches and cloisters were of white marble, forty feet high, each one made from a single block of stone. The eastern frontage was covered with heavy plates of gold which reflected the light of the rising sun with dazzling splendour. The most costly of the various offerings which adorned the temple was the great golden vine given by King Herod himself which was set up over the entrance. It was made from pure gold and each of its grape clusters was as tall as a man. All in all, the temple must have presented an overwhelming spectacle of beauty and splendour, solidity and permanence. To speak of its destruction was near blasphemy to Jewish minds, and it is interesting to note that this was one of the charges made against Jesus at his trial (Mark 14:57–58). But Jesus could read the signs of history. The Jewish nation was pressing on to its destruction, which came in the Jewish War of AD 68–70 and ended with the total destruction of the city and of the Jewish State.

Introduction to the following sections of chapter 21

For 600 years before the birth of Jesus, Jewish history had been a succession of disasters. In earlier days the Jews had hoped for a king like David to deliver them and rule over them in righteousness. But by the time Jesus was born they had long ago given up all human hope. Only a divine intervention by God himself could set things right! They divided history into two ages, the present age and the age to come. The present age was bad beyond any hope of redemption. But the age to come would be the golden age of God. In it there would be peace and prosperity for God's chosen people, who would be vindicated at last, and those who now oppressed them would be their slaves.

The age to come would be inaugurated by God himself entering human history and shattering the present order. Both the affairs of men and the natural world would be disrupted by his coming. This 'Day of the Lord' as it was called, or simply 'that Day', would be a day of terror and destruction and judgement, and the immediate period which led up to it would be one of suffering such as had never been known before. But in this travail the new age would be born.

In the period between the close of the Old Testament and the birth of Jesus there grew up a mass of literature concerning the Day of the Lord, and the age to come, which described its terrors and its judgement in strange symbols and veiled terms. Such literature was called 'apocalyptic' (from the Greek word *apocalupto* = to uncover, or to disclose). The great apocalyptic book at the end of the Old Testament era is the second half of the book of Daniel (Daniel 7–12), and the great apocalypse of the New Testament is the book of Revelation.

Alongside the belief in the Day of the Lord which they had inherited from Judaism, the Apostles believed in the second coming of Christ. Jesus himself had taught that he would return in glory, though he said that nobody, not even himself, knew or could know the time (Mark 13:32). It is easy to understand how the teaching concerning the Day of the Lord and our Lord's teaching about his return in glory became intertwined in the minds of the early Christians. It is also easy to understand how the first disciples expected Christ's return almost any day. The impact of his life and death, and the experience of his resurrection, must have been so great that it seemed to them that there was nothing left to happen in this world. Surely it had reached its consummation and was ready to be brought to its end. The earliest of the writings in the New Testament are dominated by the expectation of the immediate return of Christ. (See especially 1

Thessalonians 4:18–5:11, and 1 Corinthians 7:29–31 and 10:11.)

The third strand which is woven into this chapter in St Luke is the fall of Jerusalem. With deep insight into the spiritual and political realities of his day, Jesus had prophesied that Jerusalem would be destroyed and her people scattered. When this came, it must have seemed like the end of the world, and the sufferings that preceded it were so terrible that as it approached it is easy to understand how men linked it in their minds with the Day of the Lord and the coming of Christ in glory. All these strands are woven together in the rest of chapter 21, to which we now turn.

Troubles and Persecutions

Jacob and Moses, Joshua, Samuel and David, and many others of the great figures in Israel's history, had assembled their sons or disciples when their death drew near and delivered to them a farewell discourse. This section, and those which follow, can be thought of as a farewell discourse of Jesus in which he looks forward to the things which are to come and warns his disciples of the trials and sufferings that lie ahead. It applied originally to those who were with him in the days of his flesh, but it has brought strength and hope to many generations of Christians under persecution, and will do yet.

Jesus Speaks of the Destruction of Jerusalem

The destruction of Jerusalem took place in AD 70 at the end of one of the most frightful sieges in all history, towards the end of which the inhabitants were actually reduced to cannibalism. The Church historian Eusebius tells us that in AD 68 before the siege began the Christians in the city fled to Pella in Peraea in response to a revelation from God – and one would think with the warning of Jesus also in mind.

The Coming of the Son of Man

Terrible as the persecutions and sufferings just described will be, they are not the signs of the end. This will be heralded by events of an altogether different kind. The imagery of this paragraph is drawn from apocalyptic literature (see p. 131) and from the Old Testament (cf. Joel 2:10 and 3:15, Ezekiel 32:7-8). 'The roar of the sea and the raging tides' (verse 25) refers to more than ordinary storms. To the Jews, the sea was the great reservoir of evil (cf. Revelation 13:1). God had bound it at creation and said, 'Thus far shall you come and no farther.' (See Job 38:8-11) But he had still to secure his complete and final conquest over it.[2]

'The powers in space' (verse 26) probably refers to the angelic beings created by God who were allowed to preside over the destinies of the Gentile nations. For these to be driven from their courses would denote the break-up of the established world order of civil and international relations.

The picture of the Son of Man coming with the clouds of heaven is taken from the book of Daniel (7:13-14), where the beast-like kingdoms of tyranny are conquered and one like a Son of Man (i.e. a human figure in contrast to the beasts) comes with the clouds of heaven and receives from the Ancient of Days (i.e. from God) an *everlasting* kingdom over *all* peoples and nations and languages.

St Luke makes a small but significant and very wonderful alteration to his source in Mark 13:26 (and behind Mark, in Daniel 7:13). The Son of Man in Mark comes '*in the* clouds' (or '*with the* clouds' in Daniel) 'with great power and glory'. He comes here 'in a cloud'. This is the gentle cloud of the presence of God which had overshadowed Jesus and his disciples at the Transfiguration (9:34) and which received Jesus and hid him from their sight as he ascended into heaven (Acts 1:9). It is the same cloud of God's presence which guided and protected the children of Israel as they journeyed through the wilderness (Exodus 14:19 and 34:5, Numbers 9:16-23). The

2. It is interesting to note that in the vision of heaven in Revelation 4:6 the sea in front of the throne of God is as clear as glass – it has been stilled. In the final vision of the new heaven and the new earth in Revelation 21:1, 'the sea vanished', it was no more!

end of the world and all the convulsions of it, says St Luke, will be overshadowed by the guiding and protecting cloud of God's presence which has been with his people from the beginning.

The Lesson of the Fig Tree

There are certain things that go inseparably together, like the new green growth of spring and the coming of summer which it heralds. Even so, the final tribulations will herald the coming of Christ in glory. The statement that all this will happen in the lifetime of the first generation of disciples 'before the people now living have all died', has caused much discussion.

(1) It could be that Jesus originally delivered this little parable with regard to the fall of Jerusalem, which did happen in the lifetime of the first generation of Christians, and that the gospel writers mistakenly applied it to the last things as well.

(2) It could be that Jesus expected his return in glory within the lifetime of his first disciples and that he was wrong. Perhaps we should be much less touchy than many of us are about admitting the human ignorance of Jesus. If he was fully and perfectly human, he must have shared the ignorance and fallibility that belong to humanity in regard to future events.

(3) It could be that we have here an example of what is called 'prophetic perspective'. The Hebrews did not have quite the same attitude to time as we have. Even the Hebrew language does not have tenses in the same way that modern languages do. Things to the Hebrew mind were either complete or incomplete. If *God* had decided something, it could be regarded as already complete, so certain was it, even if it had not actually happened. The prophets often stressed the certainty of some future happening by stressing how close it was – 'it is at the very door!' So, to the Jewish mind, Jesus's stress on the closeness of his coming would not carry the same meaning in regard to time as it does for us, but would rather convey the *certainty* of the event.

The Need to Watch

The lesson we are to learn from this section, and Jesus teaches it in a number of the parables, is watchfulness and readiness. We are to live our lives in such a way that all the great moments of life (and death!) when they come, as well as that last great moment, will find us 'in Christ' and ready. We shall not then be taken unawares and unprepared. But it cannot be said too strongly that speculation about the day and the hour of Christ's coming is both futile and harmful. It is not within our knowledge, and it is not intended to be (cf. Mark 13:32–33).

The Plot against Jesus (chapter 22)

The Feast of Unleavened Bread was not strictly the same as the Passover. The seven days of unleavened bread were from the fifteenth to the twenty-first of the month Nisan (Leviticus 23:5–6). The Passover lambs were killed on the afternoon of the fourteenth of Nisan, and eaten that same night. According to Jewish reckoning the new day began at sunset, so the Passover was eaten as the days of unleavened bread began.

Passover was the greatest of all the Jewish feasts. It commemorated the deliverance of Israel out of slavery in Egypt (Exodus 12). On that night the angel of death slew the firstborn of the Egyptians but 'passed over' the houses of the Israelites whose door posts were smeared with the blood of a lamb. The Israelites left Egypt in such haste that there was no time to bake bread with leaven (i.e. yeast). They took instead a kind of biscuit which could be baked quickly and is called in Deuteronomy 'the bread of affliction' (Deuteronomy 16:3).

Every year the Jews gathered in families (as they still do) to celebrate God's great act which had delivered them from bondage and created them into a nation. The head of the house rehearsed the story of the Exodus, and the Passover lamb was eaten, everybody standing, loins girt and staff in hand, to symbolize the flight from Egypt on that first Passover night. Jews scattered all over the world kept Passover, but it was the ambition of every Jew to celebrate it at least once in his lifetime in Jerusalem. So the city was always packed to capacity at Passover-time.

Judas Agrees to Betray Jesus

The chief priests wanted to find some way of arresting Jesus quietly. He was a very popular figure with the people, and it took only a tiny spark to kindle the flames of rioting in the overcrowded city. Judas gave the authorities what they were looking for, an insider's knowledge of Jesus's movements. Many pilgrims camped out all round Jerusalem during Passover, and Judas gave the priests the essential information that Jesus went to a garden called Gethsemane on the slopes of the Mount of Olives. There, at night, he could be taken without causing any fuss.

Why Judas should have betrayed his Lord is one of the world's unsolved mysteries. Did he realize that the end had come and hope to save his own skin by turning king's evidence? Or did he think that he could force Jesus's hand and make him take the expected role of the Messiah who would lead Israel victorious against her enemies? We shall never know and we have not even a certain knowledge of his end to guide our thinking. St Matthew tells us that he brought the money back to the priests and then went and committed suicide, which suggests that he had never intended things to turn out as they did, and was bitterly repentant (Matthew 27:3–5). But St Luke in his second volume (Acts 1:18) says that he bought a field with the money (the Greek word can also mean a small farm), where he fell down and died by an act of divine judgement, his bowels bursting out. This suggests that he was impenitent to the end.

Here in his gospel St Luke simply says 'Satan went into Judas', and that is the deepest diagnosis of all, and the certain one. He gave himself to the powers of evil. Many people today think that when we have understood a man's character and actions in terms of his childhood background, his psychological complexes and his physical make-up, we have understood everything about him. But deeper than all this, and operating through it, is the cosmic struggle against the power of darkness. It was to this power that Judas yielded, and it is this power that Jesus conquered in his life and in his death.

Satan, who after the temptation had left Jesus for a while, now returns through Judas to join the final battle. Only St Luke tells us that Satan 'left him *for a while*' (4:13 and cf. also 22:28).

Jesus Prepares to Eat the Passover Meal

There is every reason to think that Jesus had arranged beforehand for his last meal with his disciples. A man carrying a jar of water would be as conspicuous in Jerusalem as the proverbial 'man wearing a white carnation' on an English railway station, for it was a woman's work to carry water.

The larger houses in Palestine had an upper room which was approached by an outside stairway. In this room the disciples are to make ready for Jesus's last supper with them.

The Lord's Supper

There has been much discussion as to whether or not the Last Supper was a Passover meal. According to the fourth gospel Jesus is actually dying on the Cross as the Paschal (i.e. Passover) lambs are being slain in the temple (see John 18:28 and 19:14). Jesus is truly 'the Lamb of God, who takes away the sin of the world' as John the Baptist proclaims at the beginning of that gospel (John 1:29). St Paul in 1 Corinthians 5:7 seems to support this view. The Passover meal, then, according to the fourth gospel took place *after* Jesus was crucified.

The suggestion in Mark and Luke is that the Last Supper was the Passover meal, though it is not completely impossible to take it otherwise.

Our translation prints the second half of verse 19 and verse 20 in square brackets. This is because some very important manuscripts of Luke do not contain these verses. Many scholars think that they were inserted in the manuscripts that do contain them to harmonize the text of Luke with that of Mark 14:22–24 and with 1 Corinthians 11:23–25. If these verses did not form part of the original text of the gospel as St Luke himself wrote it, then he gives us the order, first the blessing of the cup and second the blessing of the bread. This is the reverse order to the one given in Mark, which has become traditional in the Church. But St Luke's order is the one suggested in 1 Corinthians 10:16 and 10:21. It is also the order given in an early Jewish-Christian book called the Didache, which was written at the end of the first century. It may well be that in the early decades of the Church things had not yet taken the firm shape of later tradition.

Here we have merely scratched the surface of complicated problems concerning the Last Supper, which some people find fascinating and others boring and hairsplitting! But what has been said may help us to see that we cannot be dogmatic as Christians have so often and so sadly been about our own tradition of belief and practice at holy communion, as though our tradition is wholly right and every other wholly wrong.

This much may be said in general terms about the witness of the New Testament as a whole. (1) Jesus deliberately linked his death with the great feast of the Passover. It was to bring deliverance from the slavery of sin. (2) The Last Supper looked forward (as the Passover itself did) to God's final reign of righteousness and peace in the coming Kingdom (22:16 and 18). Every time we eat the bread and drink the cup, we do it 'until the Lord comes' (1 Corinthians 11:26). (3) Jesus intended his followers to 'Do this in remembrance of me.' In doing it we are made one with him; united with him in his death and fed and sustained by him in this present life in order that finally we may be united with him in his glory (Romans 6:5).

The Argument about Greatness

When a formal meal was held there was a slave by the door with towel and basin to wash the dirt of the street off the guests' feet as they came in. But this was a secret meeting. The disciples would slip in quietly one by one so as not to be noticed. The towel and basin would be there, but no servant to perform the menial task. Was each man too proud to wash his own feet, much less be servant to the rest, and was this what set the argument going about who was the greatest? St John tells us that during supper Jesus himself took the towel and basin and did for them all what none would stoop to do for himself (John 13:4–17).

The promise that his disciples will share his Kingdom is couched in the familiar imagery of the Messianic banquet. They are also to rule over Israel.[3] But only those who have learned the meaning of humility and service here on earth are fit to rule in heaven.

Jesus Predicts Peter's Denial

The contrast between singular and plural (thee and you) was clearer in the older English versions of the Bible than in modern translations. Jesus says that Satan will test them all (plural) but that he has prayed for Peter (singular) that his faith will not fail.

The character of Peter is an interesting study, and it is a witness to the honesty and reliability of the New Testament that wherever we meet him, in the gospels, in Acts, in the epistles, he is always recognizably the same person. Peter is impulsive, warm, open-hearted. 'Don't just wash my feet,' he blurts out to Jesus at the Last Supper, 'wash me from head to foot.' He runs to the tomb with John on Easter Day, but whereas John hesitates on the threshold, Peter bursts straight inside. In the emotion of meeting Cornelius the Gentile, he throws his Jewish scruples to the winds and eats what is put before him. But later, in a Jewish environment again, he backs down under criticism. One of Peter's great weaknesses is that when he is isolated and under attack, his courage fails. So here, he is brave enough to follow Jesus after his

---

3. In the Old Testament 'Judges' were rulers rather than judges in the modern sense. See, for instance, the book of Judges, which is a book about tribal rulers and leaders.

arrest to the High Priest's house – right into the lion's den as it were. But there, alone and surrounded by enemies, his courage fails him.

We must notice three things. First, that though Peter denied Jesus, his faith did not fail as Judas's faith failed. It was against his own heart, against his real self that he did it. It was through weakness and fear and it did not have the free consent of his will. Second, we must notice the hope that Jesus gives him, in the very prediction of his denial. 'When you turn back to me, you must strengthen your brothers.' Jesus has no illusions about Peter. He knows the sincerity of his brave words, and he knows the weakness that will bring them to no effect. Jesus knows Peter through and through, and he still believes in him. His failure will not make any difference to Jesus's love and trust in him. Third, it is interesting to notice that this is the only time in the gospels where Jesus addresses him directly by the name which he himself had given him – Peter. 'I tell you, Peter, the cock will not crow today until you have said three times that you do not know me.' This is very significant when we remember the importance which names have in the Bible, and the way in which they indicate a man's character. Peter is the new man Simon is becoming through his relationship with Jesus: the strong man, the rock man (the Greek word *petros* means a stone or large boulder), the leader of the Apostles. 'You will still be Peter to me,' even this bitter and humiliating failure which Jesus foresees will become by his prayers and forgiveness a part of the making of the new man, Peter.

Purse, Bag, and Sword

Jesus now reminds them of the sunny days in Galilee when they went out on their mission (9:2–6). They could rely entirely then on willing hospitality. But now, every man's hand will be against them as it is against him. The command to sell their coats to buy swords is not of course to be taken literally. It is another example of the way in which Jesus used startling images to bring people up short and drive his point home (cf. 14:26, 17:6, 18:25). The disciples do take him literally! His reply to them does not mean that two swords will be sufficient, but indicates a dismissal of the subject – as we dismiss something by saying, 'That's enough!' (cf. 1 Kings 19:4 and Mark 14:41).

Verse 37 contains another of the great 'musts' (see p. 88) of St Luke's gospel. The scripture, 'He was included with criminals' (Isaiah 53:12) *must* come true of Jesus. For St Luke the death of Jesus was the inevitable outcome of his life. He was included with the criminals at the end because he had always chosen to be with them in his life. It was the inevitable price of being the friend of tax collectors and sinners.

Jesus Prays

St Luke gives a much shorter account of Jesus's agony in the garden than St Mark, and he obviously has his Gentile readers in mind. He omits the Aramaic word 'Abba' ('Abba, Father' – Mark 14:36) which non-Christian Gentiles would not understand. Again, in St Luke Jesus kneels to pray, like a Gentile. Jews normally stood for prayer or, in great emotion, prostrated themselves (cf. Mark 14:35).

Our translator puts verses 43 and 44 in square brackets because some of the oldest and most important manuscripts omit them. There is a very interesting background to this omission. The earliest heresy[4] in the Church was to deny the real and full humanity of Jesus. The 'Docetists', as they were called, denied that there was in Jesus any physical weakness, any human emotions, particularly of anger or fear, and any human ignorance. Such things did not seem to them to 'fit in' with his divinity. The two verses in question are precisely the ones which record Jesus's human agony and stress in the garden. With these verses left out, Jesus appears to be calm and resigned.

Now it was above all the great Church of Alexandria

4. A heresy is an opinion (literally a 'private' opinion) which finally came to be condemned by the whole Church as false teaching.

which found the full humanity of Jesus so difficult to accept – and it was in Alexandria that the most important of the early manuscripts which omit these verses originated. With these points in mind, we conclude with the New English Bible that these two verses are the authentic words of St Luke and should remain in the text. Further support for this view is given by the fact that verse 44 contains more medical words and phrases than any other verse in the gospel – and St Luke, as we know, was a doctor.

St Mark shows us the sorrow of Jesus in Gethsemane 'so great that it almost crushes me' (Mark 14:34). St Luke shows us the fear. 'In great anguish he prayed even more fervently; his sweat was like drops of blood falling to the ground.' The Greek word *agonia* – anguish (from which our word agony comes) – means 'great fear'. The present writer remembers a friend telling him how, during the final seconds before the famous battle of Alamein began, he looked up from his watch to the officer who stood next to him and saw that although the desert night was close to freezing, great beads of sweat were running down his forehead. That is fear, and that is what Jesus suffered in the garden. He also suffered sorrow, the culmination of the heartbroken sorrow which made him weep over Jerusalem (19:41–44), for in rejecting him, he knew that his own people – God's chosen people – were rejecting God himself with a finality that might never be reversed. Was there an agony of doubt as well? We too find it hard to accept the full humanity of Jesus. The idea shocks many of us. But if Jesus was fully and truly human, he walked by faith as we walk by faith. He did not know the end from the beginning. Did he not have any agonizing doubts? Was it really God's will that his disciples should be left leaderless and that his own life should end in complete rejection? Was there no possible compromise that could provide a way forward? Was all this really the will of God? Sorrow, fear, the testing of his faith, all these must have been elements in the agony of Jesus in the garden.

But deeper than all these was the struggle between God

and the forces of evil. The crucial battle upon which the destiny of all creation hung was now being joined. It was the hour of the power of darkness (verse 53).

Jesus returns to the disciples to find them asleep, so great was their grief. This is true to human nature for the last stage of emotional exhaustion, when mind and body can take no more, is sleep.

The Arrest of Jesus

It was common for a disciple to greet his Rabbi with a kiss. According to Mark (14:44), Judas had arranged this as a signal. Unlike Matthew and Mark, Luke suggests that Jesus did not accept the kiss of Judas. Again, in Matthew and Mark the wounding of the High Priest's slave takes place after the arrest, and not before it as in Luke. Only St Luke (the doctor!) out of all four gospels records that Jesus healed the man. Matthew and Mark suggest that the arrest was made by a large crowd, almost a mob, sent by the Priests. Only St Luke (verse 52) suggests that it included representatives of the Sanhedrin and officials of the temple guard.

Note on the Trials of Jesus

There are many variations of detail in the accounts of the trials of Jesus given in the four gospels:

Mark (followed by Matthew) gives three trials.

(1) An irregular one during the night, before the Sanhedrin, at which Jesus is found worthy of death for blasphemy.

(2) A consultation of the Sanhedrin in the morning to regularize the (illegal) proceedings of the night before and to formulate the charges they will bring when they take him before Pilate to ask for the death sentence.

(3) The trial before Pilate, who yields to pressure and sentences Jesus to be crucified. The actual charges are not given.

Luke gives three trials, but they are not the same as Mark's.

(1) The first trial is in the morning before the Sanhedrin. No evidence is taken. Jesus is regarded as having con-

demned himself by a veiled admission that he is the Son of God.

(2) The trial before Pilate, at which detailed charges are made.

(3) Learning that Jesus is from Galilee, Pilate sends him for the so-called trial before Herod who returns him to Pilate for sentence.

John gives three trials again, but they are different, especially as there is no trial before the Sanhedrin.

(1) Jesus is taken before Annas, the former High Priest, and still the power behind the throne.

(2) Annas sends him to Caiaphas who was the actual High Priest at the time.

(3) Jesus is taken to Pilate who wants the Sanhedrin to try him. But the Jews object that they are not allowed to pass the death sentence. Under pressure Pilate condemns Jesus to death.

Thus there is agreement on the broad outlines of what happened. (1) There was a preliminary examination of Jesus during the night. (2) There was a more formal Jewish trial during the morning. (3) There was a trial before Pilate who reluctantly passed the death sentence.

The many variations between the gospels bear impressive witness to the honesty and integrity of their writers. St Matthew and St Luke both knew Mark, and used it extensively in writing their own gospels. The writer of the fourth gospel seems to have known Luke, and probably Mark as well. Thus each writer could have harmonized his own account to the others, and made sure that there was no discrepancy. But no, they each have respect for their own sources of information about the shattering events of the trials and Crucifixion which happened with such confusing speed, and like honest witnesses, each tells us what he knows; and as is always the case with honest witnesses there are variations of detail, but a broad overall agreement on the main points that matter. Here we shall of course follow St Luke and only mention the other gospels where necessary.

Peter Denies Jesus

The nights in Jerusalem are cold at Passover-time, and while Jesus is in the High Priest's house, the servants light a fire in the courtyard. By the light of it Peter is recognized. According to St Luke it is by a girl, and then by a man, and again by a second man. Only St Luke tells us that the Lord turned around and looked straight at Peter after his third denial. As J. A. Findlay says, linking John 1:42 with this verse, 'In two looks of Jesus is written the history of Peter's soul.'

Jesus Mocked and Beaten

According to Mark the mocking took place after the first trial and was by the members of the Sanhedrin. But in Luke it is the Jewish guards who mock him to pass the time during the long night of waiting before the morning trial. This seems more likely. They blindfold him and then hit him, saying, 'Prophesy for us, Messiah! Guess who hit you!' (22:64 and cf. Matthew 26:67)

Jesus before the Council

The examination before the Sanhedrin is not really a trial, for they have already decided his guilt. Its purpose is purely to frame the charges which they will lay against him before Pilate. Jesus will not give a plain answer to the question whether or not he is the Messiah because it means something so different to him from what it means to them, and they are not prepared to listen to him, or to believe him. But his veiled answer 'You say that I am' is enough to satisfy them.

Jesus before Pilate (chapter 23)

The Jews knew that Pilate would not be interested in the religious charge of blasphemy, therefore political charges must be framed. They are three, in ascending order of seriousness. (1) He is misleading and stirring up the people. (2) He is telling them not to pay the poll tax to Caesar. (3) He is claiming to be the Christ – a king.

They knew that these charges were totally untrue. The tragic irony of them is that if they had been true, the Jewish leaders would not have been bringing him to Pilate, they would have been supporting him.

Pilate takes up the most serious of the charges and questions Jesus about being a king. He is quickly satisfied that he poses no danger to the Empire, and makes his first attempt to acquit Jesus, 'I find no reason to condemn this man.' But the Jews will have none of this. They insist that from Galilee, right through Judea to Jerusalem, he has fomented rioting among the people.

Jesus before Herod

Galilee was in the jurisdiction of Herod Antipas. St Luke alone tells us that when Pilate heard that Jesus was from Galilee he remitted the case to Herod who was in Jerusalem for the Passover. St Luke may have had access to special information here through Joanna, the wife of Chuza, Herod's steward. (See 8:3.) This was an act of courtesy on Pilate's part, much appreciated by Herod, and the means of healing the estrangement which had existed between the two men. He had been wanting to see Jesus for a long time (9:9 and 13:31). It was also a perfectly reasonable thing to do in the cause of justice, because if there was a Galilean background to the case, Herod would know it, whereas Pilate did not.

But is this really the first sign of the fatal weakness in Pilate's character? He can see that Jesus does not constitute any threat to the Empire and that the Jews have framed the charges for hidden motives of their own. But he is an experienced enough ruler to see the ugliness of their mood and to sense trouble ahead. To shift it on to Herod's shoulders would be a welcome way out.

So to Herod they go; the priests accuse Jesus and Herod plies him with many questions, but Jesus will not give him even one word in reply. Herod with his soldiers behind him mocks him and then sends 'King Jesus' back to Pilate arrayed in a fine robe as a joke. The charge is preposterous! Significantly, St Luke does not mention any mocking by the Roman soldiers. In this gospel only

Jews mock Jesus (22:63 and 23:11). See Introduction, p. 11.

Jesus Sentenced to Death

Having heard the case himself and received the advice of Herod, Pilate is ready to give his decision publicly. 'I will have him whipped, then, and let him go.' A light flogging to act as a warning was a common procedure in such cases. (Cf. Acts 16:22 and 22:25.) This is Pilate's second attempt to release Jesus.

Verse 17 is printed in square brackets because it was not in the original text of Luke. It is easy to see how it came to be inserted by some scribe, for without it, Barabbas comes in very abruptly. According to the best manuscripts of Matthew, his full name was Jesus Barabbas, so the question is which Jesus will they have, Jesus Barabbas or Jesus the Christ? Barabbas seems to have been something of a popular hero who had been involved in anti-Roman activities and riots.

It is a well-known psychological fact that in a large crowd emotion, especially of an aggressive kind, is heightened and intelligence and reason are diminished. The crowd is soon demanding Barabbas's release and calling for Jesus to be crucified. Shouting above the din, Pilate makes his third attempt to set Jesus free. But they have found a slogan and are beginning to call out in chorus, 'To the cross with him!' Pilate makes one last attempt, and of all the hopeless things to do, he tries to reason with them. But it is too late for that, the light of reason and of humanity has by now been quenched. Only the chorus comes roaring back, wave after wave of it, growing in intensity with every cry, 'To the cross! To the cross! To the cross!'

In the next verses St Luke stresses again and again the way in which Pilate is dissociated from what happens. He passed the sentence that *they* were asking for. He set free the man *they* wanted, and turned Jesus over to them to do as *they* wished. The fourth gospel tells us that blackmail was added to the pressures that were brought to bear on Pilate. In the Roman Empire any province had the right to report its governor to Rome for mis-government, and this is what the Jewish leaders threaten to do. 'If you set him free that means that you are not the Emperor's friend! Anyone who claims to be a king is the Emperor's enemy!' (John 19:12).

There was demanded from Pilate courage of the very highest order, such as St Paul and some others of the world's great men and women have possessed. But Pilate was just an ordinary man like us!

Jesus Nailed to the Cross

A criminal normally carried the patibulum or cross-bar of his own cross to the place of execution. The whole cross would have been much too heavy to be carried by one man. According to Mark, Jesus was scourged before being taken out to be crucified, and after this terrible experience he was too weak to carry the heavy cross-bar alone. The Roman army had power to impress any citizen into temporary service (cf. Matthew 5:41). This was done by tapping him on the shoulder with the flat of a spear. Simon from faraway Cyrene was impressed in this way. By a slight change in the Greek from Mark, St Luke makes the incident carry a rich symbolic meaning. He does not just carry the cross for Jesus as in Mark, but becomes the first disciple to obey Jesus's command to 'take up his cross and come after me' (cf. 9:23 and 14:27).

It is typical of St Luke to mention the women. The wailing party normally assembled after a death, but here the women are anticipating the funeral rites by raising his death wail now. To a Jewish woman barrenness was both a sorrow and one of the greatest disgraces. The suffering that is coming on Jerusalem will be so great that women will count themselves fortunate if they are barren. The words, 'People will say to the mountains, "Fall on us!" and to the hills, "Hide us!" ' are a quotation from the description of God's judgement on Israel in the book of Hosea (Hosea 10:8). The suffering which is coming on Jerusalem is not some unfortunate disaster, but the judgement of God upon it.

Verse 31 is a proverbial saying, and as with many

proverbs it is hard to say exactly what it means in a particular context. Perhaps it means something like, 'If things like this are done now to one who is innocent, what will it be like when the end comes, for those who are guilty!'

The prayer 'Forgive them, Father! They don't know what they are doing', occurs only in Luke and is not included in some of the oldest manuscripts of the gospel. But it is so truly in the spirit of Jesus that most scholars accept it as authentic, and certain texts in Acts support it. (E.g. Acts 3:17–19, 7:59–60, and less directly Acts 2:36–38 and 13:26.) It is fitting that St Luke should be the person to preserve this saying, for throughout his gospel he has stressed the universal extent of God's forgiveness which is without any limit or condition.

Crucifixions were normally carried out by a detachment of four Roman soldiers. They were allowed to share out the prisoner's clothes among themselves. The most valuable item was the long outer robe which could not be divided. It was probably this that they threw dice for.

In this gospel the wine is offered by the soldiers and is part of the mockery. (Cf. Matthew 27:34 and Mark 15:23.) St Luke seems to have misunderstood his information here. There was a guild of women in Jerusalem who provided wine mingled with myrrh as a soporific draught to ease the terrible sufferings of the crucified. It is this which was offered to Jesus and which he refused.

St Luke tells us more than the other gospels about the two criminals who were crucified at the same time. One rails at Jesus as the priests and others are doing, 'Aren't you the Messiah? Save yourself and us!' But the other rebukes him and, turning to Jesus, says, 'Remember me, Jesus, when you come as King!' This is the only time in all the gospels when our Lord is addressed as Jesus, without any title before his name or after it. Had this man known Jesus as a boy at Nazareth? Had they both gone to the same synagogue school and played together? It may be so. Jesus answers his faith with the promise, 'Today you will be in Paradise with me.'

Paradise was originally a Persian word which stood for the walled garden of a Persian king. When the Old Testament was translated into Greek, this was the word which was used for the garden of Eden, and when Jews used the word it was no doubt the garden of Eden that was in their minds. It then came to stand for the future bliss of the righteous, and in 2 Corinthians 12:3 St Paul uses it in this way as the equivalent of heaven.

The early (and official) Jewish belief about the afterlife was that all men wait in Sheol until the general resurrection at the end of the world. Then will come the final judgement and the apportioning of rewards and punishments. But alongside this there had grown up by the time of Jesus another belief, that the souls of the righteous after death go immediately to their reward. It is this more popular view that lies behind Jesus's promise to the dying criminal.[5]

The Death of Jesus

St Luke uses the word *ekliponton* from which our word 'eclipse' comes for the darkening of the sun. It cannot have been literally an eclipse because this is astronomically impossible when the moon is at the full at Passovertime. Commentators have mentioned the black sirocco which blows in Jerusalem in April, darkening the sky. But probably the best explanation of this passage and the one which is spiritually most meaningful is that in the ancient world it was universally believed that events of momentous importance in the affairs of men were accompanied by portents in the natural world as well – all nature was in sympathy. Among the Jews this belief was associated especially with the coming Day of the Lord. (See pp. 130–131.)

> *I will show portents in the sky and on earth,*
> *blood and fire and columns of smoke;*
> *the sun shall be turned into darkness*
> *and the moon into blood*

5. And also behind the story of the rich man and Lazarus (16:19–31, see especially verse 22).

before the great and terrible day of the Lord comes.
Then everyone who invokes the Lord by name
shall be saved.

(Joel 2:30–32)

In the gospels this belief is most fully expressed by St Matthew, who tells us that as Jesus died, 'The earth shook, the rocks split apart, the graves broke open, and many of God's people who had died were raised to life. They left the graves; and after Jesus rose from death they went into the Holy City, where many people saw them.' (Matthew 27:51–53) We would perhaps say after our own dull fashion that the death of Jesus 'was of cosmic significance'. The Bible writers put exactly the same point in a much more picturesque and poetic way!

The curtain (or veil) hanging in the temple screened off the Holy of Holies which was in the very centre of the temple. Only the High Priest himself was allowed to enter into this innermost presence of God, and even he only once each year on the Day of Atonement.[6] But now no more Days of Atonement will be necessary and the veil between God and man has been removed. In Christ, access to God is open; 'We have, then, brothers, complete freedom to go into the Most Holy Place by means of the death of Jesus. He opened for us a new way, a living way, through the curtain.' (Hebrews 10:19–20)

The prayer 'In your hands I place my spirit!' is taken from Psalm 31:5. Jesus begins it with his own characteristic and intimate address to God, 'Father'. William Barclay says that this was the bedtime prayer that Jewish mothers taught their children. If this is so, its use here is another of those little touches which give the gospels such a ring of truth, for as every parish priest knows, when people are dying they return to the childhood foundations of their faith. That is why the Lord's Prayer has such power to sustain us in our last extremity. It is the prayer we learned in earliest childhood. So Jesus lays

6. For a description of the ritual of the Day of Atonement, see Leviticus 16.

down his head upon the cross and gives up his spirit into his Father's hands.

The last word at the cross comes from the Roman soldier in charge of the crucifixion. It is characteristic of St Luke, whose whole gospel is full of praise, to say that 'he praised God saying . . .' and St Luke is right, for whenever we come to see the truth and accept it, we praise God.

Pilate the Roman Governor had pronounced Jesus innocent, and now the Roman officer in charge of the execution pronounces the same verdict.[7]

Only St Luke tells us that the crowd, when they saw how Jesus died, regretted what they had done. This again is so true to life. Theirs was not the cold and calculated malice of the priests and Pharisees. They had been used, swayed by the emotions of the moment, and now they know that they have done a wicked thing and they are sorry for it.

The Burial of Jesus

The Romans left the bodies of criminals hanging for the vultures unless relatives or friends asked for the body to bury it. The Jews always did ask, for the Law commanded that the bodies of those hanged for crime should be buried the same day (Deuteronomy 21:22–23).

Joseph of Arimathea is one of those pious Jews on the fringe of St Luke's gospel story who were 'waiting for the coming of the Kingdom of God'. The short description of him reminds us straight away of Zechariah and Elizabeth (1:6) and Simeon (2:25). Joseph is linked with Nicodemus. They were both members of the Sanhedrin, the Supreme Jewish Council, and had not approved of its way of dealing with Jesus (verse 51 and see also John 7:50–52). The Sabbath began at sundown – about 6 p.m. – which did not leave enough time to complete the burial rites. So they hurriedly wrap the body of Jesus in a shroud and place it in Joseph's rock-hewn tomb. It is a *new* tomb, unused, unblemished, and therefore fit for its

7. Both the Common Bible and the New English Bible translate 'this man was innocent.'

sacred use. (Cf. the description of the donkey in 19:30, 'You will find a colt tied up *that has never been ridden.*') The women take note of the place so that they can come back at the earliest possible moment when the Sabbath is ended to complete the embalming of the body. The earliest moment is dawn on Sunday, the first day of the week.

The Resurrection (chapter 24)

The women rested on the Sabbath in obedience to the Law. At dawn on the Sunday morning they came to the tomb. A rock-hewn tomb was like a small cave. The body was wrapped in yards and yards of linen strips like bandages. Between the layers was myrrh and other spices used in embalming. It was then laid to rest on a stone shelf. The tomb was sealed by a large circular stone which was rolled along a channel to cover the entrance. They find that the stone has been rolled away and the tomb is empty.

There are differences between the gospels as to whom the women saw. In Mark it is a young man, in Matthew an angel, in John two angels (though not at the first visit), and in Luke two men in shining garments.

St Luke says that two men appeared with Jesus at the Transfiguration (9:30) and two men in white stood by the disciples at the Ascension (Acts 1:10), and he introduces them with exactly the same words in each case, 'and suddenly two men . . . stood by them'. Surely this is a deliberate linking of the three great revelations of the glory of Christ, made with all the subtle artistry which we can expect from St Luke?

The names of the women are also given differently: in Mark it is Mary Magdalene, Mary the mother of James, and Salome; in Matthew it is Mary Magdalene and the other Mary; John only mentions Mary Magdalene; Luke has Mary Magdalene, Mary the mother of James, and Joanna (whom he has mentioned before at 8:3), but he also mentions 'other women with them'. None of these differences is of any importance.

Much more important is it that St Luke has changed

Mark's 'He is going to Galilee ahead of you; there you will see him' (Mark 16:7) to 'Remember what he said to you while he was in Galilee' (verse 6). St Luke has done this so that he can change the place of the Resurrection appearances. According to Mark and Matthew they take place in Galilee; according to John they are mainly in Jerusalem, though one is in Galilee; but according to Luke they are all in or near Jerusalem, and the disciples do not leave the city until after Pentecost.

There is no need to try to reconcile these differences. As we have said before, St Luke and his readers did not suffer from our obsession with literal details and 'scientific accuracy'! (See pp. 107–108.) St Luke is presenting an over-all view of the beginnings of Christianity. Jesus had begun his work in Galilee. He had come to Jerusalem the capital city and the centre of the Jewish religion. There he had been crucified and there he had been raised from the dead and from there the message had gone out to all the world, now reaching even Rome itself. This is the broad canvas which St Luke is painting, and with an artist's eye he chooses the necessary stories to establish the Resurrection.[8]

The Walk to Emmaus

There must have been many more appearances of the risen Christ than are recorded in the gospels (cf. 1 Corinthians 15:5–7). This one is recorded only by St Luke, and it is of singular beauty and power. The suspense and sadness, the excitement and the climactic joy which we share with the two disciples as we read it draw us into the actual experience of Easter Day.

Emmaus was probably the modern Koloniyeh which is about four miles outside Jerusalem on the Jaffa road. Cleopas (short for Cleopatros) may well be the same person as the Clopas mentioned in John 19:25 whose wife Mary stood by the cross of Jesus. If this is so, it is

8. Dr Bratcher has often indicated by square brackets words that are not in the best manuscripts. But here he fails us! See the Common Bible and the New English Bible for the omissions which should be made in verses 3 and 6. The whole of verse 12 should be omitted.

likely that she is the unnamed second disciple in our story, for their invitation to Jesus to stay with them (verse 29) suggests that they lived together. Perhaps their home was at Emmaus.

They had believed that Jesus was a great prophet – and they still do. They had hoped that he was the Messiah, but this hope has been shattered by his crucifixion. How could the Messiah be crucified? Strange rumours are abroad about visions of angels and his body having disappeared, but nobody has seen *him*, they say wistfully.

The Old Testament was very important to both Jews and Christians, but they viewed it in entirely different ways. The Jews had been expecting a nationalist Messiah who would lead conquering Israel to victory over the Gentiles. It was this hope which the crucifixion had shattered once and for all for the disciples.

Christ offers to these two on the road to Emmaus a fundamentally new interpretation of the scriptures. God's purpose is to create a people who are dedicated to his service. In a wicked world this must mean suffering, for it is only through suffering willingly borne that evil is defeated. This is what the Songs of the Servant in chapters 40–55 of the book of Isaiah are about. This is the meaning of the book of Hosea, and of the life of Jeremiah. The same great truth underlies all God's dealings with Israel recorded throughout the scriptures. This is the key that unlocks their meaning, and this is the key to understanding the Messiah, for the Messiah sums up and represents in himself the whole vocation of Israel; 'Was it not necessary for the Messiah to suffer these things and enter his glory?'[9] Suddenly their hearts are on fire. The whole of the Old Testament shines with a new light for them.

By early afternoon in the east, the best part of the day is thought to be over, and the two disciples press Christ to stay the night with them. At the meal he, the guest, suddenly takes the place of host and asks the blessing, and in the moment of their recognition he vanishes from

9. Greek – *Must* not the Messiah have suffered . . . This is the ninth of St Luke's ten great 'musts'. See p. 88.

their sight. There is still time before nightfall to hurry back to Jerusalem. They arrive, bursting with their news, to find that the Lord has also appeared to Simon Peter (cf. 1 Corinthians 15:5).

Jesus Appears to His Disciples

It is surprising that when Jesus appeared the disciples should be frightened, for this was not his first appearance. There are echoes of John 20:19–20 in this passage, but in John the Lord is greeted with joy not fear. There is also perhaps a faint suggestion of Galilee and the appearance recorded in John 21:1–13 in the eating of the fish.

Christ now does for the assembled disciples what he had already done for the two on the road to Emmaus. He opens their minds to understand the purpose of God throughout the long history of Israel, and the divine way of achieving that purpose. The way through suffering to glory is clearly shown throughout it all. Once they can understand this they can see how it had to be focused and fulfilled in him the Messiah. (See *The Walk to Emmaus* above.) When it happened only he had seen it – and with the eye of faith. Now they can look back and see it too. They have been eye-witnesses of it all and now they must bear witness to the ends of the earth, calling men to 'the change of heart which leads to forgiveness of sins in his name'.

Verse 49 begins to look forward to the opening of the Acts of the Apostles. The power of God will come upon them – and it is Christ who will send the promised power. The head that once was crowned with thorns is crowned with glory now.

Jesus Is Taken up to Heaven

It is necessary for St Luke to bring the earthly life of Jesus to its conclusion, so he includes a brief mention of Jesus's final parting from the disciples. This prepares for the account of the Ascension which he will give in the opening chapter of his second volume, the Acts of the

Apostles,[10] and it makes a perfect link, for the Ascension is both an end and a beginning.

The story began in the temple in Jerusalem, and from the temple it will soon start again on its way to Rome and to the ends of the earth. It began with the praise of Zechariah and Elizabeth and Mary and the angels, and it ends with the disciples praising God with great joy. At least, so ends St Luke's first volume, the praise will never end.

10. The words 'and was taken up into heaven' in verse 51 should almost certainly be omitted. See the New English Bible and the Jerusalem Bible. The words 'worshipped him and . . .' in verse 52 should also be omitted. See the Common Bible, the New English Bible, etc. These are later additions to the gospel and spoil the transition to the book of Acts.

APPENDIX

What Happened at Easter?

Whatever happened on Easter Day transformed the disciples. On Good Friday they were broken men, afraid and without hope. During the next few weeks they were transformed, filled with an irrepressible joy and an indestructible courage. One of the remarkable things is that the Resurrection of Jesus was against all their expectations. The disciples on Easter morning, the two on the road to Emmaus, and St Thomas, all refused to believe it when they were first told about it (cf. Luke 24: 11, Luke 24:24, and John 20:25).

The case on which we have most evidence is that of St Paul. He hated Jesus and all that he stood for. He believed him to be a bogus Messiah and a deceiver of the people, and he was on his way to Damascus to round up some Christians when Jesus, whose crucifixion he had so much approved of, appeared to him with shattering effect. A blinding light shone on him and he heard a voice saying, 'I am Jesus whom you persecute.' (Cf. the three accounts in Acts 9:3–8, 22:6–11, 26:12–18.)

It was a spiritual experience. The light could not have been captured on a photographic film, nor the voice recorded on a tape recorder, but that does not mean that it was any the less real or objective. It was a personal encounter with the living Christ. St Paul was blinded and shattered by it and his whole life was turned upside down. From then on he spent the rest of his days proclaiming Jesus as Saviour and Lord, risen from the dead and alive for evermore. The evidence of all the disciples is the same. Jesus 'appeared' to them in a personal encounter as their living Lord and claimed them for his service. The earliest accounts suggest that this was a *spiritual* experience. The stories of a physical resurrection and of the empty tomb seem to belong to a later tradition.

It is not possible to date the books of the New Testamĕnt exactly, but within a few years either way we can say that St Paul wrote twenty to twenty-five years after the crucifixion, Mark was written thirty-five years after, Luke fifty years after, Matthew fifty-five years after, and the fourth gospel about sixty-five years after the event. Thus, St Paul is our earliest witness by far, and he tells us that he is reporting the evidence of those who were Christians before him, so in St Paul's letters we are in very close contact with the events themselves. (Cf. 1 Corinthians 15:3.)

It is noteworthy that St Paul never mentions the empty tomb and does not seem to know of it. He also does not seem to know any tradition of a physical resurrection of Jesus. Indeed, the arguments he uses in chapter 15 of his first letter to the Corinthians seem rather to deny a physical resurrection. He was writing to meet a crisis of belief in the Church. People were saying that there is no resurrection of the dead (15:12). We must note carefully his answer to this. If Jesus was not raised he says, the bottom has dropped out of the Christian gospel, for the Resurrection of Jesus is of central importance to it. Had he known anything of a physical resurrection of Jesus, or of the empty tomb, it is inconceivable that he would not have mentioned it to establish the truth of the Resurrection.

But not only does he not mention it, he argues that Christ's Resurrection is the first fruits of our own, and is our assurance that we too shall be raised. The implication is that Christ's Resurrection is of the same kind as ours will be. But if the physical body of Jesus was miraculously raised from the tomb, then obviously Jesus did not share our full human experience of the dissolution of the body, and we cannot share his experience of resurrection, for manifestly our bodies are either reduced to ashes at the crematorium or dissolve through the years into the earth from which they came.

St Paul had been brought up as a Pharisee within Judaism, and the belief which he assimilated was the resurrection of the physical body. But when he takes up the question of how the dead are raised, he has clearly come to quite different beliefs as a result of his conversion to Christianity (1 Corinthians 15:35f). What is made of flesh and blood cannot share in God's Kingdom, he says, and what is mortal cannot possess immortality. There is a continuity between this life and the next, but there is also a break. It is a mystery which is beyond our knowledge, but an illustration which sheds some light on the mystery is the relation of a plant to its seed. The seed is buried in the ground and suffers dissolution. From it comes the plant which has a different kind of body from the seed, yet there is a continuity and a connection between the two (1 Corinthians 15:35–41).

So it is, says St Paul, with the resurrection of the dead. The body which is put in the grave is not raised as a physical body – 'what is made of flesh and blood cannot share in God's Kingdom, and what is mortal cannot possess immortality.' (verse 50) When it is raised it will be a spiritual body. 'There is, of course, a physical body, so there has to be a spiritual body.' (verse 44)

But what of the stories of the empty tomb in the gospels? The Jews spoke of two kinds of exposition of scripture. There was 'Halakah', the pedestrian and literal commentary which drew from it the rules for daily living, and there was 'Haggadah', the exposition which brought out the spiritual meaning which lay beneath the surface of events and gave them their significance and meaning. This was regarded as a legitimate field for the use of creative imagination. It was more poetic, a sort of theological reflection or meditation. The birth stories and resurrection stories in Luke are 'Haggadah' rather than 'Halakah'. They breathe a different atmosphere from the rest of the gospel. Angels visible in human form appear to the chief people in the story. Heavenly choirs sing glory to God. The stories in the gospels about the appearances of Christ combine the early traditions about a spiritual body, such as St Paul speaks of, with later traditions which tell of a physical body which could be touched, and which could eat bread and broiled fish. Jesus invites them to 'Feel me, and you will see, because a ghost doesn't have flesh and bones, as you can see I have.' (Luke 24:39)

This is in complete contrast to St Paul's conviction that flesh and blood cannot share in God's Kingdom, and what is mortal cannot possess immortality. For if the body of the risen Christ could be handled and if he truly ate food, then this is not true: flesh and blood did share in God's Kingdom, and what is mortal did possess immortality.

The element of poetic 'Haggadah' in Matthew is stronger than in Luke and includes an earthquake and an angel descending from heaven whose appearance was like lightning and his clothes white as snow. He rolls away the stone, and before him the guards become as dead men. The resurrection stories in John are a superb meditation, which on the surface seem to suggest a physical resurrection but at a deeper level show how the physical has been transcended by Jesus and must be transcended by his disciples too.

But if the earliest witness to the Resurrection is to a spiritual encounter, and if no interest was shown either by Christians or by their opponents until many years later, in an empty tomb or the physical rising of Jesus, why did such an interest show itself when the gospels were written, some fifty years after the event?

The answer may well be that it was partly the influence of Judaism with its strong belief in a physical resurrection. Furthermore, the early Christians searched the Old Testament for passages which could be interpreted as referring to Christ. Passages such as Psalm 16 which is quoted in Acts 2:25–28, and again in Acts 13:35–37, 'You will not abandon my soul in the world of the dead', '*You will not allow your devoted servant to suffer decay*' had a profound influence on their thinking and would suggest that the Resurrection of Jesus ought to be thought of in physical terms. Again, whereas the Greeks tended to think that the most real things were ideas, or 'universal truths', to the Jews, it was 'things' which 'actually existed' which were the most real. That is why heaven is described in the book of Revelation in such a material way, as a city made of pure gold, whose foundation-stones are set with precious stones (Revelation 21:18f). It is the Jewish way of saying, '*It's real.*' In the same way, to describe the Resurrection of Jesus in physical terms was one way of saying, '*He really did conquer death.*'

Finally, towards the end of the New Testament era, heresies – that is, false teachings – were beginning to be spread abroad which denied the full humanity of Jesus and said that his body was not real flesh and blood. The Church had to counter these vigorously.[1]

Of course, the reasons offered above do not amount to conclusive proof. The most compelling reasons for believing that the Resurrection of Jesus was a spiritual reality, spiritually perceived, are religious ones, not historical. It is not God's way to provide objective cast-iron proof. That is why Jesus rejected the temptation to swoop down from the pinnacle of the temple to 'prove' his Messiahship. Faith is an *essential* element in our relationship to God. In our century, 'Science' has made many Christians ashamed of faith, and the ordinary man in the street has the idea that faith is somehow inferior to 'proof'. It is time that we reasserted that it is impossible to understand the deep spiritual truths for which our world is pining without faith. Why did Jesus not appear to Pilate or Caiaphas, or to the Pharisees? Because they had not the faith that was needed to see him. It was not just a matter of physical sight. If Jesus had risen literally and physically from the tomb, it would take away that essential element of faith response. It is interesting that in St Matthew's account of Jesus's appearance in Galilee, which seems to come from an early strand of tradition, he says, 'When they saw him they worshipped him, *even though some of them doubted.*' (Matthew 28:17) How could they have doubted if he had been there *in the flesh*?

The resurrecting of a physical body is not what the Christian hope is about. The risen Christ is not a revived corpse. He lives with the fullness of God in the power of an indestructible life (cf. Hebrews 7:16). As St Paul saw so clearly, the Resurrection of Christ is the assurance

1. These heresies were called Docetism and Gnosticism.

that we too shall rise from the dead. This implies that Jesus 'had to become like his brothers in every way'. (Hebrews 2:17) This means that he experienced the whole course of our life from birth to death, and what lies beyond death. But if his body was raised physically and did not see corruption, then he did not experience the whole of our human destiny, and he was not made like his brethren in this important respect. But if the physical body of Jesus suffered the same kind of dissolution as ours, then he is truly made one with us, and we with him, and we can believe with St Paul that 'Christ was raised to life – the first fruits of the harvest of the dead . . . What is sown in the earth as a perishable thing is raised imperishable. Sown in humiliation, it is raised in glory; sown in weakness, it is raised in power; sown as an animal body, it is raised as a spiritual body.'[2] In all this, as he was made one with us, so shall we be made one with him. Thanks be to God.

In writing this Appendix I should like to express my gratitude to Professor G. W. H. Lampe whose contribution to the book *The Resurrection* (by G. W. H. Lampe and D. M. MacKinnon, A. R. Mowbray and Co. Ltd, 1966) has done so much to deepen my own faith and has given the Resurrection of Jesus a living and contemporary reality for me which it never had before.

2. Quoted from 1 Corinthians 15, verses 20 and 42 in the New English Bible translation.

THE GOSPEL OF LUKE

Introduction

1 Dear Theophilus:
Many have done their best to write a report of the things that have taken place among us. ²They wrote what we have been told by those who saw these things from the beginning and proclaimed the message. ³And so, your Excellency, because I have carefully studied all these matters from their beginning, I thought it good to write an orderly account for you. ⁴I do this so that you will know the full truth of all those matters which you have been taught.

The Birth of John the Baptist Announced

⁵During the time when Herod was king of the land of Israel, there was a priest named Zechariah, who belonged to the priestly order of Abijah. His wife's name was Elizabeth; she also belonged to a priestly family. ⁶They both lived good lives in God's sight, and obeyed fully all the Lord's commandments and rules. ⁷They had no children because Elizabeth could not have any, and she and Zechariah were both very old.

⁸One day Zechariah was doing his work as a priest before God, taking his turn in the daily service. ⁹According to the custom followed by the priests, he was chosen by lot to burn the incense on the altar. So he went into the temple of the Lord, ¹⁰while the crowd of people outside prayed during the hour of burning the incense. ¹¹An angel of the Lord appeared to him, standing at the right side of the altar where the incense was burned. ¹²When Zechariah saw him he was troubled and felt afraid. ¹³But the angel said to him, "Don't be afraid, Zechariah! God has heard your

Don't be afraid, Zechariah!

prayer, and your wife Elizabeth will bear you a son. You are to name him John. [14]How glad and happy you will be, and how happy many others will be when he is born! [15]He will be a great man in the Lord's sight. He must not drink any wine or strong drink. From his very birth he will be filled with the Holy Spirit. [16]He will bring back many of the people of Israel to the Lord their God. [17]He will go ahead of him, strong and mighty like the prophet Elijah. He will bring fathers and children together again; he will turn the disobedient people back to the way of thinking of the righteous; he will get the Lord's people ready for him."

[18]Zechariah said to the angel, "How shall I know if this is so? I am an old man and my wife also is old."

[19]"I am Gabriel," the angel answered. "I stand in the presence of God, who sent me to speak to you and tell you this good news. [20]But you have not believed my message, which will come true at the right time. Because you have not believed you will be unable to speak; you will remain silent until the day my promise to you comes true."

[21]In the meantime the people were waiting for Zechariah, wondering why he was spending such a long time in the temple. [22]When he came out he could not speak to them, and so they knew that he had seen a vision in the temple. Unable to say a word, he made signs to them with his hands.

[23]When his period of service in the temple was over, Zechariah went back home. [24]Some time later his wife Elizabeth became pregnant, and did not leave the house for five months. [25]"Now at last the Lord has helped me in this way," she said. "He has taken away my public disgrace!"

The Birth of Jesus Announced

[26]In the sixth month of Elizabeth's pregnancy God sent the angel Gabriel to a town in Galilee named Nazareth. [27]He had a message for a girl promised in marriage to a man named Joseph, who was a descendant of King David. The girl's name was Mary. [28]The angel came to her and said, "Peace be with you! The Lord is with you, and has greatly blessed you!"

²⁹Mary was deeply troubled by the angel's message, and she wondered what his words meant. ³⁰The angel said to her, "Don't be afraid, Mary, because God has been gracious to you. ³¹You will become pregnant and give birth to a son, and you will name him Jesus. ³²He will be great and will be called the Son of the Most High God. The Lord God will make him a king, as his ancestor David was, ³³and he will be the king of the descendants of Jacob forever; his kingdom will never end!"

³⁴Mary said to the angel, "I am a virgin. How, then, can this be?"

³⁵The angel answered, "The Holy Spirit will come on you, and God's power will rest upon you. For this reason the holy child will be called the Son of God. ³⁶Remember your relative Elizabeth. It is said that she cannot have children; but she herself is now six months pregnant, even though she is very old. ³⁷For there is not a thing that God cannot do."

³⁸"I am the Lord's servant," said Mary; "may it happen to me as you have said." And the angel left her.

Mary Visits Elizabeth

³⁹Soon afterwards Mary got ready and hurried off to the hill country, to a town in Judea. ⁴⁰She went into Zechariah's house and greeted Elizabeth. ⁴¹When Elizabeth heard Mary's greeting, the baby moved within her. Elizabeth was filled with the Holy Spirit, ⁴²and spoke in a loud voice, "You are the most blessed of all women, and blessed is the child you will bear! ⁴³Why should this great thing happen to me, that my Lord's mother comes to visit me? ⁴⁴For as soon as I heard your greeting, the baby within me jumped with gladness. ⁴⁵How happy are you to believe that the Lord's message to you will come true!"

Mary's Song of Praise

⁴⁶Mary said,
> "My heart praises the Lord;
> ⁴⁷ my soul is glad because of God my Saviour,
> ⁴⁸ because he has remembered me, his lowly servant!
> From now on all people will call me happy,

49 because of the great things the Mighty
        God has done for me.
    His name is holy;
50   he shows mercy to those who fear him,
        from one generation to another.
51 He stretched out his mighty arm
        and scattered the proud with all their
        plans.
52 He brought down mighty kings from their
        thrones,
        and lifted up the lowly.
53 He filled the hungry with good things,
        and sent the rich away with empty
        hands.
54 He kept the promise he made to our
        ancestors,
        and came to the help of his servant
        Israel;
55 he remembered to show mercy to Abra-
        ham
        and to all his descendants forever!"

56Mary stayed about three months with Elizabeth,
and then went back home.

The Birth of John the Baptist

57The time came for Elizabeth to have her baby, and
she gave birth to a son. 58Her neighbours and relatives
heard how wonderfully good the Lord had been to her,
and they all rejoiced with her.

59When the baby was a week old they came to circum-
cise him; they were going to name him Zechariah, his
father's name. 60But his mother said, "No! His name
will be John."

61They said to her, "But you don't have any relative
with that name!" 62Then they made signs to his father,
asking him what name he would like the boy to have.

63Zechariah asked for a writing pad and wrote, "His
name is John." How surprised they all were! 64At that
moment Zechariah was able to speak again, and he
started praising God. 65The neighbours were all filled
with fear, and the news about these things spread
through all the hill country of Judea. 66Everyone who

heard of it thought about it and asked, "What is this child going to be?" It was plain that the Lord's power was with him.

Zechariah's Prophecy

⁶⁷John's father Zechariah was filled with the Holy Spirit, and he spoke God's message,

⁶⁸ "Let us praise the Lord, the God of Israel!
He came to the help of his people and set them free.
⁶⁹ He provided a mighty Saviour for us,
who is a descendant of his servant David.
⁷⁰ Long ago by means of his holy prophets he said this:
⁷¹   he promised to save us from our enemies,
and from the power of all those who hate us.
⁷² He said he would show mercy to our ancestors,
and remember his sacred covenant.
⁷³⁻⁷⁴ He made a solemn promise to our ancestor Abraham,
and vowed that he would rescue us from our enemies,
and allow us to serve him without fear;
⁷⁵ to be holy and righteous before him,
all the days of our life.

⁷⁶ "You, my child, will be called a prophet of the Most High God.
You will go ahead of the Lord
to prepare his road for him;
⁷⁷ to tell his people that they will be saved,
by having their sins forgiven.
⁷⁸ Our God is merciful and tender.
He will cause the bright dawn of salvation to rise on us,
⁷⁹   and shine from heaven on all those who live in the dark shadow of death,
to guide our steps into the path of peace."

⁸⁰The child grew and developed in body and spirit. He lived in the desert until the day when he would appear publicly to the people of Israel.

The Birth of Jesus
(Also Matt. 1.18–25)

2 At that time Emperor Augustus sent out an order for all the citizens of the Empire to register themselves for the census. ²When this first census took place, Quirinius was the governor of Syria. ³Everyone, then, went to register himself, each to his own town.

⁴Joseph went from the town of Nazareth, in Galilee, to Judea, to the town named Bethlehem, where King David was born. Joseph went there because he was a descendant of David. ⁵He went to register himself with

Everyone, then, went to register himself

Mary, who was promised in marriage to him. She was pregnant, ⁶and while they were in Bethlehem, the time came for her to have her baby. ⁷She gave birth to her first son, wrapped him in cloths and laid him in a manger—there was no room for them to stay in the inn.

The Shepherds and the Angels

⁸There were some shepherds in that part of the country who were spending the night in the fields, taking care of their flocks. ⁹An angel of the Lord appeared to them, and the glory of the Lord shone over them. They were terribly afraid, ¹⁰but the angel said to them, "Don't be

afraid! I am here with good news for you, which will bring great joy to all the people. ¹¹This very day in David's town your Saviour was born—Christ the Lord! ¹²What will prove it to you is this: you will find a baby wrapped in cloths and lying in a manger."

¹³Suddenly a great army of heaven's angels appeared with the angel, singing praises to God,

¹⁴ "Glory to God in the highest heaven,
and peace on earth to those with whom
he is pleased!"

¹⁵When the angels went away from them back into heaven, the shepherds said to one another, "Let us go to Bethlehem and see this thing that has happened, that the Lord has told us."

¹⁶So they hurried off and found Mary and Joseph, and saw the baby lying in the manger. ¹⁷When the shepherds saw him they told them what the angel had said about this child. ¹⁸All who heard it were filled with wonder at what the shepherds told them. ¹⁹Mary remembered all these things and thought deeply about them. ²⁰The shepherds went back, singing praises to God for all they had heard and seen; it had been just as the angel had told them.

Glory to God in the highest heaven

Jesus Is Named

²¹A week later, when the time came for the baby to be circumcised, he was named Jesus, the name which the angel had given him before he had been conceived.

Jesus Is Presented in the Temple

²²The time came for Joseph and Mary to do what the Law of Moses commanded and perform the ceremony of purification. So they took the child to Jerusalem to present him to the Lord, ²³as written in the law of the Lord, "Every firstborn male shall be dedicated to the Lord." ²⁴They also went to offer a sacrifice of a pair of doves or two young pigeons, as required by the law of the Lord.

²⁵Now there was a man living in Jerusalem whose name was Simeon. He was a good and God-fearing man, and was waiting for Israel to be saved. The Holy Spirit was with him, ²⁶and he had been assured by the Holy Spirit that he would not die before he had seen the Lord's promised Messiah. ²⁷Led by the Spirit, Simeon went into the temple. When the parents brought the child Jesus into the temple to do for him what the Law required, ²⁸Simeon took the child in his arms, and gave thanks to God:

²⁹ "Now, Lord, you have kept your promise,
and you may let your servant go in peace.
³⁰ With my own eyes I have seen your salvation,
³¹   which you have prepared in the presence of all peoples:
³² A light to reveal your way to the Gentiles,
and bring glory to your people Israel."

³³The child's father and mother were amazed at the things Simeon said about him. ³⁴Simeon blessed them and said to Mary, his mother, "This child is chosen by God for the destruction and the salvation of many in Israel. He will be a sign from God which many people will speak against, ³⁵and so reveal their secret thoughts.

And sorrow, like a sharp sword, will break your own heart."

³⁶There was a prophetess named Anna, daughter of Phanuel, of the tribe of Asher. She was an old woman who had been married for seven years, ³⁷and then had been a widow for eighty-four years. She never left the temple; day and night she worshipped God, fasting and praying. ³⁸That very same hour she arrived and gave thanks to God, and spoke about the child to all who were waiting for God to redeem Jerusalem.

The Return to Nazareth

³⁹When they had finished doing all that was required by the law of the Lord, they returned to Galilee, to their home town of Nazareth. ⁴⁰The child grew and became strong; he was full of wisdom, and God's blessings were with him.

The Boy Jesus in the Temple

⁴¹Every year the parents of Jesus went to Jerusalem for the Feast of Passover. ⁴²When Jesus was twelve years old, they went to the feast as usual. ⁴³When the days of the feast were over, they started back home, but the boy Jesus stayed in Jerusalem. His parents did not know this; ⁴⁴they thought that he was with the group, so they travelled a whole day, and then started looking for him among their relatives and friends. ⁴⁵They did not find him, so they went back to Jerusalem looking for him. ⁴⁶On the third day they found him in the temple, sitting with the Jewish teachers, listening to them and asking questions. ⁴⁷All who heard him were amazed at his intelligent answers. ⁴⁸His parents were amazed when they saw him, and his mother said to him, "Son, why have you done this to us? Your father and I have been terribly worried trying to find you."

⁴⁹He answered them, "Why did you have to look for me? Didn't you know that I had to be in my Father's house?" ⁵⁰But they did not understand what he said to them.

⁵¹So Jesus went back with them to Nazareth, where he was obedient to them. His mother treasured all these

They found him in the temple

things in her heart. ⁵²And Jesus grew, both in body and in wisdom, gaining favour with God and men.

The Preaching of John the Baptist
(Also Matt. 3.1–12; Mark 1.1–8; John 1.19–28)

3 It was the fifteenth year of the rule of Emperor Tiberius; Pontius Pilate was governor of Judea, Herod was ruler of Galilee, and his brother Philip ruler of the territory of Iturea and Trachonitis; Lysanias was ruler of Abilene, ²and Annas and Caiaphas were high priests. It was at this time that the word of God came to John, the son of Zechariah, in the desert. ³So John went throughout the whole territory of the Jordan River. "Turn away from your sins and be baptized," he preached, "and God will forgive your sins." ⁴As the prophet Isaiah had written in his book,

"Someone is shouting in the desert:
'Get the Lord's road ready for him;
make a straight path for him to travel!
⁵ All low places must be filled up,
all hills and mountains levelled off.
The winding roads must be made
straight,
and the rough paths made smooth.
⁶ All mankind will see God's salvation!' "

[7]Crowds of people came out to John to be baptized by him. "You snakes!" he said to them. "Who told you that you could escape from God's wrath that is about to come? [8]Do the things that will show that you have turned from your sins. And don't start saying among yourselves, 'Abraham is our ancestor.' I tell you that God can take these rocks and make descendants for Abraham! [9]The axe is ready to cut down the trees at the roots; every tree that does not bear good fruit will be cut down and thrown in the fire."

[10]The people asked him, "What are we to do, then?"

[11]He answered, "Whoever has two shirts must give one to the man who has none, and whoever has food must share it."

[12]Some tax collectors came to be baptized, and they asked him, "Teacher, what are we to do?"

[13]"Don't collect more than is legal," he told them.

[14]Some soldiers also asked him, "What about us? What are we to do?"

He said to them, "Don't take money from anyone by force or accuse anyone falsely. Be content with your pay."

[15]People's hopes began to rise, and they began to wonder about John, thinking that perhaps he might be the Messiah. [16]So John said to all of them, "I baptize you with water, but one who is much greater than I is coming. I am not good enough even to untie his sandals. He will baptize you with the Holy Spirit and fire. [17]He has his winnowing shovel with him, to thresh out all the grain and gather the wheat into his barn; but he will burn the chaff in a fire that never goes out."

[18]In many different ways John urged the people as he preached the Good News to them. [19]But John spoke against Governor Herod, because he had married Herodias, his brother's wife, and had done many other evil things. [20]Then Herod did an even worse thing by putting John in prison.

The Baptism of Jesus
(Also Matt. 3.13–17; Mark 1.9–11)

[21]After all the people had been baptized, Jesus also was baptized. While he was praying, heaven was opened, [22]and the Holy Spirit came down upon him in

bodily form, like a dove. And a voice came from heaven, "You are my own dear Son. I am well pleased with you."

The Genealogy of Jesus
(Also Matt. 1.1–17)

²³When Jesus began his work he was about thirty years old; he was the son, so people thought, of Joseph, who was the son of Heli, ²⁴the son of Matthat, the son of Levi, the son of Melchi, the son of Jannai, the son of Joseph, ²⁵the son of Mattathias, the son of Amos, the son of Nahum, the son of Esli, the son of Naggai, ²⁶the son of Maath, the son of Mattathias, the son of Semein, the son of Josech, the son of Joda, ²⁷the son of Joanan, the son of Rhesa, the son of Zerubbabel, the son of Shealtiel, the son of Neri, ²⁸the son of Melchi, the son of Addi, the son of Cosam, the son of Elmadam, the son of Er, ²⁹the son of Joshua, the son of Eliezer, the son of Jorim, the son of Matthat, the son of Levi, ³⁰the son of Simeon, the son of Judah, the son of Joseph, the son of Jonam, the son of Eliakim, ³¹the son of Melea, the son of Menna, the son of Mattatha, the son of Nathan, the son of David, ³²the son of Jesse, the son of Obed, the son of Boaz, the son of Salmon, the son of Nahshon, ³³the son of Amminadab, the son of Admin, the son of Arni, the son of Hezron, the son of Perez, the son of Judah, ³⁴the son of Jacob, the son of Isaac, the son of Abraham, the son of Terah, the son of Nahor, ³⁵the son of Serug, the son of Reu, the son of Peleg, the son of Eber, the son of Shelah, ³⁶the son of Cainan, the son of Arphaxad, the son of Shem, the son of Noah, the son of Lamech, ³⁷the son of Methuselah, the son of Enoch, the son of Jared, the son of Mahalaleel, the son of Cainan, ³⁸the son of Enos, the son of Seth, the son of Adam, the son of God.

The Temptation of Jesus
(Also Matt. 4.1–11; Mark 1.12–13)

4 Jesus returned from the Jordan full of the Holy Spirit, and was led by the Spirit into the desert, ²where he was tempted by the Devil for forty days. In all that time he ate nothing, so that he was hungry when it was over.

³The Devil said to him, "If you are God's Son, order this stone to turn into bread."

⁴Jesus answered, "The scripture says, 'Man cannot live on bread alone.'"

⁵Then the Devil took him up and showed him in a second all the kingdoms of the world. ⁶"I will give you all this power, and all this wealth," the Devil told him. "It was all handed over to me and I can give it to anyone I choose. ⁷All this will be yours, then, if you kneel down before me."

⁸Jesus answered, "The scripture says, 'Worship the Lord your God and serve only him!'"

⁹Then the Devil took him to Jerusalem and set him on the highest point of the temple, and said to him, "If you are God's Son, throw yourself down from here. ¹⁰For the scripture says, 'God will order his angels to take good care of you.' ¹¹It also says, 'They will hold you up with their hands so that not even your feet will be hurt on the stones.'"

¹²Jesus answered him, "The scripture says, 'You must not put the Lord your God to the test.'"

¹³When the Devil finished tempting Jesus in every way, he left him for a while.

Jesus Begins His Work in Galilee
(Also Matt. 4.12–17; Mark 1.14–15)

¹⁴Then Jesus returned to Galilee, and the power of the Holy Spirit was with him. The news about him spread throughout all that territory. ¹⁵He taught in their synagogues and was praised by all.

Jesus Rejected at Nazareth
(Also Matt. 13.53–58; Mark 6.1–6)

¹⁶Then Jesus went to Nazareth, where he had been brought up, and on the Sabbath day he went as usual to the synagogue. He stood up to read the Scriptures, ¹⁷and was handed the book of the prophet Isaiah. He unrolled the scroll and found the place where it is written,

¹⁸ "The Spirit of the Lord is upon me,
because he has chosen me to preach the
Good News to the poor.
He has sent me to proclaim liberty to
the captives,

and recovery of sight to the blind;
to set free the oppressed,
   19   and announce the year when the Lord
will save his people."

²⁰Jesus rolled up the scroll, gave it back to the attendant, and sat down. All the people in the synagogue had their eyes fixed on him. ²¹He began speaking to them, "This passage of scripture has come true today, as you heard it being read."

²²They were all well impressed with him, and marvelled at the beautiful words that he spoke. They said, "Isn't he the son of Joseph?"

²³He said to them, "I am sure that you will quote this proverb to me, 'Doctor, heal yourself.' You will also say to me, 'Do here in your own home town the same things we were told happened in Capernaum.' ²⁴I tell you this," Jesus added. "A prophet is never welcomed in his own home town. ²⁵Listen to me: it is true that there were many widows in Israel during the time of Elijah, when there was no rain for three and a half years and there was a great famine throughout the whole land. ²⁶Yet Elijah was not sent to a single one of them, but only to a widow of Zarephath, in the territory of Sidon. ²⁷And there were many lepers in Israel during the time of the prophet Elisha; yet not one of them was made clean, but only Naaman the Syrian."

²⁸All the people in the synagogue were filled with anger when they heard this. ²⁹They rose up, dragged Jesus out of town and took him to the top of the hill on which their town was built, to throw him over the cliff. ³⁰But he walked through the middle of the crowd and went his way.

A Man with an Evil Spirit
(Also Mark 1.21–28)

³¹Then Jesus went to Capernaum, a town in Galilee, where he taught the people on the Sabbath. ³²They were all amazed at the way he taught, because his words had authority. ³³There was a man in the synagogue who had the spirit of an evil demon in him; he screamed out in a loud voice, ³⁴"Ah! What do you want with us, Jesus of Nazareth? Are you here to destroy us? I know who you are: you are God's holy messenger!"

³⁵Jesus commanded the spirit, "Be quiet, and come out of the man!" The demon threw the man down in front of them and went out of him without doing him any harm.

³⁶They were all amazed, and said to one another, "What kind of words are these? With authority and power this man gives orders to the evil spirits, and they come out!" ³⁷And the report about Jesus spread everywhere in that region.

Jesus Heals Many People
(Also Matt. 8.14–17; Mark 1.29–34)

³⁸Jesus left the synagogue and went to Simon's home. Simon's mother-in-law was sick with a high fever, and they spoke to Jesus about her. ³⁹He went and stood at her bedside, and gave a command to the fever. The fever left her, and she got up at once and began to wait on them.

⁴⁰After sunset, all who had friends who were sick with various diseases brought them to Jesus; he placed his hands on every one of them and healed them all. ⁴¹Demons, also, went out from many people, screaming, "You are the Son of God!"

Jesus commanded them and would not let them speak, because they knew that he was the Messiah.

Jesus Preaches in the Synagogues
(Also Mark 1.35–39)

⁴²At daybreak Jesus left the town and went off to a lonely place. The people started looking for him, and when they found him they tried to keep him from leaving. ⁴³But he said to them, "I must preach the Good News of the Kingdom of God in other towns also, because that is what God sent me to do."

⁴⁴So he preached in the synagogues all over the country.

Jesus Calls the First Disciples
(Also Matt. 4.18–22; Mark 1.16–20)

5 One time Jesus was standing on the shore of Lake Gennesaret while the people pushed their way up to him to listen to the word of God. ²He saw two boats pulled up on the beach; the fishermen had left them and

Let your nets down for a catch

were washing the nets. ³Jesus got into one of the boats —it belonged to Simon—and asked him to push off a little from the shore. Jesus sat in the boat and taught the crowd.

⁴When he finished speaking, he said to Simon, "Push the boat out further to the deep water, and you and your partners let your nets down for a catch."

⁵"Master," Simon answered, "we worked hard all night long and caught nothing. But if you say so, I will let down the nets." ⁶They let the nets down and caught such a large number of fish that the nets were about to break. ⁷So they motioned to their partners in the other boat to come and help them. They came and filled both boats so full of fish that they were about to sink. ⁸When Simon Peter saw what had happened, he fell on his knees before Jesus and said, "Go away from me, Lord! I am a sinful man!"

⁹He and the others with him were all amazed at the large number of fish they had caught. ¹⁰The same was true of Simon's partners, James and John, the sons of Zebedee. Jesus said to Simon, "Don't be afraid; from now on you will be catching men."

¹¹They pulled the boats on the beach, left everything and followed Jesus.

Jesus Makes a Leper Clean
(Also Matt. 8.1–4; Mark 1.40–45)

¹²Once Jesus was in a certain town where there was a man who was covered with leprosy. When he saw Jesus, he threw himself down and begged him, "Sir, if you want to, you can make me clean!"

¹³Jesus reached out and touched him. "I do want to," he answered. "Be clean!" At once the leprosy left the man. ¹⁴Jesus ordered him, "Don't tell this to anyone, but go straight to the priest and let him examine you; then offer the sacrifice, as Moses ordered, to prove to everyone that you are now clean."

¹⁵But the news about Jesus spread all the more widely, and crowds of people came to hear him and be healed from their diseases. ¹⁶But he would go away to lonely places, where he prayed.

Let him down on his bed into the middle of the group

Jesus Heals a Paralysed Man
(Also Matt. 9.1–8; Mark 2.1–12)

¹⁷One day when Jesus was teaching, some Pharisees and teachers of the Law were sitting there who had come from every town in Galilee and Judea, and from

Jerusalem. The power of the Lord was present for Jesus to heal the sick. [18]Some men came carrying a paralysed man on a bed, and they tried to take him into the house and lay him before Jesus. [19]Because of the crowd, however, they could find no way to take him in. So they carried him up on the roof, made an opening in the tiles, and let him down on his bed into the middle of the group in front of Jesus. [20]When Jesus saw how much faith they had, he said to the man, "Your sins are forgiven you, my friend."

· [21]The teachers of the Law and the Pharisees began to say to themselves, "Who is this man who speaks against God in this way? No man can forgive sins; God alone can!"

[22]Jesus knew their thoughts and said to them, "Why do you think such things? [23]Is it easier to say, 'Your sins are forgiven you,' or to say, 'Get up and walk'? [24]I will prove to you, then, that the Son of Man has authority on earth to forgive sins." So he said to the paralysed man, "I tell you, get up, pick up your bed, and go home!"

[25]At once the man got up before them all, took the bed he had been lying on, and went home, praising God. [26]They were all completely amazed! Full of fear, they praised God, saying, "What marvellous things we have seen today!"

Jesus Calls Levi
(Also Matt. 9.9–13; Mark 2.13–17)

[27]After this, Jesus went out and saw a tax collector named Levi, sitting in his office. Jesus said to him, "Follow me." [28]Levi got up, left everything and followed him.

[29]Then Levi had a big feast in his house for Jesus, and there was a large number of tax collectors and other people at the table with them. [30]Some Pharisees and teachers of the Law who belonged to their group complained to Jesus' disciples. "Why do you eat and drink with tax collectors and outcasts?" they asked.

[31]Jesus answered them, "People who are well do not need a doctor, but only those who are sick. [32]I have not come to call the respectable people to repent, but the outcasts."

The Question about Fasting
(Also Matt. 9.14–17; Mark 2.18–22)

³³Some people said to Jesus, "The disciples of John fast frequently and offer up prayers, and the disciples of the Pharisees do the same; but your disciples eat and drink."

³⁴Jesus answered, "Do you think you can make the guests at a wedding party go without food as long as the bridegroom is with them? Of course not! ³⁵But the time will come when the bridegroom will be taken away from them, and they will go without food in those days."

³⁶Jesus told them this parable also, "No one tears a piece off a new coat to patch up an old coat. If he does, he will have torn the new coat, and the piece of new cloth will not match the old. ³⁷Nor does anyone pour new wine into used wineskins. If he does, the new wine will burst the skins, the wine will pour out, and the skins will be ruined. ³⁸No! New wine should be poured into fresh skins! ³⁹And no one wants new wine after drinking old wine. 'The old is better,' he says."

The Question about the Sabbath
(Also Matt. 12.1–8; Mark 2.23–28)

6 Jesus was walking through some wheat fields on a Sabbath day. His disciples began to pick the heads of wheat, rub them in their hands, and eat the grain. ²Some Pharisees said, "Why are you doing what our Law says you cannot do on the Sabbath?"

³Jesus answered them, "Haven't you read what David did when he and his men were hungry? ⁴He went into the house of God, took the bread offered to God, ate it, and gave it also to his men. Yet it is against our Law for anyone to eat it except the priests."

⁵And Jesus concluded, "The Son of Man is Lord of the Sabbath."

The Man with a Crippled Hand
(Also Matt. 12.9–14; Mark 3.1–6)

⁶On another Sabbath Jesus went into a synagogue and taught. A man was there whose right hand was crippled. ⁷Some teachers of the Law and Pharisees wanted some

reason to accuse Jesus of doing wrong; so they watched him very closely to see if he would cure on the Sabbath. [8]But Jesus knew their thoughts and said to the man with the crippled hand, "Stand up and come here to the front." The man got up and stood there. [9]Then Jesus said to them, "I ask you: What does our Law allow us to do on the Sabbath? To help or to harm? To save a man's life or destroy it?" [10]He looked round at them all, then said to the man, "Stretch out your hand." He did so, and his hand became well again.

[11]But they were filled with rage and began to discuss among themselves what they could do to Jesus.

Jesus Chooses the Twelve Apostles
(Also Matt. 10.1–4; Mark 3.13–19)

[12]At that time Jesus went up a hill to pray, and spent the whole night there praying to God. [13]When day came he called his disciples to him and chose twelve of them, whom he named apostles: [14]Simon (whom he also named Peter) and his brother Andrew; James and John, Philip and Bartholomew, [15]Matthew and Thomas, James, the son of Alphaeus and Simon (who was called the Patriot), [16]Judas, the son of James and Judas Iscariot, who became the traitor.

Jesus Teaches and Heals
(Also Matt. 4.23–25)

[17]Coming down from the hill with them, Jesus stood on a level place with a large number of his disciples. A great crowd of people was there from all over Judea, and from Jerusalem, and from the coast cities of Tyre and Sidon; [18]they came to hear him and to be healed of their diseases. Those who were troubled by evil spirits also came and were healed. [19]All the people tried to touch him, for power was going out from him and healing them all.

Happiness and Sorrow
(Also Matt. 5.1–12)

[20]Jesus looked at his disciples and said,
　　"Happy are you poor;
　　　　the Kingdom of God is yours!
[21]"Happy are you who are hungry now;

you will be filled!
"Happy are you who weep now;
   you will laugh!

22"Happy are you when men hate you, and reject you,
and insult you, and say that you are evil, because of the
Son of Man! 23Be glad when that happens, and dance for
joy, because a great reward is kept for you in heaven.
For their ancestors did the very same things to the
prophets.

24 "But how terrible for you who are rich
   now;
   you have had your easy life!
25 "How terrible for you who are full now;
   you will go hungry!
"How terrible for you who laugh now;
   you will mourn and weep!

26"How terrible when all men speak well of you; because their ancestors said the very same things to the
false prophets."

Love for Enemies
(Also Matt.5.38–48; 7.12a)

27"But I tell you who hear me: Love your enemies, do
good to those who hate you, 28bless those who curse
you, and pray for those who mistreat you. 29If anyone
hits you on one cheek, let him hit the other one too; if
someone takes your coat, let him have your shirt as well.
30Give to everyone who asks you for something, and
when someone takes what is yours, do not ask for it
back. 31Do for others just what you want them to do for
you.

32"If you love only the people who love you, why
should you receive a blessing? Even sinners love those
who love them! 33And if you do good only to those who
do good to you, why should you receive a blessing? Even
sinners do that! 34And if you lend only to those from
whom you hope to get it back, why should you receive
a blessing? Even sinners lend to sinners, to get back the
same amount! 35No! Love your enemies and do good to
them; lend and expect nothing back. You will have a
great reward, and you will be sons of the Most High
God. For he is good to the ungrateful and the wicked.
36Be merciful, just as your Father is merciful."

Lend and expect nothing back

Judging Others
(Also Matt. 7.1–5)

³⁷"Do not judge others, and God will not judge you; do not condemn others, and God will not condemn you; forgive others, and God will forgive you. ³⁸Give to others, and God will give to you: you will receive a full measure, a generous helping, poured into your hands— all that you can hold. The measure you use for others is the one God will use for you."

³⁹And Jesus told them this parable, "One blind man cannot lead another one; if he does, both will fall into a ditch. ⁴⁰No pupil is greater than his teacher; but every pupil, when he has completed his training, will be like his teacher.

⁴¹"Why do you look at the speck in your brother's eye, but pay no attention to the log in your own eye? ⁴²How can you say to your brother, 'Please, brother, let me take that speck out of your eye,' yet not even see the log in your own eye? You hypocrite! Take the log out of your own eye first, and then you will be able to see and take the speck out of your brother's eye."

A Tree and Its Fruit
(Also Matt. 7.16–20; 12.33–35)

⁴³"A healthy tree does not bear bad fruit, nor does a poor tree bear good fruit. ⁴⁴Every tree is known by the fruit it bears; you do not pick figs from thorn bushes, or

gather grapes from bramble bushes. ⁴⁵A good man brings good out of the treasure of good things in his heart; a bad man brings bad out of his treasure of bad things. For a man's mouth speaks what his heart is full of."

The Two House Builders
(Also Matt. 7.24–27)

⁴⁶"Why do you call me, 'Lord, Lord,' and don't do what I tell you? ⁴⁷Everyone who comes to me, and listens to my words, and obeys them—I will show you what he is like. ⁴⁸He is like a man who built a house: he dug deep and laid the foundation on the rock. The river flooded over and hit that house but could not shake it, because it had been well built. ⁴⁹But the one who hears my words and does not obey them is like a man who built a house on the ground, without laying a foundation; when the flood hit that house it fell at once—what a terrible crash that was!"

Jesus Heals a Roman Officer's Servant
(Also Matt. 8.5–13)

7 When Jesus had finished saying all these things to the people, he went to Capernaum. ²A Roman officer there had a servant who was very dear to him; the man was sick and about to die. ³When the officer heard about Jesus, he sent to him some Jewish elders to ask him to come and heal his servant. ⁴They came to Jesus and begged him earnestly, "This man really deserves your help. ⁵He loves our people and he himself built a synagogue for us."

⁶So Jesus went with them. He was not far from the house when the officer sent friends to tell him, "Sir, don't trouble yourself. I do not deserve to have you come into my house, ⁷neither do I consider myself worthy to come to you in person. Just give the order and my servant will get well. ⁸I, too, am a man placed under the authority of superior officers, and I have soldiers under me. I order this one, 'Go!' and he goes; I order that one, 'Come!' and he comes; and I order my slave, 'Do this!' and he does it."

⁹Jesus was surprised when he heard this; he turned round and said to the crowd following him, "I have

never found such faith as this, I tell you, not even in Israel!"

¹⁰The messengers went back to the officer's house and found his servant well.

Jesus Raises a Widow's Son

¹¹Soon afterwards Jesus went to a town named Nain; his disciples and a large crowd went with him. ¹²Just as he arrived at the gate of the town, a funeral procession was coming out. The dead man was the only son of a woman who was a widow, and a large crowd from the city was with her. ¹³When the Lord saw her his heart was filled with pity for her and he said to her, "Don't cry." ¹⁴Then he walked over and touched the coffin, and the men carrying it stopped. Jesus said, "Young man! Get up, I tell you!" ¹⁵The dead man sat up and began to talk, and Jesus gave him back to his mother.

¹⁶Everyone was filled with fear, and they praised God, "A great prophet has appeared among us!" and, "God has come to save his people!"

¹⁷This news about Jesus went out through all the country and the surrounding territory.

The Messengers from John the Baptist
(Also Matt. 11.2–19)

¹⁸John's disciples told him about all these things. He called two of them to him ¹⁹and sent them to the Lord to ask him, "Are you the one John said was going to come, or should we expect someone else?"

²⁰When they came to Jesus they said, "John the Baptist sent us to ask, 'Are you the one he said was going to come, or should we expect someone else?'"

²¹At that very time Jesus healed many people from their sicknesses, diseases, and evil spirits, and gave sight to many blind people. ²²He answered John's messengers, "Go back and tell John what you have seen and heard: the blind can see, the lame can walk, the lepers are made clean, the deaf can hear, the dead are raised to life, and the Good News is preached to the poor. ²³How happy is he who has no doubts about me!"

²⁴After John's messengers had left, Jesus began to speak about John to the crowds, "When you went out to John in the desert, what did you expect to see? A

blade of grass bending in the wind? ²⁵What did you go out to see? A man dressed up in fancy clothes? Really, those who dress like that and live in luxury are found in palaces! ²⁶Tell me, what did you go out to see? A prophet? Yes, I tell you—you saw much more than a prophet. ²⁷For John is the one of whom the scripture says, 'Here is my messenger, says God; I will send him ahead of you to open the way for you.' ²⁸I tell you," Jesus added, "John is greater than any man ever born; but he who is least in the Kingdom of God is greater than he."

²⁹All the people and the tax collectors heard him; they were the ones who had obeyed God's righteous demands and had been baptized by John. ³⁰But the Pharisees and the teachers of the Law rejected God's purpose for themselves, and refused to be baptized by John.

³¹"Now, to what can I compare the people of this day? What are they like? ³²They are like children sitting in the market place. One group shouts to the other, 'We played wedding music for you, but you would not dance! We sang funeral songs, but you would not cry!' ³³John the Baptist came, and he fasted and drank no wine, and you said, 'He has a demon in him!' ³⁴The Son of Man came, and he ate and drank, and you said, 'Look at this man! He is a glutton and wine-drinker, a friend of tax collectors and outcasts!' ³⁵God's wisdom, however, is shown to be true by all who accept it."

Jesus at the Home of Simon the Pharisee

³⁶A Pharisee invited Jesus to have dinner with him. Jesus went to his house and sat down to eat. ³⁷There was a woman in that town who lived a sinful life. She heard that Jesus was eating in the Pharisee's house, so she brought an alabaster jar full of perfume ³⁸and stood behind Jesus, by his feet, crying and wetting his feet with her tears. Then she dried his feet with her hair, kissed them, and poured the perfume on them. ³⁹When the Pharisee who had invited Jesus saw this, he said to himself, "If this man really were a prophet, he would know who this woman is who is touching him; he would know what kind of sinful life she leads!"

⁴⁰Jesus spoke up and said to him, "Simon, I have something to tell you."

"Yes, Teacher," he said, "tell me."

⁴¹"There were two men who owed money to a moneylender," Jesus began; "one owed him fifty pounds and the other one five pounds. ⁴²Neither one could pay him back, so he cancelled the debts of both. Which one, then, will love him more?"

⁴³"I suppose," answered Simon, "that it would be the one who was forgiven more."

"Your answer is correct," said Jesus. ⁴⁴Then he turned to the woman and said to Simon, "Do you see this woman? I came into your home, and you gave me no water for my feet, but she has washed my feet with her tears and dried them with her hair. ⁴⁵You did not

She has covered my feet with perfume

welcome me with a kiss, but she has not stopped kissing my feet since I came. ⁴⁶You provided no oil for my head, but she has covered my feet with perfume. ⁴⁷I tell you, then, the great love she has shown proves that her many sins have been forgiven. Whoever has been forgiven little, however, shows only a little love."

⁴⁸Then Jesus said to the woman, "Your sins are forgiven."

⁴⁹The others sitting at the table began to say to themselves, "Who is this, who even forgives sins?"

⁵⁰But Jesus said to the woman, "Your faith has saved you; go in peace."

Women who Accompanied Jesus

8 Some time later Jesus travelled through towns and villages, preaching the Good News about the Kingdom of God. The twelve disciples went with him, ²and so did some women who had been healed of evil spirits and diseases: Mary (who was called Magdalene), from whom seven demons had been driven out; ³Joanna, the wife of Chuza who was an officer in Herod's court; Susanna, and many other women who used their own resources to help Jesus and his disciples.

The Parable of the Sower
(Also Matt. 13.1–9; Mark 4.1–9)

⁴People kept coming to Jesus from one town after another; and when a great crowd gathered, Jesus told this parable,

⁵"A man went out to sow his seed. As he scattered the seed in the field, some of it fell along the path, where it was stepped on, and the birds ate it up. ⁶Some of it fell on rocky ground, and when the plants sprouted they dried up, because the soil had no moisture. ⁷Some of the seed fell among thorns, which grew up with the plants and choked them. ⁸And some seeds fell in good soil; the plants grew and bore grain, one hundred grains each."

And Jesus concluded, "Listen, then, if you have ears to hear with!"

The Purpose of the Parables
(Also Matt. 13.10–17; Mark 4.10–12)

⁹His disciples asked Jesus what this parable meant. ¹⁰Jesus answered, "The knowledge of the secrets of the Kingdom of God has been given to you; but to the rest it comes by means of parables, so that they may look but not see, and listen but not understand."

Jesus Explains the Parable of the Sower
(Also Matt. 13.18–23; Mark 4.13–20)

¹¹"This is what the parable means: the seed is the

word of God. ¹²The seed that fell along the path stands
for those who hear; but the Devil comes and takes the
message away from their hearts to keep them from believing and being saved. ¹³The seed that fell on rocky
ground stands for those who hear the message and receive it gladly. But it does not sink deep into them; they
believe only for a while, and fall away when the time of
testing comes. ¹⁴The seed that fell among thorns stands
for those who hear; but the worries and riches and pleasures of this life crowd in and choke them, and their fruit
never ripens. ¹⁵The seed that fell in good soil stands for
those who hear the message and retain it in a good and
obedient heart, and persist until they bear fruit."

A Lamp under a Bowl
(Also Mark 4.21–25)

¹⁶"No one lights a lamp and covers it with a bowl or
puts it under a bed. Instead, he puts it on the lampstand,
so that people will see the light as they come in. ¹⁷What-
ever is hidden away will be brought out into the open,
and whatever is covered up will be found and brought
to light.
¹⁸"Be careful, then, how you listen; because whoever
has something will be given more, but whoever has
nothing will have taken away from him even the little
he thinks he has."

Jesus' Mother and Brothers
(Also Matt. 12.46–50; Mark 3.31–35)

¹⁹Jesus' mother and brothers came to him, but were
unable to join him because of the crowd. ²⁰Someone said
to Jesus, "Your mother and brothers are standing outside and want to see you."
²¹Jesus said to them all, "My mother and brothers
are those who hear the word of God and obey it."

Jesus Calms a Storm
(Also Matt. 8.23–27; Mark 4.35–41)

²²One day Jesus got into a boat with his disciples and
said to them, "Let us go across to the other side of the
lake." So they started out. ²³As they were sailing, Jesus
went to sleep. A strong wind blew down on the lake, and
the boat began to fill with water, putting them all in great

danger. ²⁴The disciples came to Jesus and woke him up, saying, "Master, Master! We are about to die!"

Jesus got up and gave a command to the wind and to the stormy water; they quietened down and there was a great calm. ²⁵Then he said to the disciples, "Where is your faith?"

But they were amazed and afraid, and said to one another, "Who is this man? He gives orders to the winds and waves, and they obey him!"

Jesus Heals a Man with Demons
(Also Matt. 8.28–34; Mark 5.1–20)

²⁶They sailed on over to the territory of the Gergesenes, which is across the lake from Galilee. ²⁷As Jesus stepped ashore, he was met by a man from the town who had demons in him. He had gone for a long time without clothes, and would not stay at home, but spent his time in the burial caves. ²⁸When he saw Jesus he gave a loud cry, fell down before him and said in a loud voice, "Jesus, Son of the Most High God! What do you want with me? I beg you, don't punish me!" ²⁹He said this because Jesus had ordered the evil spirit to go out of him. Many times it had seized him, and even though he was kept a prisoner, his hands and feet tied with chains, he would break the chains and be driven by the demon out into the desert.

³⁰Jesus asked him, "What is your name?"

"My name is 'Mob,'" he answered—because many demons had gone into him. ³¹The demons begged Jesus not to send them into the abyss.

³²A large herd of pigs was near by, feeding on the hillside. The demons begged Jesus to let them go into the pigs, and he let them. ³³So the demons went out of the man and into the pigs; the whole herd rushed down the side of the cliff into the lake and were drowned.

³⁴The men who were taking care of the pigs saw what happened, so they ran off and spread the news in the town and among the farms. ³⁵People went out to see what had happened. They came to Jesus and found the man from whom the demons had gone out sitting at the feet of Jesus, clothed, and in his right mind; and they were all afraid. ³⁶Those who had seen it told the people how the man had been cured. ³⁷Then all the people from

the territory of the Gergesenes asked Jesus to go away, because they were terribly afraid. So Jesus got into the boat and left. ³⁸The man from whom the demons had gone out begged Jesus, "Let me go with you."

But Jesus sent him away, saying, ³⁹"Go back home and tell what God has done for you."

The man went through the whole town telling what Jesus had done for him.

She told him why she had touched him

Jairus' Daughter and the Woman Who Touched Jesus' Cloak
(Also Matt. 9.18–26; Mark 5.21–43)

⁴⁰When Jesus returned to the other side of the lake the crowd welcomed him, because they had all been waiting for him. ⁴¹Then a man named Jairus arrived, an official in the local synagogue. He threw himself down at Jesus' feet and begged him to go to his home, ⁴²because his only daughter, twelve years old, was dying.

As Jesus went along, the people were crowding him from every side. ⁴³A certain woman was there who had suffered from severe bleeding for twelve years; she had spent all she had on doctors, but no one had been able to cure her. ⁴⁴She came up in the crowd behind Jesus and touched the edge of his cloak, and her bleeding stopped at once. ⁴⁵Jesus asked, "Who touched me?"

Everyone denied it, and Peter said, "Master, the people are all round you and crowding in on you."

⁴⁶But Jesus said, "Someone touched me, for I knew it when power went out of me." ⁴⁷The woman saw that she had been found out, so she came, trembling, and threw herself at Jesus' feet. There, in front of everybody, she told him why she had touched him and how she had been healed at once. ⁴⁸Jesus said to her, "My daughter, your faith has made you well. Go in peace."

⁴⁹While Jesus was saying this, a messenger came from the official's house. "Your daughter has died," he told Jairus; "don't bother the Teacher any longer."

⁵⁰But Jesus heard it and said to Jairus, "Don't be afraid; only believe, and she will be well."

⁵¹When he arrived at the house he would not let anyone go in with him except Peter, John, and James, and the child's father and mother. ⁵²Everyone there was crying and mourning for the child. Jesus said, "Don't cry; the child is not dead—she is only sleeping!"

⁵³They all made fun of him, because they knew that she was dead. ⁵⁴But Jesus took her by the hand and called out, "Get up, child!" ⁵⁵Her life returned and she got up at once; and Jesus ordered them to give her something to eat. ⁵⁶Her parents were astounded, but Jesus commanded them not to tell anyone what had happened.

Jesus Sends out the Twelve Disciples
(Also Matt. 10.5–15; Mark 6.7–13)

9 Jesus called the twelve disciples together and gave them power and authority to drive out all demons and to cure diseases. ²Then he sent them out to preach the Kingdom of God and to heal the sick. ³He said to them, "Take nothing with you for the journey: no walking stick, no beggar's bag, no food, no money, not even an extra shirt. ⁴Wherever you are welcomed, stay in the same house until you leave that town; ⁵wherever people don't welcome you, leave that town and shake the dust off your feet as a warning to them."

⁶The disciples left and travelled through all the vil-

lages, preaching the Good News and healing people
everywhere.

Herod's Confusion
(Also Matt. 14.1–12; Mark 6.14–29)

⁷Herod, the ruler of Galilee, heard about all the things
that were happening; he was very confused about it
because some people were saying, "John the Baptist has
come back to life!" ⁸Others said that Elijah had appeared, while others said that one of the prophets of long
ago had come back to life. ⁹Herod said, "I had John's
head cut off; but who is this man I hear these things
about?" And he kept trying to see Jesus.

Jesus Feeds the Five Thousand
(Also Matt. 14.13–21; Mark 6.30–44; John 6.1–14)

¹⁰The apostles came back and told Jesus everything
they had done. He took them with him and they went
off by themselves to a town named Bethsaida. ¹¹When
the crowds heard about it they followed him. He welcomed them, spoke to them about the Kingdom of God,
and healed those who needed it.

¹²When the sun had begun to set, the twelve disciples
came to him and said, "Send the people away so they
can go to the villages and farms round here and find food
and lodging, because this is a lonely place."

¹³But Jesus said to them, "You yourselves give them
something to eat."

They answered, "All we have is five loaves and two
fish. Do you want us to go and buy food for this whole
crowd?" ¹⁴(There were about five thousand men there.)

Jesus said to his disciples, "Make the people sit
down in groups of about fifty each."

¹⁵The disciples did so and made them all sit down.
¹⁶Jesus took the five loaves and two fish, looked up to
heaven, thanked God for them, broke them, and gave
them to the disciples to distribute to the people.
¹⁷They all ate and had enough; and the disciples took
up twelve baskets of what the people left over.

Peter's Declaration about Jesus
(Also Matt. 16.13–19; Mark 8.27–29)

¹⁸One time when Jesus was praying alone, the disci-

ples came to him. "Who do the crowds say I am?" he asked them.

[19]"Some say that you are John the Baptist," they answered. "Others say that you are Elijah, while others say that one of the prophets of long ago has come back to life."

[20]"What about you?" he asked them. "Who do you say I am?"

Peter answered, "You are God's Messiah."

Jesus Speaks about His Suffering and Death
(Also Matt. 16.20–28; Mark 8.30—9.1)

[21]Then Jesus gave them strict orders not to tell this to anyone, [22]and added, "The Son of Man must suffer much, and be rejected by the elders, the chief priests, and the teachers of the Law. He will be put to death, and be raised to life on the third day."

[23]And he said to all, "If anyone wants to come with me, he must forget himself, take up his cross every day, and follow me. [24]For whoever wants to save his own life will lose it; but whoever loses his life for my sake will save it. [25]Will a man gain anything if he wins the whole world but is himself lost or defeated? Of course not! [26]If a man is ashamed of me and of my teaching, then the Son of Man will be ashamed of him when he comes in his glory and the glory of the Father and of the holy angels. [27]Remember this! There are some here, I tell you, who will not die until they have seen the Kingdom of God."

The Transfiguration
(Also Matt. 17.1–8; Mark 9.2–8)

[28]About a week after he had said these things, Jesus took Peter, John, and James with him and went up a hill to pray. [29]While he was praying, his face changed its appearance and his clothes became dazzling white. [30]Suddenly two men were there talking with him. They were Moses and Elijah, [31]who appeared in heavenly glory and talked with Jesus about how he would soon fulfil God's purpose by dying in Jerusalem. [32]Peter and his companions were sound asleep, but they awoke and saw Jesus' glory and the two men who were standing

with him. ³³As the men were leaving Jesus, Peter said to him, "Master, it is a good thing that we are here. We will make three tents, one for you, one for Moses, and one for Elijah." (He really did not know what he was saying.)

³⁴While he was still speaking, a cloud appeared and covered them with its shadow; and the disciples were afraid as the cloud came over them. ³⁵A voice said from the cloud, "This is my Son, whom I have chosen —listen to him!"

³⁶When the voice stopped, there was Jesus all alone. The disciples kept quiet about all this, and told no one at that time anything they had seen.

Jesus Heals a Boy with an Evil Spirit
(Also Matt. 17.14–18; Mark 9.14–27)

³⁷The next day they went down from the hill, and a large crowd met Jesus. ³⁸A man shouted from the crowd, "Teacher! Look, I beg you, at my son—my only son! ³⁹A spirit attacks him with a sudden shout and throws him into a fit, so that he foams at the mouth; it keeps on hurting him and will hardly let him go! ⁴⁰I begged your disciples to drive it out, but they couldn't."

⁴¹Jesus answered, "How unbelieving and wrong you people are! How long must I stay with you? How long do I have to put up with you?" Then he said to the man, "Bring your son here."

⁴²As the boy was coming, the demon knocked him to the ground and threw him into a fit. Jesus gave a command to the evil spirit, healed the boy, and gave him back to his father. ⁴³All the people were amazed at the mighty power of God.

Jesus Speaks again about His Death
(Also Matt. 17.22–23; Mark 9.30–32)

The people were still marvelling at everything Jesus was doing, when he said to his disciples, ⁴⁴"Don't forget what I am about to tell you! The Son of Man is going to be handed over to the power of men." ⁴⁵But they did not know what this meant. It had been hidden from them so that they could not understand it, and they were afraid to ask him about the matter.

Who Is the Greatest?
(Also Matt. 18.1–5; Mark 9.33–37)

⁴⁶An argument came up among the disciples as to which one of them was the greatest. ⁴⁷Jesus knew what they were thinking, so he took a child, stood him by his side, ⁴⁸and said to them, "Whoever in my name welcomes this child, welcomes me; and whoever welcomes me, also welcomes the one who sent me. For he who is least among you all is the greatest."

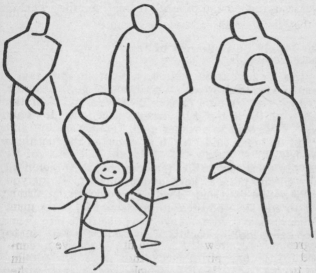

He who is least among you all is the greatest

Who Is not against You Is for You
(Also Mark 9.38–40)

⁴⁹John spoke up, "Master, we saw a man driving out demons in your name, and we told him to stop, because he doesn't belong to our group."

⁵⁰"Do not try to stop him," Jesus said to him and to the other disciples, "because whoever is not against you is for you."

A Samaritan Village Refuses to Receive Jesus

⁵¹As the days drew near when Jesus would be taken up to heaven, he made up his mind and set out on his way to Jerusalem. ⁵²He sent messengers ahead of him, who left and went into a Samaritan village to get everything ready for him. ⁵³But the people there would not receive him, because it was plain that he was going to Jerusalem. ⁵⁴When the disciples James and John saw this they said, "Lord, do you want us to call fire down from heaven and destroy them?"

⁵⁵Jesus turned and rebuked them; ⁵⁶and they went on to another village.

The Would-Be Followers of Jesus
(Also Matt. 8.19–22)

⁵⁷As they went on their way, a certain man said to Jesus, "I will follow you wherever you go."

⁵⁸Jesus said to him, "Foxes have holes, and birds have nests, but the Son of Man has no place to lie down and rest." ⁵⁹He said to another man, "Follow me."

But that man said, "Sir, first let me go back and bury my father."

⁶⁰Jesus answered, "Let the dead bury their own dead. You go and preach the Kingdom of God."

⁶¹Another man said, "I will follow you, sir; but first let me go and say good-bye to my family."

⁶²Jesus said to him, "Anyone who starts to plough and then keeps looking back is of no use for the Kingdom of God."

Jesus Sends Out the Seventy-two

10 After this the Lord chose another seventy-two men and sent them out, two by two, to go ahead of him to every town and place where he himself was about to go. ²He said to them, "There is a large harvest, but few workers to gather it in. Pray to the owner of the harvest that he will send out workers to gather in his harvest. ³Go! I am sending you like lambs among wolves. ⁴Don't take a purse, or a beggar's bag, or shoes; don't stop to greet anyone on the road. ⁵Whenever you go into a house, first say, 'Peace be with this house.' ⁶If a peace-loving man lives there, let your greeting of

peace remain on him; if not, take back your greeting of peace. [7]Stay in that same house, eating and drinking what they offer you, because a worker should be given his pay. Don't move round from one house to another. [8]Whenever you go into a town and are made welcome, eat what is set before you, [9]heal the sick in that town, and say to the people there, 'The Kingdom of God has come near you.' [10]But whenever you go into a town and are not welcomed there, go out in the streets and say, [11]'Even the dust from your town that sticks to our feet we wipe off against you; but remember this, the Kingdom of God has come near you!' [12]I tell you that on the Judgment Day God will show more mercy to Sodom than to that town!"

The Unbelieving Towns
(Also Matt. 11.20–24)

[13]"How terrible it will be for you, Chorazin! How terrible for you too, Bethsaida! If the miracles which were performed in you had been performed in Tyre and Sidon, long ago the people there would have sat down, put on sackcloth, and sprinkled ashes on themselves to show that they had turned from their sins! [14]God will show more mercy on the Judgment Day to Tyre and Sidon than to you. [15]And as for you, Capernaum! You wanted to lift yourself up to heaven? You will be thrown down to hell!"

[16]Jesus said to his disciples, "Whoever listens to you, listens to me; whoever rejects you, rejects me; and whoever rejects me, rejects the one who sent me."

The Return of the Seventy-two

[17]The seventy-two men came back in great joy. "Lord," they said, "even the demons obeyed us when we commanded them in your name!"

[18]Jesus answered them, "I saw Satan fall like lightning from heaven. [19]Listen! I have given you authority, so that you can walk on snakes and scorpions, and over all the power of the Enemy, and nothing will hurt you. [20]But don't be glad because the evil spirits obey you; rather be glad because your names are written in heaven."

Jesus Rejoices
(Also Matt. 11.25–27; 13.16–17)

²¹At that time Jesus was filled with joy by the Holy Spirit, and said, "Father, Lord of heaven and earth! I thank you because you have shown to the unlearned what you have hidden from the wise and learned. Yes, Father, this was done by your own choice and pleasure.

²²"My Father has given me all things. No one knows who the Son is except the Father, and no one knows who the Father is except the Son and those to whom the Son wants to reveal him."

²³Then Jesus turned to the disciples and said to them privately, "How fortunate you are, to see the things you see! ²⁴Many prophets and kings, I tell you, wanted to see what you see, but they could not, and to hear what you hear, but they did not."

The Parable of the Good Samaritan

²⁵A certain teacher of the Law came up and tried to trap Jesus. "Teacher," he asked, "what must I do to receive eternal life?"

²⁶Jesus answered him, "What do the Scriptures say? How do you interpret them?"

²⁷The man answered, " 'You must love the Lord your God with all your heart, with all your soul, with all your strength, and with all your mind'; and, 'You must love your fellow-man as yourself.' "

²⁸"Your answer is correct," replied Jesus; "do this and you will live."

²⁹But the teacher of the Law wanted to put himself in the right, so he asked Jesus, "Who is my fellow-man?"

³⁰Jesus answered, "There was a man who was going down from Jerusalem to Jericho, when robbers attacked him, stripped him and beat him up, leaving him half dead. ³¹It so happened that a priest was going down that road; when he saw the man he walked on by, on the other side. ³²In the same way a Levite also came there, went over and looked at the man, and then walked on by, on the other side. ³³But a certain Samaritan who was travelling that way came upon him, and when he saw the

man his heart was filled with pity. ³⁴He went over to him, poured oil and wine on his wounds and bandaged them; then he put the man on his own animal and took him to an inn, where he took care of him. ³⁵The next day he took out two silver coins and gave them to the innkeeper. 'Take care of him,' he told the innkeeper, 'and when I come back this way I will pay you back whatever you spend on him.' "

³⁶And Jesus concluded, "In your opinion, which one of these three acted like a fellow-man towards the man attacked by the robbers?"

³⁷The teacher of the Law answered, "The one who was kind to him."

Jesus replied, "You go, then, and do the same."

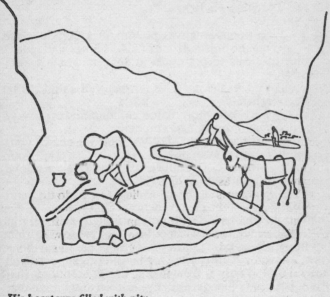

His heart was filled with pity

Jesus Visits Martha and Mary

³⁸As Jesus and his disciples went on their way, he came to a certain village where a woman named Martha welcomed him in her home. ³⁹She had a sister named Mary, who sat down at the feet of the Lord and listened to his teaching. ⁴⁰Martha was upset over all the work she had to do; so she came and said, "Lord, don't you care that my sister has left me to do all the work by myself? Tell her to come and help me!"

⁴¹The Lord answered her, "Martha, Martha! You are worried and troubled over so many things, ⁴²but just one is needed. Mary has chosen the right thing, and it will not be taken away from her."

Jesus' Teaching on Prayer
(Also Matt. 6.9–13; 7.7–11)

11 One time Jesus was praying in a certain place. When he finished, one of his disciples said to him, "Lord, teach us to pray, just as John taught his disciples."

²Jesus said to them, "This is what you should pray:
'Father:
> May your holy name be honoured;
> may your Kingdom come.
³ Give us day by day the food we need.
⁴ Forgive us our sins,
> because we forgive everyone who does us wrong.
And do not bring us to hard testing.'"

⁵And Jesus said to his disciples, "Suppose one of you should go to a friend's house at midnight and tell him, 'Friend, let me borrow three loaves of bread. ⁶A friend of mine who is on a journey has just come to my house and I haven't got any food for him!'⁷And suppose your friend should answer from inside, 'Don't bother me! The door is already locked, and my children and I are in bed. I can't get up to give you anything.' ⁸Well, what then? I tell you, even if he will not get up and give you the bread because he is your friend, yet he will get up and give you everything you need because you are not ashamed to keep on asking. ⁹And so I say to you: Ask, and you will receive; seek, and you will find; knock, and

the door will be opened to you. ¹⁰For everyone who asks will receive, and he who seeks will find, and the door will be opened to him who knocks. ¹¹Would any of you who are fathers give your son a snake when he asks for fish? ¹²Or would you give him a scorpion when he asks for an egg? ¹³As bad as you are, you know how to give good things to your children. How much more, then, the Father in heaven will give the Holy Spirit to those who ask him!"

Jesus and Beelzebul
(Also Matt. 12.22–30; Mark 3.20–27)

¹⁴Jesus was driving out a demon that could not talk; when the demon went out, the man began to talk. The crowds were amazed, ¹⁵but some of the people said, "It is Beelzebul, the chief of the demons, who gives him the power to drive them out."

¹⁶Others wanted to trap him, so they asked him to perform a miracle to show God's approval. ¹⁷But Jesus knew their thoughts and said to them, "Any country that divides itself into groups that fight each other will not last very long; a family divided against itself falls apart. ¹⁸So if Satan's kingdom has groups fighting each other, how can it last? You say that I drive out demons because Beelzebul gives me the power to do so. ¹⁹If this is how I drive them out, how do your followers drive them out? Your own followers prove that you are wrong! ²⁰No, it is rather by means of God's power that I drive out demons, which proves that the Kingdom of God has already come to you.

²¹"When a strong man, with all his weapons ready, guards his own house, all his belongings are safe. ²²But when a stronger man attacks him and defeats him, he carries away all the weapons the owner was depending on and divides up what he stole.

²³"Anyone who is not for me is really against me; anyone who does not help me gather is really scattering."

The Return of the Evil Spirit
(Also Matt. 12.43–45)

²⁴"When an evil spirit goes out of a man, it travels over dry country looking for a place to rest. If it can't

find one, it says to itself, 'I will go back to my house which I left.' [25]So it goes back and finds the house clean and all fixed up. [26]Then it goes out and brings seven other spirits even worse than itself, and they come and live there. So that man is in worse shape, when it is all over, than he was at the beginning."

True Happiness

[27]When Jesus had said this, a woman spoke up from the crowd and said to him, "How happy is the woman who bore you and nursed you!"

[28]But Jesus answered, "Rather, how happy are those who hear the word of God and obey it!"

The Demand for a Miracle
(Also Matt. 12.38–42)

[29]As the people crowded round Jesus he went on to say, "How evil are the people of this day! They ask for a miracle, but none will be given them except the miracle of Jonah. [30]In the same way that the prophet Jonah was a sign for the people of Nineveh, so the Son of Man will be a sign for the people of this day. [31]On the Judgment Day the Queen from the South will stand up and accuse the people of today, because she travelled halfway round the world to listen to Solomon's wise teaching; and there is something here, I tell you, greater than Solomon. [32]On the Judgment Day the people of Nineveh will stand up and accuse you, because they turned from their sins when they heard Jonah preach; and there is something here, I tell you, greater than Jonah!"

The Light of the Body
(Also Matt. 5.15; 6.22–23)

[33]"No one lights a lamp and then hides it or puts it under a bowl; instead, he puts it on the lampstand, so that people may see the light as they come in. [34]Your eyes are like a lamp for the body. When your eyes are clear your whole body is full of light; but when your eyes are bad your whole body will be in darkness. [35]Be careful, then, that the light in you is not darkness. [36]If, then, your whole body is full of light, with no part of it in

darkness, it will be bright all over, as when a lamp shines on you with its brightness."

Jesus Accuses the Pharisees and the Teachers of the Law
(Also Matt. 23.1–36; Mark 12.38–40)

³⁷When Jesus finished speaking, a Pharisee invited him to eat with him; so he went in and sat down to eat. ³⁸The Pharisee was surprised when he noticed that Jesus had not washed before eating. ³⁹So the Lord said to him, "Now, then, you Pharisees clean the cup and plate on the outside, but inside you are full of violence and evil. ⁴⁰Fools! Did not God, who made the outside, also make the inside? ⁴¹But give what is in your cups and plates to the poor, and everything will be clean for you.

⁴²"How terrible for you, Pharisees! You give to God one tenth of the seasoning herbs, such as mint and rue and all the other herbs, but you neglect justice and love for God. These you should practise, without neglecting the others.

⁴³"How terrible for you, Pharisees! You love the reserved seats in the synagogues, and to be greeted with respect in the market places. ⁴⁴How terrible for you! You are like unmarked graves which people walk on without knowing it."

⁴⁵One of the teachers of the Law said to him, "Teacher, when you say this you insult us too!"

⁴⁶Jesus answered, "How terrible for you, too, teachers of the Law! You put loads on men's backs which are hard to carry, but you yourselves will not stretch out a finger to help them carry those loads. ⁴⁷How terrible for you! You make fine tombs for the prophets—the very prophets your ancestors murdered.

You put loads on men's backs

⁴⁸You yourselves admit, then, that you approve of what

your ancestors did; because they murdered the prophets, and you build their tombs. [49]For this reason the Wisdom of God said, 'I will send them prophets and messengers; they will kill some of them and persecute others.' [50]So the people of this time will be punished for the murder of all the prophets killed since the creation of the world, [51]from the murder of Abel to the murder of Zechariah, who was killed between the altar and the holy place. Yes, I tell you, the people of this time will be punished for them all!

[52]"How terrible for you, teachers of the Law! You have kept the key that opens the door to the house of knowledge; you yourselves will not go in, and you stop those who are trying to go in!"

[53]When Jesus left that place the teachers of the Law and the Pharisees began to criticize him bitterly and ask him questions about many things, [54]trying to lay traps for him and catch him in something wrong he might say.

A Warning against Hypocrisy
(Also Matt. 10.26–27)

12 As thousands of people crowded together, so that they were stepping on each other, Jesus said first to his disciples, "Be on guard against the yeast of the Pharisees—I mean their hypocrisy. [2]Whatever is covered up will be uncovered, and every secret will be made known. [3]So then, whatever you have said in the dark will be heard in broad daylight, and whatever you have whispered in men's ears in a closed room will be shouted from the housetops."

Whom to Fear
(Also Matt. 10.28–31)

[4]"I tell you, my friends, do not be afraid of those who kill the body but cannot afterwards do anything worse. [5]I will show you whom to fear: fear God who, after killing, has the authority to throw into hell. Yes, I tell you, be afraid of him!

[6]"Aren't five sparrows sold for two pennies? Yet not a single one of them is forgotten by God. [7]Even the hairs of your head have all been numbered. So do not be afraid; you are worth much more than many sparrows!"

Confessing and Denying Christ
(Also Matt. 10.32–33; 12.32; 10.19–20)

⁸"I tell you: whoever declares publicly that he belongs to me, the Son of Man will do the same for him before the angels of God; ⁹but whoever denies publicly that he belongs to me, the Son of Man will also deny him before the angels of God.

¹⁰"Anyone who says a word against the Son of Man can be forgiven; but the one who says evil things against the Holy Spirit will not be forgiven.

¹¹"When they bring you to be tried in the synagogues, or before governors or rulers, do not be worried about how you will defend yourself or what you will say. ¹²For the Holy Spirit will teach you at that time what you should say."

The Parable of the Rich Fool

¹³A man in the crowd said to him, "Teacher, tell my brother to divide with me the property our father left us."

¹⁴Jesus answered him, "Man, who gave me the right to judge, or to divide the property between you two?" ¹⁵And he went on to say to them all, "Watch out, and guard yourselves from all kinds of greed; because a man's true life is not made up of the things he owns, no matter how rich he may be."

¹⁶Then Jesus told them this parable, "A rich man had land which bore good crops. ¹⁷He began to think to himself, 'I don't have a place to keep all my crops. What can I do? ¹⁸This is what I will do,' he told himself; 'I will tear my barns down and build bigger ones, where I will store the grain and all my other goods. ¹⁹Then I will say to myself, Lucky man! You have all the good things you need for many years. Take life easy, eat, drink, and enjoy yourself!' ²⁰But God said to him, 'You fool! This very night you will have to give up your life; then who will get all these things you have kept for yourself?'"

²¹And Jesus concluded, "This is how it is with those who pile up riches for themselves but are not rich in God's sight."

Trust in God
(Also Matt. 6.25–34)

²²Then Jesus said to the disciples, "This is why I tell you: do not be worried about the food you need to stay alive, or about the clothes you need for your body. ²³Life is much more important than food, and body much more important than clothes. ²⁴Look at the crows: they don't plant seeds or gather a harvest; they don't have

Do not be worried

storage rooms or barns; God feeds them! You are worth so much more than birds! ²⁵Which one of you can live a few more years by worrying about it? ²⁶If you can't manage even such a small thing, why worry about the other things? ²⁷Look how the wild flowers grow: they don't work or make clothes for themselves. But I tell you that not even Solomon, as rich as he was, had clothes as beautiful as one of these flowers. ²⁸It is God who clothes the wild grass—grass that is here today, gone tomorrow, burned up in the oven. Won't he be all the more sure to clothe you? How little faith you have! ²⁹So don't be all upset, always concerned about what you will eat and drink. ³⁰(For the heathen of this world are always concerned about all these things.) Your Father knows that you need these things. ³¹Instead, be concerned with his Kingdom, and he will provide you with these things."

Riches in Heaven
(Also Matt. 6.19–21)

³²"Do not be afraid, little flock; because your Father is pleased to give you the Kingdom. ³³Sell all your belongings and give the money to the poor. Provide for yourselves purses that don't wear out, and save your riches in heaven, where they will never decrease, because no thief can get to them, no moth can destroy them. ³⁴For your heart will always be where your riches are."

Watchful Servants

³⁵"Be ready for whatever comes, with your clothes fastened tight at the waist and your lamps lit, ³⁶like servants who are waiting for their master to come back from a wedding feast. When he comes and knocks, they will open the door for him at once. ³⁷How happy are those servants whose master finds them awake and ready when he returns! I tell you, he will fasten his belt, have them sit down, and wait on them. ³⁸How happy are they if he finds them ready, even if he should come as late as midnight or even later! ³⁹And remember this! If the man of the house knew the time when the thief would come, he would not let the thief break into his house. ⁴⁰And you, too, be ready, because the Son of Man will come at an hour when you are not expecting him."

The Faithful or the Unfaithful Servant
(Also Matt. 24.45–51)

⁴¹Peter said, "Lord, are you telling this parable to us, or do you mean it for everyone?"

⁴²The Lord answered, "Who, then, is the faithful and wise servant? He is the one whom his master will put in charge, to run the household and give the other servants their share of the food at the proper time. ⁴³How happy is that servant if his master finds him doing this when he comes home! ⁴⁴Indeed, I tell you, the master will put that servant in charge of all his property. ⁴⁵But if that servant says to himself, 'My master is taking a long time to come back,' and begins to beat the other servants, both the men and the women, and eats and drinks and

gets drunk, ⁴⁶then the master will come back some day when the servant does not expect him and at a time he does not know. The master will cut him to pieces, and make him share the fate of the disobedient.

⁴⁷"The servant who knows what his master wants him to do, but does not get himself ready and do what his master wants, will be punished with a heavy whipping; ⁴⁸but the servant who does not know what his master wants, and does something for which he deserves a whipping, will be punished with a light whipping. The man to whom much is given, of him much is required; the man to whom more is given, of him much more is required."

Jesus the Cause of Division
(Also Matt. 10.34–36)

⁴⁹"I came to set the earth on fire; how I wish it were already kindled! ⁵⁰I have a baptism to receive; how distressed I am until it is over! ⁵¹Do you suppose that I came to bring peace to the world? Not peace, I tell you, but division. ⁵²From now on a family of five will be divided, three against two, two against three. ⁵³Fathers will be against their sons, and sons against their fathers; mothers will be against their daughters, and daughters against their mothers; mothers-in-law will be against their daughters-in-law, and daughters-in-law against their mothers-in-law."

Understanding the Time
(Also Matt. 16.2–3)

⁵⁴Jesus said also to the people, "When you see a cloud coming up in the west, at once you say, 'It is going to rain,' and it does. ⁵⁵And when you feel the south wind blowing, you say, 'It is going to get hot,' and it does. ⁵⁶Hypocrites! You can look at the earth and the sky and tell what it means; why, then, don't you know the meaning of this present time?"

Settle with Your Opponent
(Also Matt. 5.25–26)

⁵⁷"Why do you not judge for yourselves the right thing to do? ⁵⁸If a man brings a lawsuit against you and takes you to court, do your best to settle the matter with

him while you are on the way, so that he won't drag you before the judge, and the judge hand you over to the police, and the police put you in jail. ⁵⁹You will not come out of there, I tell you, until you pay the last penny of your fine."

Turn from Your Sins or Die

13 At that time some people were there who told Jesus about the Galileans whom Pilate had killed while they were offering sacrifices to God. ²Jesus answered them, "Because these Galileans were killed in that way, do you think it proves that they were worse sinners than all the other Galileans? ³No! I tell you that if you do not turn from your sins, you will all die as they did. ⁴What about those eighteen in Siloam who were killed when the tower fell on them? Do you suppose this proves that they were worse than all the other people living in Jerusalem? ⁵No! I tell you that if you do not turn from your sins, you will all die as they did."

The Parable of the Unfruitful Fig Tree

⁶Then Jesus told them this parable, "A man had a fig tree growing in his vineyard. He went looking for figs on it but found none. ⁷So he said to his gardener, 'Look, for three years I have been coming here looking for figs on this fig tree and I haven't found any. Cut it down! Why should it go on using up the soil?' ⁸But the gardener answered, 'Leave it alone, sir, just this one year; I will dig a trench round it and fill it up with fertilizer. ⁹Then if the tree bears figs next year, so much the better; if not, then you will have it cut down.' "

Jesus Heals a Crippled Woman on the Sabbath

¹⁰One Sabbath day Jesus was teaching in a synagogue. ¹¹A woman was there who had an evil spirit in her that had kept her sick for eighteen years; she was bent over and could not straighten up at all. ¹²When Jesus saw her he called out to her, "Woman, you are free from your sickness!" ¹³He placed his hands on her and at once she straightened herself up and praised God.

¹⁴The official of the synagogue was angry that Jesus had healed on the Sabbath; so he spoke up and said to the people, "There are six days in which we should

work; so come during those days and be healed, but not on the Sabbath!"

[15]The Lord answered him by saying, "You hypocrites! Any one of you would untie his ox or his donkey from the stall and take it out to give it water on the Sabbath. [16]Now here is this descendant of Abraham whom Satan has kept in bonds for eighteen years; should she not be freed from her bonds on the Sabbath?" [17]His answer made all his enemies ashamed of themselves, while all the people rejoiced over every wonderful thing that he did.

Give it water on the Sabbath

The Parable of the Mustard Seed
(Also Matt. 13.31–32; Mark 4.30–32)

[18]Jesus asked, "What is the Kingdom of God like? What shall I compare it with? [19]It is like a mustard seed, which a man took and planted in his field; the plant grew and became a tree, and the birds made their nests in its branches."

The Parable of the Yeast
(Also Matt. 13.33)

[20]Again Jesus asked, "What shall I compare the Kingdom of God with? [21]It is like the yeast which a woman takes and mixes in a bushel of flour, until the whole batch of dough rises."

The Narrow Door
(Also Matt. 7.13–14, 21–23)

[22]Jesus went through towns and villages, teaching and making his way towards Jerusalem. [23]Someone asked him, "Sir, will just a few people be saved?"

Jesus answered them, [24]"Do your best to go in through the narrow door; because many people, I tell you, will try to go in but will not be able. [25]The master of the house will get up and close the door; then when you stand outside and begin to knock on the door and say, 'Open the door for us, sir!' he will answer you, 'I don't know where you come from!' 26Then you will answer back, 'We ate and drank with you; you taught in our town!' 27He will say again, 'I don't know where you come from. Get away from me, all you evildoers!' 28What crying and gnashing of teeth there will be when you see Abraham, Isaac, and Jacob and all the prophets in the Kingdom of God, while you are thrown out! 29People will come from the east and the west, from the north and the south, and sit at the table in the Kingdom of God. 30Then those who are now last will be first, and those who are now first will be last."

Jesus' Love for Jerusalem
(Also Matt. 23.37–39)

31At that same time some Pharisees came to Jesus and said to him, "You must get out of here and go somewhere else, because Herod wants to kill you."

32Jesus answered them, "Go tell that fox: 'I am driving out demons and performing cures today and tomorrow, and on the third day I shall finish my work.' 33Yet I must be on my way today, tomorrow, and the next day; it is not right for a prophet to be killed anywhere except in Jerusalem.

34"Jerusalem, Jerusalem! You kill the prophets, you stone the messengers God has sent you! How many times I wanted to put my arms round all your people, just as a hen gathers her chicks under her wings, but you would not let me! 35Now your home will be completely forsaken. You will not see me, I tell you, until the time comes when you say, 'God bless him who comes in the name of the Lord.'"

Jesus Heals a Sick Man

14 One Sabbath day Jesus went to eat a meal at the home of one of the leading Pharisees; and people were watching Jesus closely. 2A man whose legs and arms were swollen came to Jesus, 3and Jesus spoke up and asked the teachers of the Law and the Pharisees, "Does our Law allow healing on the Sabbath, or not?"

4But they would not say a thing. Jesus took the man, healed him and sent him away. 5Then he said to them, "If any one of you had a son or an ox that happened to fall in a well on a Sabbath, would you not pull him out at once on the Sabbath itself?"

⁶But they were not able to answer him about this.

Humility and Hospitality

⁷Jesus noticed how some of the guests were choosing the best places, so he told this parable to all of them, ⁸"When someone invites you to a wedding feast, do not sit down in the best place. It could happen that someone more important than you had been invited, ⁹and your host, who invited both of you, would come and say to you, 'Let him have this place.' Then you would be ashamed and have to sit in the lowest place. ¹⁰Instead, when you are invited, go and sit in the lowest place, so that your host will come to you and say, 'Come on up, my friend, to a better place.' This will bring you honour in the presence of all the other guests. ¹¹Because everyone who makes himself great will be humbled, and everyone who humbles himself will be made great."

¹²Then Jesus said to his host, "When you give a lunch or a dinner, do not invite your friends, or your brothers, or your relatives, or your rich neighbours—because they will invite you back and in this way you will be paid for what you did. ¹³When you give a feast, invite the poor, the crippled, the lame, and the blind, ¹⁴and you will be blessed; because they are not able to pay you back. You will be paid by God when the good people rise from death."

The Parable of the Great Feast
(Also Matt. 22.1–10)

¹⁵One of the men sitting at the table heard this and said to Jesus, "How happy are those who will sit at the table in the Kingdom of God!"

¹⁶Jesus said to him, "There was a man who was giving a great feast, to which he invited many people. ¹⁷At the time for the feast he sent his servant to tell his guests, 'Come, everything is ready!' ¹⁸But they all began, one after another, to make excuses. The first one told the servant, 'I bought a field, and have to go and look at it; please accept my apologies.' ¹⁹Another one said, 'I bought five pairs of oxen and am on my way to try them

out; please accept my apologies.' ²⁰Another one said, 'I have just got married, and for this reason I cannot come.' ²¹The servant went back and told all this to his master. The master of the house was furious and said to his servant, 'Hurry out to the streets and alleys of the town, and bring back the poor, the crippled, the blind, and the lame.' ²²Soon the servant said, 'Your order has been carried out, sir, but there is room for more.' ²³So the master said to the servant, 'Go out to the country roads and lanes, and make people come in, so that my house will be full. ²⁴I tell you all that none of those men who were invited will taste my dinner!' "

The Cost of Being a Disciple
(Also Matt. 10.37–38)

²⁵Great crowds of people were going along with Jesus. He turned and said to them, ²⁶"Whoever comes to me cannot be my disciple unless he hates his father and his mother, his wife and his children, his brothers and his sisters, and himself as well. ²⁷Whoever does not carry his own cross and come after me cannot be my disciple. ²⁸If one of you is planning to build a tower, he sits down first and figures out what it will cost, to see if he has enough money to finish the job. ²⁹If he doesn't, he will not be able to finish the tower after laying the foundation; and all who see what happened will make fun of him. ³⁰'This man began to build but can't finish the job!' they will say. ³¹If a king goes out with ten thousand men to fight another king, who comes against him with twenty thousand men, he will sit down first and decide if he is strong enough to face that other king. ³²If he isn't, he will send messengers to meet the other king, while he is still a long way off, to ask for terms of peace. ³³In the same way," concluded Jesus, "none of you can be my disciple unless he gives up everything he has."

Worthless Salt
(Also Matt. 5.13; Mark 9.50)

³⁴"Salt is good, but if it loses its taste there is no way to make it salty again. ³⁵It is no good for the soil or for the manure pile; it is thrown away. Listen, then, if you have ears!"

The Lost Sheep
(Also Matt. 18.12–14)

15 One time many tax collectors and outcasts came to listen to Jesus. ²The Pharisees and the teachers of the Law started grumbling, "This man welcomes outcasts and even eats with them!" ³So Jesus told them this parable,

⁴"Suppose one of you has a hundred sheep and loses one of them—what does he do? He leaves the other ninety-nine sheep in the pasture and goes looking for the one that got lost until he finds it. ⁵When he finds it, he is so happy that he puts it on his shoulders, ⁶and carries it back home. Then he calls his friends and neighbours together, and says to them, 'I am so happy I found my lost sheep. Let us celebrate!' ⁷In the same way, I tell you, there will be more joy in heaven over one sinner who repents than over ninety-nine respectable people who do not need to repent."

The Lost Coin

⁸"Or suppose a woman who has ten silver coins loses one of them—what does she do? She lights a lamp, sweeps her house, and looks carefully everywhere until she finds it. ⁹When she finds it, she calls her friends and neighbours together, and says to them, 'I am so happy I found the coin I lost. Let us celebrate!' ¹⁰In the same way, I tell you, the angels of God rejoice over one sinner who repents."

The Lost Son

¹¹Jesus went on to say, "There was a man who had two sons. ¹²The younger one said to him, 'Father, give me now my share of the property.' So the man divided the property between his two sons. ¹³After a few days the younger son sold his part of the property and left home with the

Left home with the money

money. He went to a country far away, where he wasted his money in reckless living. ¹⁴He spent everything he had. Then a severe famine spread over that country, and he was left without a thing. ¹⁵So he went to work for one of the citizens of that country, who sent him out to his farm to take care of the pigs. ¹⁶He wished he could fill himself with the bean pods the pigs ate, but no one gave him anything to eat. ¹⁷At last he came to his senses

Here I am, about to starve!

and said, 'All my father's hired workers have more than they can eat, and here I am, about to starve! ¹⁸I will get up and go to my father and say, "Father, I have sinned against God and against you. ¹⁹I am no longer fit to be called your son; treat me as one of your hired workers." ' ²⁰So he got up and started back to his father.

"He was still a long way from home when his father saw him; his heart was filled with pity and he ran, threw his arms round his son, and kissed him. ²¹'Father,' the son said, 'I have sinned against God and against you. I am no longer fit to be called your son.' ²²But the father called his servants: 'Hurry!' he said. 'Bring the best robe and put it on him. Put a ring on his finger and shoes on his feet. ²³Then go get the prize calf and kill it, and let us celebrate with a feast! ²⁴Because this son of mine was dead, but now he is alive; he was lost, but now he has been found.' And so the feasting began.

²⁵"The older son, in the meantime, was out in the field. On his way back, when he came close to the house, he heard the music and dancing. ²⁶He called one of the servants and asked him, 'What's going on?' ²⁷'Your brother came back home,' the servant answered, 'and your father killed the prize calf, because he got him back safe and sound.' ²⁸The older brother was so angry that he would not go into the house; so his father came out and begged

He has been found

him to come in. ²⁹'Look,' he answered back to his father, 'all these years I have worked like a slave for you, and I never disobeyed your orders. What have you given me? Not even a goat for me to have a feast with my friends! ³⁰But this son of yours wasted all your property on prostitutes, and when he comes back home you kill the prize calf for him!' ³¹'My son,' the father answered, 'you are always here with me and everything I have is yours. ³²But we had to have a feast and be happy, because your brother was dead, but now he is alive; he was lost, but now he has been found.' "

The Shrewd Manager

16 Jesus said to his disciples, "There was a rich man who had a manager, and he was told that the manager was wasting his master's money. ²He called him in and said, 'What is this I hear about you? Turn in a complete account of your handling of my property, because you cannot be my manager any longer.' ³'My master is going to dismiss me from my job,' the man said to himself. 'What shall I do? I am not strong enough to dig ditches, and I am ashamed to beg. ⁴Now I know what I will do! Then when my job is gone I shall have friends who will welcome me in their homes.' 'So he called in all the people who were in debt to his master. He said to the first one, 'How much do you owe my master?' '"One hundred barrels of olive oil,' he answered. 'Here is your account,' the manager told him; 'sit down and write fifty.' ⁷He said to another one, 'And you—how much do you owe?' 'A thousand bushels of wheat,' he answered. 'Here is your account,' the manager told him; 'write eight hundred.' ⁸The master of this dishonest manager praised him for doing such a shrewd thing; because the people of this world are much more shrewd in handling their affairs than the people who belong to the light.''

⁹And Jesus went on to say, "And so I tell you: make friends for yourselves with worldly wealth, so that when it gives out you will be welcomed in the eternal home. ¹⁰Whoever is faithful in small matters will be faithful in large ones; whoever is dishonest in small matters will be dishonest in large ones. ¹¹If, then, you have not been faithful in handling worldly wealth, how can you be trusted with true wealth? ¹²And if you have not been faithful with what belongs to someone else, who will give you what belongs to you?

¹³"No servant can be the slave of two masters; he will hate one and love the other; he will be loyal to one and despise the other. You cannot serve both God and money."

Some Sayings of Jesus
(Also Matt. 11.12–13; 5.31–32; Mark 10.11–12)

¹⁴The Pharisees heard all this, and they made fun of Jesus, because they loved money. ¹⁵Jesus said to them, "You are the ones who make yourselves look right in men's sight, but God knows your hearts. For what men think is of great value is worth nothing in God's sight.

¹⁶"The Law of Moses and the writings of the prophets were in effect up to the time of John the Baptist; since then the Good News about the Kingdom of God is being told, and everyone forces his way in. ¹⁷But it is easier for heaven and earth to disappear than for the smallest detail of the Law to be done away with.

¹⁸"Any man who divorces his wife and marries an-

other woman commits adultery; and the man who marries a divorced woman commits adultery."

The Rich Man and Lazarus

¹⁹"There was once a rich man who dressed in the most expensive clothes and lived in great luxury every day. ²⁰There was also a poor man, named Lazarus, full of sores, who used to be brought to the rich man's door, ²¹hoping to fill himself with the bits of food that fell from the rich man's table. Even the dogs would come and lick his sores. ²²The poor man died and was carried by the angels to Abraham's side, at the feast in heaven; the rich man died and was buried. ²³He was in great pain in Hades; and he looked up and saw Abraham, far away, with Lazarus at his side. ²⁴So he called out, 'Father Abraham! Take pity on me, and send Lazarus to dip his finger in some water and cool off my tongue, because I am in great pain in this fire!' ²⁵But Abraham said, 'Remember, my son, that in your lifetime you were given all the good things, while Lazarus got all the bad things; but now he is enjoying himself here, while you are in pain. ²⁶Besides all that, there is a deep pit lying between us, so that those who want to cross over from here to you cannot do it, nor can anyone cross over to us from where you are.' ²⁷The rich man said, 'Well, father, I beg you, send Lazarus to my father's house, ²⁸where I have five brothers; let him go and warn them so that they, at least, will not come to this place of pain.' ²⁹Abraham said, 'Your brothers have Moses and the prophets to warn them; let your brothers listen to what they say.' ³⁰The rich man answered, 'That is not enough, father Abraham! But if someone were to rise from death and go to them, then they would turn from their sins.' ³¹But Abraham said, 'If they will not listen to Moses and the prophets, they will not be convinced even if someone were to rise from death.' "

Sin

(Also Matt. 18.6–7, 21–22; Mark 9.42)

17 Jesus said to his disciples, "Things that make people fall into sin are bound to happen; but how terrible for the one who makes them happen! ²It would

be better for him if a large millstone were tied round his neck and he were thrown into the sea, than for him to cause one of these little ones to sin. ³Be on your guard!

"If your brother sins, rebuke him, and if he repents, forgive him. ⁴If he sins against you seven times in one day, and each time he comes to you saying, 'I repent,' you must forgive him."

Faith

⁵The apostles said to the Lord, "Make our faith greater."

⁶The Lord answered, "If you had faith as big as a mustard seed, you could say to this mulberry tree, 'Pull yourself up by the roots and plant yourself in the sea!' and it would obey you."

A Servant's Duty

⁷"Suppose one of you has a servant who is ploughing or looking after the sheep. When he comes in from the field, do you say to him, 'Hurry along and eat your meal'? ⁸Of course not! Instead, you say to him, 'Get my supper ready, then put on your apron and wait on me while I eat and drink; after that you may eat and drink.' ⁹The servant does not deserve thanks for obeying orders, does he? ¹⁰It is the same with you; when you have done all you have been told to do, say, 'We are ordinary servants; we have only done our duty.'"

Jesus Makes Ten Lepers Clean

¹¹As Jesus made his way to Jerusalem he went between Samaria and Galilee. ¹²He was going into a village when he was met by ten lepers. They stood at a distance ¹³and shouted, "Jesus! Master! Have pity on us!"

¹⁴Jesus saw them and said to them, "Go and let the priests examine you."

On the way they were made clean. ¹⁵One of them, when he saw that he was healed, came back, praising God in a loud voice. ¹⁶He threw himself to the ground at Jesus' feet, thanking him. The man was a Samaritan. ¹⁷Jesus spoke up, "There were ten men made clean;

where are the other nine? [18]Why is this foreigner the only one who came back to give thanks to God?" [19]And Jesus said to him, "Get up and go; your faith has made you well."

Where are the other nine?

The Coming of the Kingdom
(Also Matt. 24.23–28, 37–41)

[20]Some Pharisees asked Jesus when the Kingdom of God would come. His answer was, "The Kingdom of God does not come in such a way as to be seen. [21]No one will say, 'Look, here it is!' or, 'There it is!'; because the Kingdom of God is within you."

[22]Then he said to the disciples, "The time will come when you will wish you could see one of the days of the Son of Man, but you will not see it. [23]There will be those who will say to you, 'Look, over there!' or, 'Look, over here!' But don't go out looking for it. [24]As the lightning flashes across the sky and lights it up from one side to

the other, so will the Son of Man be in his day. [25]But first he must suffer much and be rejected by the people of this day. [26]As it was in the time of Noah, so shall it be in the days of the Son of Man. [27]Everybody kept on eating and drinking, men and women married, up to the very day Noah went into the ark and the Flood came and killed them all. [28]It will be as it was in the time of Lot. Everybody kept on eating and drinking, buying and selling, planting and building. [29]On the day Lot left Sodom, fire and sulphur rained down from heaven and killed them all. [30]That is how it will be on the day the Son of Man is revealed.

[31]"The man who is on the roof of his house on that day must not go down into the house to get his belongings that are there; in the same way, the man who is out in the field must not go back to the house. [32]Remember Lot's wife! [33]Whoever tries to save his own life will lose it; whoever loses his life will save it. [34]On that night, I tell you, there will be two men sleeping in one bed: one will be taken away, the other left behind. [35]Two women will be grinding meal together: one will be taken away, the other left behind. [[36]Two men will be in the field: one will be taken away, the other left behind.]"

[37]The disciples asked him, "Where, Lord?"

Jesus answered, "Where there is a dead body the vultures will gather."

The Parable of the Widow and the Judge

18 Then Jesus told them this parable, to teach them that they should always pray and never become discouraged. [2]"There was a judge in a certain town who neither feared God nor respected men. [3]And there was a widow in that same town who kept coming to him and pleading for her rights: 'Help me against my opponent!' [4]For a long time the judge was not willing, but at last he said to himself, 'Even though I don't fear God or respect men, [5]yet because of all the trouble this widow is giving me I will see to it that she gets her rights; or else she will keep on coming and finally wear me out!' "

[6]And the Lord continued, "Listen to what that corrupt judge said. [7]Now, will God not judge in favour of his own people who cry to him for help day and night?

Will he be slow to help them? 8I tell you, he will judge in their favour, and do it quickly. But will the Son of Man find faith on earth when he comes?"

The Parable of the Pharisee and the Tax Collector

9Jesus also told this parable to people who were sure of their own goodness and despised everybody else. 10"Two men went up to the temple to pray; one was a Pharisee, the other a tax collector. 11The Pharisee stood apart by himself and prayed, 'I thank you, God, that I am not greedy, dishonest, or immoral, like everybody else; I thank you that I am not like that tax collector. 12I fast two days every week, and I give you one tenth of all my income.' 13But the tax collector stood at a distance and would not even raise his face to heaven, but beat on his breast and said, 'God, have pity on me, a sinner!' 14I tell you," said Jesus, "this man, and not the other, was in the right with God when he went home. Because everyone who makes himself great will be humbled, and everyone who humbles himself will be made great."

Jesus Blesses Little Children
(Also Matt. 19.13–15; Mark 10.13–16)

15Some people brought their babies to Jesus to have him place his hands on them. But the disciples saw them and scolded them for doing so. 16But Jesus called the children to him, and said, "Let the children come to me, and do not stop them, because the Kingdom of God belongs to such as these. 17Remember this! Whoever does not receive the Kingdom of God like a child will never enter it."

The Rich Man
(Also Matt. 19.16–30; Mark 10.17–31)

18A Jewish leader asked Jesus, "Good Teacher, what must I do to receive eternal life?"

19"Why do you call me good?" Jesus asked him. "No one is good except God alone. 20You know the commandments: 'Do not commit adultery; do not murder; do not steal; do not lie; honour your father and mother.' "

²¹The man replied, "Ever since I was young I have obeyed all these commandments."

²²When Jesus heard this, he said to him, "You still need to do one thing. Sell all you have and give the money to the poor, and you will have riches in heaven; then come and follow me." ²³But when the man heard this he became very sad, because he was very rich.

²⁴Jesus saw that he was sad and said, "How hard it is for rich people to enter the Kingdom of God! ²⁵It is much harder for a rich man to enter the Kingdom of God than for a camel to go through the eye of a needle."

²⁶The people who heard him asked, "Who, then, can be saved?"

²⁷Jesus answered, "What is impossible for men is possible for God."

²⁸Then Peter said, "Look! We have left our homes to follow you."

²⁹"Yes," Jesus said to them, "and I tell you this: anyone who leaves home or wife or brothers or parents or children for the sake of the Kingdom of God ³⁰will receive much more in this present age, and eternal life in the age to come."

Jesus Speaks a Third Time about His Death
(Also Matt. 20.17–19; Mark 10.32–34)

³¹Jesus took the twelve disciples aside and said to them, "Listen! We are going to Jerusalem where everything the prophets wrote about the Son of Man will come true. ³²He will be handed over to the Gentiles, who will make fun of him, insult him, and spit on him. ³³They will whip him and kill him, but on the third day he will rise to life."

³⁴The disciples did not understand any of these things; the meaning of the words was hidden from them, and they did not know what Jesus was talking about.

Jesus Heals a Blind Beggar
(Also Matt. 20.29–34; Mark 10.46–52)

³⁵Jesus was coming near Jericho, and a certain blind man was sitting by the road, begging. ³⁶When he heard the crowd passing by he asked, "What is this?"

³⁷"Jesus of Nazareth is passing by," they told him.

³⁸He cried out, "Jesus! Son of David! Have mercy on me!"

³⁹The people in front scolded him and told him to be quiet. But he shouted even more loudly, "Son of David! Have mercy on me!"

⁴⁰So Jesus stopped and ordered that the blind man be brought to him. When he came near, Jesus asked him, ⁴¹"What do you want me to do for you?"

"Sir," he answered, "I want to see again."

⁴²Then Jesus said to him, "See! Your faith has made you well."

⁴³At once he was able to see, and he followed Jesus, giving thanks to God. When the crowd saw it, they all praised God.

Jesus and Zacchaeus

19 Jesus went on into Jericho and was passing through. ²There was a chief tax collector there, named Zacchaeus, who was rich. ³He was trying to see

He was a little man

who Jesus was, but he was a little man and could not see
Jesus because of the crowd. ⁴So he ran ahead of the
crowd and climbed a sycamore tree to see Jesus, who
would be going that way. ⁵When Jesus came to that
place he looked up and said to Zacchaeus, "Hurry down,
Zacchaeus, because I must stay in your house today."

⁶Zacchaeus hurried down and welcomed him with
great joy. ⁷All the people who saw it started grumbling,
"This man has gone as a guest to the home of a sinner!"

⁸Zacchaeus stood up and said to the Lord, "Listen,
sir! I will give half my belongings to the poor; and if I
have cheated anyone, I will pay him back four times as
much."

⁹Jesus said to him, "Salvation has come to this house
today; this man, also, is a descendant of Abraham. ¹⁰For
the Son of Man came to seek and to save the lost."

The Parable of the Gold Coins
(Also Matt. 25.14–30)

¹¹While the people were listening to this, Jesus continued and told them a parable. He was now almost at
Jerusalem, and they supposed that the Kingdom of God
was just about to appear. ¹²So he said, "There was a
nobleman who went to a country far away to be made
king and then come back home. ¹³Before he left, he
called his ten servants and gave them each a gold coin
and told them, 'See what you can earn with this while
I am gone.' ¹⁴Now, his countrymen hated him, and so
they sent messengers after him to say, 'We don't want
this man to be our king.'

¹⁵"The nobleman was made king and came back. At
once he ordered his servants, to whom he had given
the money, to appear before him in order to find out
how much they had earned. ¹⁶The first one came and
said, 'Sir, I have earned ten gold coins with the one
you gave me.' ¹⁷'Well done,' he said; 'you are a good
servant! Since you were faithful in small matters, I will
put you in charge of ten cities.' ¹⁸The second servant
came and said, 'Sir, I have earned five gold coins with
the one you gave me.' ¹⁹To this one he said, 'You will
be in charge of five cities.' ²⁰Another servant came and
said, 'Sir, here is your gold coin; I kept it hidden in a
handkerchief. ²¹I was afraid of you, because you are a

hard man. You take what is not yours, and reap what you did not plant.' ²²He said to him, 'You bad servant! I will use your own words to condemn you! You know that I am a hard man, taking what is not mine and reaping what I have not planted. ²³Well, then, why didn't you put my money in the bank? Then I would have received it back with interest when I returned.' ²⁴Then he said to those who were standing there, 'Take the gold coin away from him and give it to the servant who has ten coins.' ²⁵They said to him, 'Sir, he already has ten coins!' ²⁶'I tell you,' he replied, 'that to every one who has, even more will be given; but the one who does not have, even the little that he has will be taken away from him. ²⁷Now, as for these enemies of mine who did not want me to be their king: bring them here and kill them before me!' "

The Master needs it

The Triumphant Entry into Jerusalem
(Also Matt. 21.1–11; Mark 11.1–11; John 12.12–19)

²⁸Jesus said this and then went on to Jerusalem ahead of them. ²⁹As he came near Bethphage and Bethany, at the Mount of Olives, he sent two disciples ahead ³⁰with

these instructions, "Go to the village there ahead of you; as you go in you will find a colt tied up that has never been ridden. Untie it and bring it here. ³¹If someone asks you, 'Why are you untying it?' tell him, 'The Master needs it.'"

³²They went on their way and found everything just as Jesus had told them. ³³As they were untying the colt, its owners said to them, "Why are you untying it?"

³⁴"The Master needs it," they answered, ³⁵and took the colt to Jesus. Then they threw their cloaks over the animal and helped Jesus get on. ³⁶As he rode on, they spread their cloaks on the road.

³⁷When he came near Jerusalem, at the place where the road went down the Mount of Olives, the large crowd of his disciples began to thank God and praise him in loud voices for all the great things that they had seen: ³⁸"God bless the king who comes in the name of the Lord! Peace in heaven, and glory to God!"

³⁹Then some of the Pharisees spoke up from the crowd to Jesus. "Teacher," they said, "command your disciples to be quiet!"

⁴⁰Jesus answered, "If they keep quiet, I tell you, the stones themselves will shout."

Jesus Weeps over Jerusalem

⁴¹He came closer to the city and when he saw it he wept over it, ⁴²saying, "If you only knew today what is needed for peace! But now you cannot see it! ⁴³The days will come upon you when your enemies will surround you with barricades, blockade you, and close in on you from every side. ⁴⁴They will completely destroy you and the people within your walls; not a single stone will they leave in its place, because you did not recognise the time when God came to save you!"

Jesus Goes to the Temple
(Also Matt. 21.12–17; Mark 11.15–19; John 2.13–22)

⁴⁵Jesus went into the temple and began to drive out the merchants, ⁴⁶saying to them, "It is written in the Scriptures that God said, 'My house will be called a house of prayer.' But you have turned it into a hideout for thieves!"

God bless the king who comes in the name of the Lord!

⁴⁷Jesus taught in the temple every day. The chief priests, the teachers of the Law, and the leaders of the people wanted to kill him, ⁴⁸but they could not find how to do it, because all the people kept listening to him, not wanting to miss a single word.

The Question about Jesus' Authority
(Also Matt. 21.23–27; Mark 11.27–33)

20 One day, when Jesus was in the temple teaching the people and preaching the Good News, the chief priests and the teachers of the Law, together with the elders, came ²and said to him, "Tell us, what right do you have to do these things? Who gave you the right to do them?"

³Jesus answered them, "Now let me ask you a question. Tell me, ⁴did John's right to baptize come from God or from men?"

⁵They started to argue among themselves, "What shall we say? If we say, 'From God,' he will say, 'Why, then, did you not believe John?' ⁶But if we say, 'From men,' this whole crowd here will stone us, because they are convinced that John was a prophet." ⁷So they answered, "We don't know where it came from."

⁸And Jesus said to them, "Neither will I tell you, then, by what right I do these things."

The Parable of the Tenants in the Vineyard
(Also Matt. 21.33–46; Mark 12.1–12)

⁹Then Jesus told the people this parable, "A man planted a vineyard, rented it out to tenants, and then left home for a long time. ¹⁰When the time came for harvesting the grapes, he sent a slave to the tenants to receive from them his share of the harvest. But the tenants beat the slave and sent him back without a thing. ¹¹So he sent another slave; but the tenants beat him also, treated him shamefully, and sent him back without a thing. ¹²Then he sent a third slave; the tenants hurt him, too, and threw him out. ¹³Then the owner of the vineyard said, 'What shall I do? I will send my own dear son; surely they will respect him!' ¹⁴But when the tenants saw him they said to one another, 'This is the owner's son. Let us kill him, and his property will be ours!' ¹⁵So they threw him out of the vineyard and killed him.

"What, then, will the owner of the vineyard do to the tenants?" Jesus asked. ¹⁶"He will come and kill those men, and turn over the vineyard to other tenants."

When the people heard this they said, "Surely not!"

¹⁷Jesus looked at them and asked, "What, then, does this scripture mean?

'The very stone which the builders rejected
turned out to be the most important
stone.'

¹⁸Everyone who falls on that stone will be cut to
pieces; and if the stone falls on someone, it will crush
him to dust."

The Question about Paying Taxes
(Also Matt. 22.15–22; Mark 12.13–17)

¹⁹The teachers of the Law and the chief priests tried
to arrest Jesus on the spot, because they knew that he
had told this parable against them; but they were afraid
of the people. ²⁰So they watched for the right time. They
bribed some men to pretend they were sincere, and sent
them to trap Jesus with questions, so they could hand
him over to the authority and power of the Governor.
²¹These spies said to Jesus, "Teacher, we know that
what you say and teach is right. We know that you pay
no attention to a man's status, but teach the truth about
God's will for man. ²²Tell us, is it against our Law for
us to pay taxes to the Roman Emperor, or not?"

²³But Jesus saw through their trick and said to them,
²⁴"Show me a silver coin. Whose face and name are
these on it?"

"The Emperor's," they answered.

²⁵So Jesus said, "Well, then, pay to the Emperor
what belongs to him, and pay to God what belongs to
God."

²⁶They could not catch him in a thing there before
the people, so they kept quiet, amazed at his answer.

The Question about Rising from Death
(Also Matt. 22.23–33; Mark 12.18–27)

²⁷Some Sadducees came to Jesus. (They are the ones
who say that people will not rise from death.) They
asked him, ²⁸"Teacher, Moses wrote this law for us: 'If
a man dies and leaves a wife, but no children, that man's
brother must marry the widow so they can have children
for the dead man.' ²⁹Once there were seven brothers; the
oldest got married, and died without having children.
³⁰Then the second one married the woman, ³¹and then
the third. The same thing happened to all seven—they

died without having children. ³²Last of all, the woman died. ³³Now, on the day when the dead rise to life, whose wife will she be? All seven of them had married her."

³⁴Jesus answered them, "The men and women of this age marry, ³⁵but the men and women who are worthy to rise from death and live in the age to come do not marry. ³⁶They are like angels and cannot die. They are the sons of God, because they have risen from death. ³⁷And Moses clearly proves that the dead are raised to life. In the passage about the burning bush he speaks of the Lord as 'the God of Abraham, the God of Isaac, and the God of Jacob.' ³⁸This means that he is the God of the living, not of the dead, because all are alive to him."

³⁹Some of the teachers of the Law spoke up, "A good answer, Teacher!" ⁴⁰For they did not dare ask him any more questions.

The Question about the Messiah
(Also Matt. 22.41–46; Mark 12.35–37)

⁴¹Jesus said to them, "How can it be said that the Messiah will be the descendant of David? ⁴²Because David himself says in the book of Psalms,

'The Lord said to my Lord:
Sit here at my right side,
43   until I put your enemies as a footstool
under your feet.'

⁴⁴David, then, called him 'Lord.' How can the Messiah be David's descendant?"

Jesus Warns against the Teachers of the Law
(Also Matt. 23.1–36; Mark 12.38–40)

⁴⁵As all the people listened to him, Jesus said to his disciples, ⁴⁶"Watch out for the teachers of the Law, who like to walk around in their long robes, and love to be greeted with respect in the market place; who choose the reserved seats in the synagogues and the best places at feasts; ⁴⁷who take advantage of widows and rob them of their homes, and then make a show of saying long prayers! Their punishment will be all the worse!"

The Widow's Offering
(Also Mark 12.41–44)

21 Jesus looked round and saw rich men dropping their gifts in the temple treasury, ²and he also saw a very poor widow dropping in two little copper coins. ³He said, "I tell you that this poor widow put in more than all the others. ⁴For the others offered their gifts from what they had to spare of their riches; but she, poor as she is, gave all she had to live on."

She, poor as she is, gave all she had to live on

Jesus Speaks of the Destruction of the Temple
(Also Matt. 24.1–2; Mark 13.1–2)

⁵Some of them were talking about the temple, how beautiful it looked with its fine stones and the gifts offered to God. Jesus said, ⁶"All this you see—the time will come when not a single stone here will be left in its place; every one will be thrown down."

Troubles and Persecutions
(Also Matt. 24.3–14; Mark 13.3–13)

⁷"Teacher," they asked, "when will this be? And what will happen to show that the time has come for it to take place?"

⁸Jesus said, "Watch out; don't be fooled. Because many men will come in my name saying, 'I am he!' and, 'The time has come!' But don't follow them. ⁹Don't be

afraid when you hear of wars and revolutions; such things must happen first, but they do not mean that the end is near."

[10]He went on to say, "Countries will fight each other, kingdoms will attack one another. [11]There will be terrible earthquakes, famines, and plagues everywhere; there will be awful things and great signs from the sky. [12]Before all these things take place, however, you will be arrested and persecuted; you will be handed over to trial in synagogues and be put in prison; you will be brought before kings and rulers for my sake. [13]This will be your chance to tell the Good News. [14]Make up your minds ahead of time not to worry about how you will defend yourselves; [15]because I will give you such words and wisdom that none of your enemies will be able to resist or deny what you say. [16]You will be handed over by your parents, your brothers, your relatives, and your friends; they will put some of you to death. [17]Everyone will hate you because of me. [18]But not a single hair from your heads will be lost. [19]Stand firm, because this is how you will save yourselves."

Jesus Speaks of the Destruction of Jerusalem
(Also Matt. 24.15–21; Mark 13.14–19)

[20]"When you see Jerusalem surrounded by armies, then you will know that soon she will be destroyed. [21]Then those who are in Judea must run away to the hills; those who are in the city must leave, and those who are out in the country must not go into the city. [22]For these are 'The Days of Punishment,' to make come true all that the Scriptures say. [23]How terrible it will be in those days for women who are pregnant, and for mothers with little babies! Terrible distress will come upon this land, and God's wrath will be against this people. [24]Some will be killed by the sword, and others taken as prisoners to all countries; and the heathen will trample over Jerusalem until their time is up."

The Coming of the Son of Man
(Also Matt. 24.29–31; Mark 13.24–27)

[25]"There will be signs in the sun, the moon, and the stars. On earth, whole countries will be in despair, afraid

of the roar of the sea and the raging tides. [26]Men will faint from fear as they wait for what is coming over the whole earth; for the powers in space will be driven from their courses. [27]Then the Son of Man will appear, coming in a cloud with great power and glory. [28]When these things begin to happen, stand up and raise your heads, because your salvation is near."

The Lesson of the Fig Tree
(Also Matt. 24.32–35; Mark 13.28–31)

[29]Then Jesus told them this parable, "Remember the fig tree and all the other trees. [30]When you see their leaves beginning to appear you know that summer is near. [31]In the same way, when you see these things happening, you will know that the Kingdom of God is about to come.

[32]"Remember this! All these things will take place before the people now living have all died. [33]Heaven and earth will pass away; my words will never pass away."

The Need to Watch

[34]"Watch yourselves! Don't let yourselves become occupied with too much feasting and strong drink, and the worries of this life, or that Day may come on you suddenly. [35]For it will come like a trap upon all men over the whole earth. [36]Be on watch and pray always that you will have the strength to go safely through all these things that will happen, and to stand before the Son of Man."

[37]Jesus spent those days teaching in the temple, and when evening came he would go out and spend the night on the Mount of Olives. [38]All the people would go to the temple early in the morning to listen to him.

The Plot against Jesus
(Also Matt. 26.1–5; Mark 14.1–2; John 11.45–53)

22 The time was near for the Feast of Unleavened Bread, which is called the Passover. [2]The chief priests and the teachers of the Law were trying to find some way of killing Jesus; because they were afraid of the people.

Judas Agrees to Betray Jesus
(Also Matt. 26.14–16; Mark 14.10–11)

³Then Satan went into Judas, called Iscariot, who was one of the twelve disciples. ⁴So Judas went off and spoke with the chief priests and the officers of the temple guard about how he could hand Jesus over to them. ⁵They were pleased and offered to pay him money. ⁶Judas agreed to it and started looking for a good chance to betray Jesus to them without the people knowing about it.

Jesus Prepares to Eat the Passover Meal
(Also Matt. 26.17–25; Mark 14.12–21; John 13.21–30)

⁷The day came during the Feast of Unleavened Bread when the lambs for the Passover meal had to be killed. ⁸Jesus sent Peter and John with these instructions, "Go and get our Passover meal ready for us to eat."

⁹"Where do you want us to get it ready?" they asked him.

¹⁰He said, "Listen! As you go into the city a man carrying a jar of water will meet you. Follow him into the house that he enters, ¹¹and say to the owner of the house: 'The Teacher says to you, Where is the room where my disciples and I will eat the Passover meal?' ¹²He will show you a large furnished room upstairs, where you will get everything ready."

¹³They went off and found everything just as Jesus had told them, and prepared the Passover meal.

The Lord's Supper
(Also Matt. 26.26–30; Mark 14.22–26; 1 Cor. 11.23–25)

¹⁴When the hour came, Jesus took his place at the table with the apostles. ¹⁵He said to them, "I have wanted so much to eat this Passover meal with you before I suffer! ¹⁶For I tell you, I will never eat it until it is given its full meaning in the Kingdom of God."

¹⁷Then Jesus took the cup, gave thanks to God, and said, "Take this and share it among yourselves; ¹⁸for I tell you that I will not drink this wine from now on until the Kingdom of God comes."

¹⁹Then he took the bread, gave thanks to God, broke it, and gave it to them, saying, "This is my body [which

is given for you. Do this in memory of me." 20In the
same way he gave them the cup, after the supper, saying,
"This cup is God's new covenant sealed with my blood
which is poured out for you.]

21"But, look! The one who betrays me is here at the
table with me! 22Because the Son of Man will die as God
has decided it; but how terrible for that man who betrays
him!"

23Then they began to ask among themselves which
one of them it could be who was going to do this.

The Argument about Greatness

24An argument came up among the disciples as to
which one of them should be thought of as the greatest.
25Jesus said to them, "The kings of this world have
power over their people, and the rulers are called
'Friends of the People.' 26But this is not the way it is
with you; rather, the greatest one among you must be
like the youngest, and the leader must be like the servant. 27Who is greater, the one who sits down to eat or
the one who serves him? The one who sits down, of
course. But I am among you as one who serves.

28"You have stayed with me all through my trials;
29and just as my Father has given me the right to rule,
so I will make the same agreement with you. 30You will
eat and drink at my table in my Kingdom, and you will
sit on thrones to judge the twelve tribes of Israel."

Jesus Predicts Peter's Denial
(Also Matt. 26.31–35; Mark 14.27–31; John 13.36–38)

31"Simon, Simon! Listen! Satan has received permis-
sion to test all of you, as a farmer separates the wheat
from the chaff. 32But I have prayed for you, Simon, that
your faith will not fail. And when you turn back to me,
you must strengthen your brothers."

33Peter answered, "Lord, I am ready to go to prison
with you and to die with you!"

34"I tell you, Peter," Jesus answered, "the cock will
not crow today until you have said three times that you
do not know me."

Simon, Simon! Listen!

Purse, Bag, and Sword

³⁵Then Jesus said to them, "When I sent you out that time without purse, bag, or shoes, did you lack anything?"

"Not a thing," they answered.

³⁶"But now," Jesus said, "whoever has a purse or a bag must take it; and whoever does not have a sword must sell his coat and buy one. ³⁷For I tell you this: the scripture that says, 'He was included with criminals,' must come true about me. Because that which was written about me is coming true."

³⁸The disciples said, "Look! Here are two swords, Lord!"

"That is enough!" he answered.

Jesus Prays on the Mount of Olives
(Also Matt. 26.36–46; Mark 14.32–42)

³⁹Jesus left the city and went, as he usually did, to the Mount of Olives; and the disciples went with him. ⁴⁰When he came to the place he said to them, "Pray that you will not fall into temptation."

⁴¹Then he went off from them, about the distance of a stone's throw, and knelt down and prayed. ⁴²"Father," he said, "if you will, take this cup away from me. Not my will, however, but your will be done." [⁴³An angel from heaven appeared to him and strengthened him. ⁴⁴In great anguish he prayed even more fervently; his

sweat was like drops of blood, falling to the ground.]

⁴⁵Rising from his prayer, he went back to the disciples and found them asleep, worn out by their grief. ⁴⁶And he said to them, "Why are you sleeping? Get up, and pray that you will not fall into temptation."

The Arrest of Jesus
(Also Matt. 26.47–56; Mark 14.43–50; John 18.3–11)

⁴⁷Jesus was still speaking when a crowd arrived. Judas, one of the twelve disciples, was leading them, and he came up to Jesus to kiss him. ⁴⁸But Jesus said, "Is it with a kiss, Judas, that you betray the Son of Man?"

⁴⁹When the disciples who were with Jesus saw what was going to happen, they said, "Shall we strike with our swords, Lord?" ⁵⁰And one of them struck the High Priest's slave and cut off his right ear.

⁵¹But Jesus said, "Enough of this!" He touched the man's ear and healed him.

⁵²Then Jesus said to the chief priests and the officers of the temple guard and the elders who had come there to get him, "Did you have to come with swords and clubs, as though I were an outlaw? ⁵³I was with you in the temple every day, and you did not try to arrest me. But this is your hour to act, when the power of darkness rules."

Peter Denies Jesus
(Also Matt. 26.57–58, 69–75; Mark 14.53–54, 66–72; John 18.12–18, 25–27)

⁵⁴They arrested Jesus and took him away into the house of the High Priest; and Peter followed from a distance. ⁵⁵A fire had been lit in the centre of the court-yard, and Peter joined those who were sitting round it. ⁵⁶When one of the servant girls saw him sitting there at the fire, she looked straight at him and said, "This man too was with him!"

⁵⁷But Peter denied it, "Woman, I don't even know him!"

⁵⁸After a little while, a man noticed him and said, "You are one of them, too!"

But Peter answered, "Man, I am not!"

⁵⁹And about an hour later another man insisted

This man too was with him!

strongly, "There isn't any doubt that this man was with him, because he also is a Galilean!"

⁶⁰But Peter answered, "Man, I don't know what you are talking about!"

At once, while he was still speaking, a cock crowed. ⁶¹The Lord turned round and looked straight at Peter, and Peter remembered the Lord's words, how he had said, "Before the cock crows today, you will say three times that you do not know me." ⁶²Peter went out and wept bitterly.

Jesus Mocked and Beaten
(Also Matt. 26.67–68; Mark 14.65)

⁶³The men who were guarding Jesus made fun of him and beat him. ⁶⁴They blindfolded him and asked him, "Who hit you? Guess!" ⁶⁵And they said many other insulting things to him.

Jesus before the Council
(Also Matt. 26.59–66; Mark 14.55–64; John 18.19–24)

⁶⁶When day came, the elders of the Jews, the chief priests, and the teachers of the Law met together, and Jesus was brought to their Council. ⁶⁷"Tell us," they said, "are you the Messiah?"

He answered, "If I tell you, you will not believe me, ⁶⁸and if I ask you a question you will not answer. ⁶⁹But from now on the Son of Man will be seated at the right side of the Almighty God."

⁷⁰They all said, "Are you, then, the Son of God?"
He answered them, "You say that I am."
⁷¹And they said, "We don't need any witnesses! We
ourselves have heard his very own words!"

Jesus before Pilate
(Also Matt. 27.1–2, 11–14; Mark 15.1–5; John 18.28–38)

23 The whole group rose up and took Jesus before
Pilate, ²where they began to accuse him, "We
caught this man misleading our people, telling them not
to pay taxes to the Emperor and claiming that he himself
is Christ, a king."

³Pilate asked him, "Are you the king of the Jews?"
"You say it," answered Jesus.

⁴Then Pilate said to the chief priests and the crowds,
"I find no reason to condemn this man."

⁵But they insisted even more strongly, "He is starting
a riot among the people all through Judea with his teaching. He began in Galilee, and now has come here."

Jesus before Herod

⁶When Pilate heard this he asked, "Is this man a
Galilean?" ⁷When he learned that Jesus was from the
region ruled by Herod, he sent him to Herod, who was
also in Jerusalem at that time. ⁸Herod was very pleased
when he saw Jesus, because he had heard about him and
had been wanting to see him for a long time. He was
hoping to see Jesus perform some miracle. ⁹So Herod
asked Jesus many questions, but Jesus did not answer a
word. ¹⁰The chief priests and the teachers of the Law
stepped forward and made strong accusations against
Jesus. ¹¹Herod and his soldiers made fun of Jesus and
treated him with contempt. They put a fine robe on him
and sent him back to Pilate. ¹²On that very day Herod
and Pilate became friends; they had been enemies before
this.

Jesus Sentenced to Death
(Also Matt. 27.15–26; Mark 15.6–15; John 18.39—19.16)

¹³Pilate called together the chief priests, the leaders,
and the people, ¹⁴and said to them, "You brought this
man to me and said that he was misleading the people.

Now, I have examined him here in your presence, and I have not found him guilty of any of the crimes you accuse him of. [15]Nor did Herod find him guilty, because he sent him back to us. There is nothing this man has done to deserve death. [16]I will have him whipped, then, and let him go."

[[17]At each Passover Feast Pilate had to set free one prisoner for them.] [18]The whole crowd cried out, "Kill him! Set Barabbas free for us!" [19](Barabbas had been put in prison for a riot that had taken place in the city, and for murder.)

[20]Pilate wanted to set Jesus free, so he called out to the crowd again. [21]But they shouted back, "To the cross with him! To the cross!"

[22]Pilate said to them the third time, "But what crime has he committed? I cannot find anything he has done to deserve death! I will have him whipped and set him free."

[23]But they kept on shouting at the top of their voices that Jesus should be nailed to the cross; and finally their shouting won. [24]So Pilate passed the sentence on Jesus that they were asking for. [25]He set free the man they wanted, the one who had been put in prison for riot and murder, and turned Jesus over to them to do as they wished.

Jesus Nailed to the Cross
(Also Matt. 27.32–44; Mark 15.21–32; John 19.17–27)

[26]They took Jesus away. As they went, they met a man named Simon, from Cyrene, who was coming into the city from the country. They seized him, put the cross on him and made him carry it behind Jesus.

[27]A large crowd of people followed him; among them were some women who were weeping and wailing for him. [28]Jesus turned to them and said, "Women of Jerusalem! Don't cry for me, but for yourselves and your children. [29]For the days are coming when people will say, 'How lucky are the women who never had children, who never bore babies, who never nursed them!' [30]That will be the time when people will say to the mountains, 'Fall on us!' and to the hills, 'Hide us!' [31]For if such things as these are done when the wood is green, what will it be like when it is dry?"

Put the cross on him and made him carry it

³²They took two others also, both of them criminals, to be put to death with Jesus. ³³When they came to the place called "The Skull," they nailed Jesus to the cross there, and the two criminals, one on his right and one on his left. ³⁴Jesus said, "Forgive them, Father! They don't know what they are doing."

They divided his clothes among themselves by throwing dice. ³⁵The people stood there watching, while the Jewish leaders made fun of him, "He saved others; let him save himself, if he is the Messiah whom God has chosen!"

³⁶The soldiers also made fun of him; they came up to him and offered him cheap wine, ³⁷and said, "Save yourself, if you are the king of the Jews!"

³⁸These words were written above him: "This is the King of the Jews."

³⁹One of the criminals hanging there hurled insults at him, "Aren't you the Messiah? Save yourself and us!"

⁴⁰The other one, however, rebuked him, saying, "Don't you fear God? We are all under the same sentence. ⁴¹Ours, however, is only right, because we are getting what we deserve for what we did; but he has done no wrong." ⁴²And he said to Jesus, "Remember me, Jesus, when you come as King!"

⁴³Jesus said to him, "I tell you this: today you will be in Paradise with me."

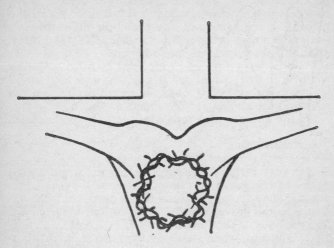

He said this and died

The Death of Jesus
(Also Matt. 27.45–56; Mark 15.33–41; John 19.28–30)

⁴⁴It was about twelve o'clock when the sun stopped shining and darkness covered the whole country until three o'clock; ⁴⁵and the curtain hanging in the temple was torn in two. ⁴⁶Jesus cried out in a loud voice, "Father! In your hands I place my spirit!" He said this and died.

⁴⁷The army officer saw what had happened, and he praised God, saying, "Certainly he was a good man!"

⁴⁸When the people who had gathered there to watch the spectacle saw what happened, they all went back home, beating their breasts. ⁴⁹All those who knew Jesus personally, including the women who had followed him from Galilee, stood off at a distance to see these things.

The Burial of Jesus
(Also Matt. 27.57–61; Mark 15.42–47; John 19.38–42)

⁵⁰⁻⁵¹There was a man named Joseph, from the Jewish town of Arimathea. He was a good and honourable man, and waited for the coming of the Kingdom of God. Although a member of the Council, he had not agreed

with their decision and action. ⁵²He went into the presence of Pilate and asked for the body of Jesus. ⁵³Then he took the body down, wrapped it in a linen sheet, and placed it in a grave which had been dug out of the rock —a grave which had never been used. ⁵⁴It was Friday, and the Sabbath was about to begin.

⁵⁵The women who had followed Jesus from Galilee went with Joseph and saw the grave and how Jesus' body was placed in it. ⁵⁶Then they went back home and prepared the spices and ointments for his body.

On the Sabbath they rested, as the Law commanded.

The Resurrection
(Also Matt. 28.1–10; Mark 16.1–8; John 20.1–10)

24 Very early on Sunday morning the women went to the grave carrying the spices they had prepared. ²They found the stone rolled away from the entrance to the grave, ³so they went in; but they did not find the body of the Lord Jesus. ⁴They stood there puzzled about this, when suddenly two men in bright shining clothes stood by them. ⁵Full of fear, the women bowed down to the ground, as the men said to them, "Why are you looking among the dead for one who is alive? ⁶He is not here; he has been raised. Remember what he said to you while he was in Galilee: ⁷'The Son of Man must be handed over to sinful men, be nailed to the cross and rise to life on the third day.'"

Told all these things

⁸Then the women remembered his words, ⁹returned from the grave, and told all these things to the eleven

disciples and all the rest. [10]The women were Mary Magdalene, Joanna, and Mary the mother of James; they
and the other women with them told these things to the
apostles. [11]But the apostles thought that what the
women said was nonsense, and did not believe them.
[12]But Peter got up and ran to the grave; he bent down
and saw the grave cloths and nothing else. Then he went
back home wondering at what had happened.

The Walk to Emmaus
(Also Mark 16.12–13)

[13]On that same day two of them were going to a
village named Emmaus, about seven miles from Jerusalem, [14]and they were talking to each other about all
the things that had happened. [15]As they talked and discussed, Jesus himself drew near and walked along with
them; [16]they saw him, but somehow did not recognize
him. [17]Jesus said to them, "What are you talking about,
back and forth, as you walk along?"

They stood still, with sad faces. [18]One of them, named
Cleopas, asked him, "Are you the only man living in
Jerusalem who does not know what has been happening
there these last few days?"

[19]"What things?" he asked.

"The things that happened to Jesus of Nazareth,"
they answered. "This man was a prophet, and was considered by God and by all the people to be mighty in
words and deeds. [20]Our chief priests and rulers handed
him over to be sentenced to death, and he was nailed to
the cross. [21]And we had hoped that he would be the one
who was going to redeem Israel! Besides all that, this is
now the third day since it happened. [22]Some of the
women of our group surprised us; they went at dawn to
the grave, [23]but could not find his body. They came back
saying they had seen a vision of angels who told them
that he is alive. [24]Some of our group went to the grave
and found it exactly as the women had said; but they did
not see him."

[25]Then Jesus said to them, "How foolish you are, how
slow you are to believe everything the prophets said!
[26]Was it not necessary for the Messiah to suffer these
things and enter his glory?" [27]And Jesus explained to
them what was said about him in all the Scriptures,

beginning with the books of Moses and the writings of all the prophets.

²⁸They came near the village to which they were going, and Jesus acted as if he were going farther; ²⁹but they held him back, saying, "Stay with us; the day is almost over and it is getting dark." So he went in to stay with them. ³⁰He sat at table with them, took the bread, and said the blessing; then he broke the bread and gave it to them. ³¹Their eyes were opened and they recognized him; but he disappeared from their sight. ³²They said to each other, "Wasn't it like a fire burning in us when he talked to us on the road and explained the Scriptures to us?"

³³They got up at once and went back to Jerusalem, where they found the eleven disciples gathered together with the others ³⁴and saying, "The Lord is risen indeed! He has appeared to Simon!"

³⁵The two then explained to them what had happened on the road, and how they had recognized the Lord when he broke the bread.

Jesus Appears to His Disciples
(Also Matt. 28.16–20; Mark 16.14–18; John 20.19–23; Acts 1.6–8)

³⁶While they were telling them this, suddenly the Lord himself stood among them and said to them, "Peace be with you."

³⁷Full of fear and terror, they thought that they were seeing a ghost. ³⁸But he said to them, "Why are you troubled? Why are these doubts coming up in your minds? ³⁹Look at my hands and my feet and see that it is I, myself. Feel me, and you will see, because a ghost doesn't have flesh and bones, as you can see I have."

⁴⁰He said this and showed them his hands and his feet. ⁴¹They still could not believe, they were so full of joy and wonder; so he asked them, "Do you have anything to eat here?" ⁴²They gave him a piece of cooked fish, ⁴³which he took and ate before them.

⁴⁴Then he said to them, "These are the very things I told you while I was still with you: everything written about me in the Law of Moses, the writings of the prophets, and the Psalms had to come true."

⁴⁵Then he opened their minds to understand the Scriptures, ⁴⁶and said to them, "This is what is written:

that the Messiah must suffer, and rise from death on the third day, 47and that in his name the message about repentance and the forgiveness of sins must be preached to all nations, beginning in Jerusalem. 48You are witnesses of these things. 49And I myself will send upon you what my Father has promised. But you must wait in the city until the power from above comes down upon you."

Jesus Is Taken up to Heaven
(Also Mark 16.19–20; Acts 1.9–11)

50Then he led them out of the city as far as Bethany, where he raised his hands and blessed them. 51As he was blessing them, he departed from them and was taken up into heaven. 52They worshipped him and went back into Jerusalem, filled with great joy, 53and spent all their time in the temple giving thanks to God.

He raised his hands and blessed them

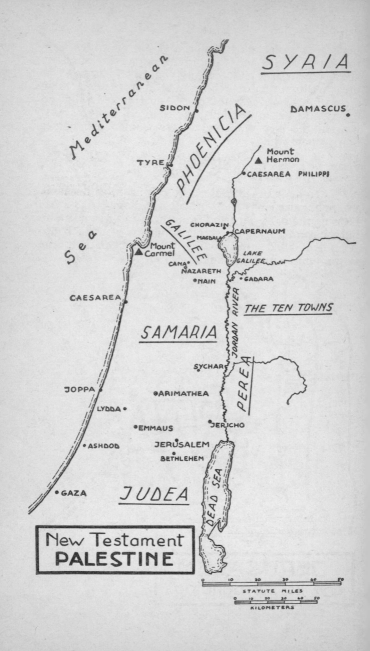

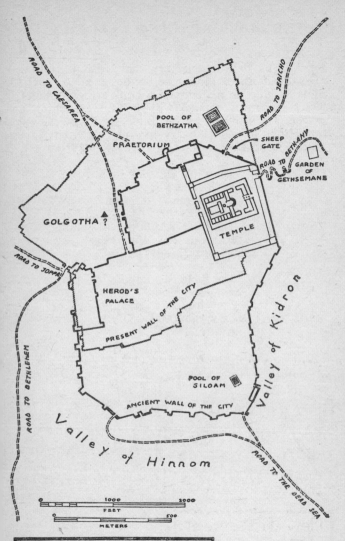

ROAD TO CAESAREA

ROAD TO JERICHO

POOL OF
BETHZATHA

PRAETORIUM

SHEEP
GATE

ROAD TO BETHANY

GARDEN
OF
GETHSEMANE

GOLGOTHA ?

TEMPLE

ROAD TO JOPPA

HEROD'S
PALACE

PRESENT WALL OF THE CITY

Valley of Kidron

ROAD TO BETHLEHEM

POOL OF
SILOAM

ANCIENT WALL OF THE CITY

Valley of Hinnom

ROAD TO THE DEAD SEA

1000   2000
FEET

500
METERS

JERUSALEM
and its surroundings

THE BIBLE READING FELLOWSHIP

Readers of this commentary may wish to follow a regular pattern of Bible reading, designed to cover the Bible roughly on the basis of a book a month. Suitable Notes (send for details) with helpful exposition and prayers are provided by the Bible Reading Fellowship three times a year (January to April, May to August, September to December), and are available from:

UK   The Bible Reading Fellowship,
St Michael's House,
2 Elizabeth Street, London, SW1W 9RQ

USA   The Bible Reading Fellowship,
P.O. Box 299, Winter Park,
Florida 32789, USA

AUSTRALIA   The Bible Reading Fellowship,
Jamieson House,
Constitution Avenue, Reid,
Canberra, ACT 2601,
Australia

Also available in the Fontana Religious Series

How Modern Should Theology Be?
HELMUT THIELICKE

'Thielicke touches on basic theological issues for today, but he does it with such a light hand, and with such graphic powers of illustration that I really cannot recall any other modern preacher who is so much *au fait* with modern theological questions.'   *Ronald Gregor Smith*

Strange Victory
GORDON W. IRESON

The Gospel, we are told, is Good News. What of? When we invite a man to become a Christian, what exactly are we offering to him, and asking him? These are some of the questions this book seeks to answer.

Companion to the Good News
JOSEPH RHYMER and ANTHONY BULLEN

More than 30 million people have bought *Good News for Modern Man* since it was first published. This 'Companion' has been written to help people understand the New Testament.

Apologia Pro Vita Sua
J. H. NEWMAN

A passionate defence of Cardinal Newman's own intellectual and spiritual integrity by a man who had been under continuous attack for many years.

Also available in the Fontana Religious Series

Something Beautiful for God
MALCOLM MUGGERIDGE

'For me, Mother Teresa of Calcutta embodies Christian love in action. Her face shines with the love of Christ on which her whole life is centred. *Something Beautiful for God* is about her and the religious order she has instituted.'

Malcolm Muggeridge

Instrument of Thy Peace
ALAN PATON

'Worthy of a permanent place on the short shelf of enduring classics of the life of the Spirit.'

Henry P. van Dusen, Union Theological Seminary

Sing A New Song
THE PSALMS IN TODAY'S ENGLISH VERSION

These religious poems are of many kinds: there are hymns of praise and worship of God; prayers for help, protection, and salvation; pleas for forgiveness; songs of thanksgiving for God's blessings; and petitions for the punishment of enemies. This translation of the *Psalms in Today's English Version* has the same freshness and clarity of language, the same accuracy of scholarship based on the very best originals available as *Good News for Modern Man* and *The New Testament in Today's English Version*.

The Gospel According to Peanuts
ROBERT L. SHORT

This book has made a lasting appeal to people of all denominations and none. It has been read and enjoyed by literally millions of people. A wonderfully imaginative experiment in Christian communication.